A History of Business in Medieval Europe, 1200–1550, demolishes the widely held view that the phrase "medieval business" is an oxymoron. The authors review the entire range of business in medieval western Europe, probing its Roman and Christian heritage to discover the economic and political forces that shaped the organization of agriculture, manufacturing, construction, mining, transportation, and marketing. Then they deal with the responses of businessmen to the devastating plagues, famines, and warfare that beset Europe in the late Middle Ages. The remarkable success in coping with this hostile new environment was "a harvest of adversity" that prepared the way for the economic expansion of the sixteenth century.

Two main themes run through the book. First, the force and direction of business development in this period stemmed primarily from the demands of the elite. Second, the lasting legacy of medieval businessmen was less their skillful adaptations of imported inventions than their brilliant innovations in business organization.

Edwin S. Hunt is a retired businessman and former adjunct professor of history at the University of Cincinnati. He is the author of *The Medieval Super-companies*.

James M. Murray is Associate Professor of History at the University of Cincinnati. He is the author of *Notarial Instruments in Flanders, 1280–1452*.

Cambridge Medieval Textbooks

A HISTORY OF BUSINESS
IN MEDIEVAL EUROPE, 1200–1550

A HISTORY OF BUSINESS
IN MEDIEVAL EUROPE,
1200–1550

EDWIN S. HUNT   JAMES M. MURRAY

CAMBRIDGE
UNIVERSITY PRESS

CAMBRIDGE UNIVERSITY PRESS
Cambridge, New York, Melbourne, Madrid, Cape Town, Singapore, São Paulo

Cambridge University Press
32 Avenue of the Americas, New York, NY 10013-2473, USA

www.cambridge.org
Information on this title: www.cambridge.org/9780521495813

First published 1999
6th printing 2006

Printed in the United States of America

A catalog record for this publication is available from the British Library.

Library of Congress Cataloging in Publication Data

A history of business in medieval Europe, 1200–1550 / Edwin S. Hunt,
James M. Murray.
p.   cm.
Includes bibliographical references and index.
ISBN 0-521-49581-4 (hc.). – ISBN 0-521-49923-2 (pbk.)
1. Europe – Commerce – History.   2. Banks and banking – Europe – History.
3. Europe – Economic conditions.   4. Economic history – Medieval, 500–1500.
I. Hunt, Edwin S.   II. Murray, James M., 1954– .
HF3495.H57   1999
330.94'01 – dc21   98-38599

ISBN-13   978-0-521-49581-3 hardback
ISBN-10   0-521-49581-4 hardback

ISBN-13   978-0-521-49923-1 paperback
ISBN-10   0-521-49923-2 paperback

CONTENTS

Contents

ILLUSTRATIONS

INTRODUCTION

Definitions are the first order of business for any book, particularly one whose title contains such slippery terms as "business" and "Europe." A second order is to forewarn the reader that there are two distinct divisions that must be recognized in this history, one geographical and the other temporal. And the third is to emphasize that this is a business history, not an economic history.

In this book, business will be dealt with in its broadest sense, that is, any activity involving exchange between two or more parties – in country or town, and on a local, regional, or international scale. Our coverage will therefore range from the organization of small artisanal workshops to the operations of large international manufacturers and marketers. And it will deal extensively with the vital role in business of medieval governments of all sorts. The Europe whose business we will be examining is somewhat more restricted in scope, being limited to those territories contemporaries called Western Christendom, including the Iberian peninsula as it became Christianized. Stated another way, we will be looking at what is commonly known as western Europe, plus Poland and Hungary. We will, however, also be discussing the activities of European businessmen wherever they took place, especially in North Africa and the Near East.

The geographic division is necessary in order to recognize the significant differences between northern and southern Europe in the evolution of business practice. First, what we will be calling "north" or "northwest" will include the British Isles, Scandinavia, the Low Countries, Germany, and north and central France. The "south" will consist of Italy, Iberia, and southern France. Poland, Bohemia, Hungary, and

Switzerland do not fall into either of these categories and will always be cited specifically. In broad terms, the south was more sophisticated and innovative than the north with regard to corporate organization, financial devices, and accounting techniques for most of our period. But there were also numerous differences within each of these regions, so that it is misleadingly simplistic to lump all the south and all the north into single units of analysis. To be sure, it can be said that the evolution of banking and accounting procedures was more or less simultaneous throughout the cities of Italy, Provence, and Catalonia, but business organization developed very differently in each of those locations. For example, enterprise units in Venice were relatively small, closely regulated, and dominated by state policy, whereas in Tuscany, although businesses were closely identified with government, some of them became quite large and operated more or less independently. Similarly, in the north, enterprises in the Low Countries and England were not very large by Italian standards but maintained a degree of independence, while those of the German Hanse became highly regulated and dominated by the town and princely governments of the league. In this sense, Robert Lopez's vision of the north and south as mirror images of each other is insightful, despite the obvious differences.

The Black Death of 1347–50 marks the halfway point of our period and our book. Yet the plague's importance, we will argue, was as much symbolic as real, epitomizing a period of severe disruptions lasting throughout most of the fourteenth century. In this reign of "King Death" recurring famines, plagues, and endemic warfare profoundly affected the demography, psychology, and economy of western Europe, to which business had to adapt. Thus, in Part I we attempt to describe various components of business activity as practiced in the High Middle Ages, and to trace, however briefly, the evolution of each. Here was a business environment characterized by the need to provide necessities and luxuries for increasingly populous towns and increasingly prosperous rural magnates from increasingly long distances. Part II is the story, first of the successful adaptation of business to an extended period of calamity, and then of the pursuit of opportunities to secure low-cost sources of goods wherever they might be found.

The overriding theme of this book is that medieval business was driven from beginning to end by the continuous demands of the elite. To be sure, there will be plenty of evidence for mass markets, for example in foodstuffs and textiles, but these developed as a consequence of the urbanization that resulted from the expansion of trade. The initial thrust came from the elite's dietary preferences, inherited from Mediterranean and Christian cultures, and from their insatiable desire for luxuries of food, clothing, and ornamentation. These pressures stimulated exchange and the need for business specialists to provide or procure the goods. Thus, we depart somewhat from tradition as we argue that elitist demands affected, directly or indirectly, virtually all businesses, rather than just those dealing in luxury goods. At the beginning of the thirteenth century, the point where our history begins, it is the ruling classes and their bureaucracies (which included businessmen) that largely determined how surpluses were spent, whether on cathedrals, castles, infrastructure, or luxuries. And although purchasing power began to spread among more people, especially after the Black Death, the demands of governments continued to influence the direction of investment and thus of innovation. These demands became increasingly accompanied by reams of enforcing regulations. At the end of our story, governments are vigorously engaged in controlling trade at all levels, but with diminishing success.

Chronology presents an inevitable problem in a book covering the many facets of business activity across a wide geographical area. The history of medieval business is not an orderly march over the centuries; the innovations and practices that we shall discuss do not fit into tidy time frames. Rather, each kind of business evolved over lengthy periods in different ways at different paces in different parts of our territory. Thus, our subject requires a business-by-business approach, each with its own chronology, especially in the first part of the book, where we must frequently reach back to ancient Mediterranean civilizations and the early Middle Ages to provide adequate background and perspective.

The selection of 1200–1550 as the prime period of enquiry might seem odd to economic historians accustomed to studying the spectacular rise and decline of commerce during the High and late Middle Ages. Starting with the commercial revolution near its apogee rather than at its beginning enables us to focus on the adaptations that businessmen in different lines of endeavor in different parts of Europe had made to take advantage of the long economic expansion. And extending the survey some fifty years beyond 1500, the conventional closing date of the Middle Ages, makes it possible to highlight the evolution of some extremely important business innovations and their direct linkage to some of the spectacular developments, good and bad, of the early modern period. These included large-scale mining, mass-market fisheries, new financing mechanisms, and slave-worked plantations, to name a few. This somewhat unconventional approach enables us to take full advantage of recent research and interpretations and separates this work from the older syntheses of economic historians such as Robert Lopez and Harry Miskimin, who regarded the fourteenth and fifteenth centuries as an economic wasteland. Our closing date also coincides roughly with the last years before the flow of precious metals from the New World profoundly changed the economies of western Europe.

We strive throughout the book to observe the distinction between economic and business history. Seeking to imitate the lengthy magnificence of the *Cambridge Economic History of Europe* would be foolish, although the economic environment and changes in it are of course crucial to this survey. Consideration of developments in politics, warfare, technology, and social attitudes is also important, as all of these forces presented problems and opportunities to medieval businessmen who had to find a variety of ways of coping with them day by day. But business must remain the window through which we view the larger changes of European economy and society. It provides a quite different vision of the late Middle Ages from even those economic historians such as Carlo Cipolla who share our disagreement with the depression theory for that period. Cipolla's analysis stresses per capita economic improvement; the business window highlights the qualitative changes that laid the basis for the sixteenth-century expansion.

Pursuing our subject – even closely defined – across a culturally diverse territory over a 350-year period in a short format has forced considerable economies in the selection of representative data. Thus much interesting and important material has been omitted, and significant geographical areas and commercial endeavors have been given short shrift. And although we have cited certain business or cultural practices derived from Rome, Byzantium, and Islam that we believe to be relevant to the medieval story, we have avoided overburdening this book by venturing very deeply into those business histories. Some may find the lacunae too numerous, or the choices ill-made. Nonetheless, if our account brings a new and coherent picture of the vitality, variety, and adaptability of business activity in medieval Europe, it will have served its purpose.

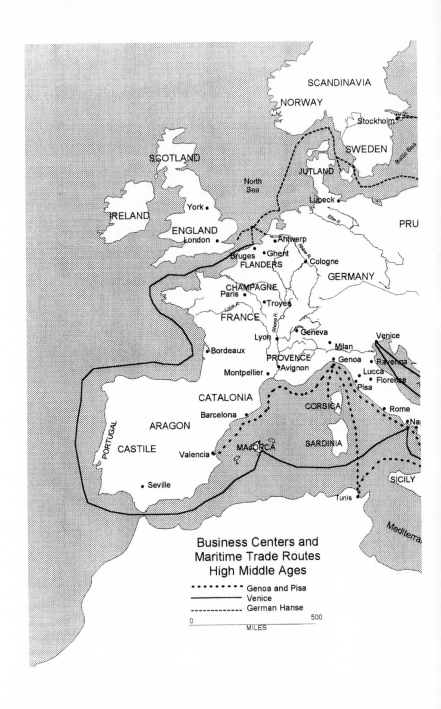

SCANDINAVIA

NORWAY

Stockholm

SWEDEN

JUTLAND

North Sea

Lübeck

PRU

York

IRELAND

ENGLAND

London

Antwerp

Bruges • Ghent

Cologne

FLANDERS

GERMANY

CHAMPAGNE

Paris

Troyes

FRANCE

Geneva

Venice

Lyon

Milan

Bordeaux

Genoa

Ravenna

PROVENCE

Avignon

Lucca

Florence

Montpellier

Pisa

CATALONIA

Barcelona

CORSICA

Rome

ARAGON

MAJORCA

SARDINIA

Na

CASTILE

Valencia

PORTUGAL

Seville

Tunis

SICILY

Business Centers and
Maritime Trade Routes
High Middle Ages

•••••••• Genoa and Pisa
———— Venice
– – – – German Hanse

0   500

MILES

Mediterra

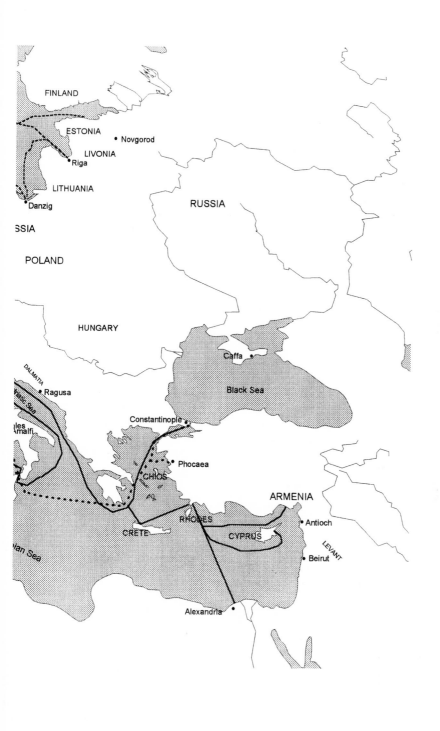

PART I

BEFORE THE BLACK DEATH: PROGRESS AND PROBLEMS

•

I

ECONOMICS, CULTURE, AND GEOGRAPHY OF EARLY MEDIEVAL TRADE

•

I saw a swelling tide of mobilized wealth, which seigneurial exactions channeled into the dwelling-places of the rich, and that new wealth fostered a taste for luxury and expenditure that laid the groundwork for the takeoff, for that crucial turning point in the European economy that inaugurated the age of the businessman . . .[1]

A world without business is as unimaginable in our fin de siècle age as one without light or air. Moreover, "doing business" has come to be an activity that bridges night and day, land and sea, and even airless space. Business is now all-embracing and, as it seems to some, all-consuming. This was not always so, and one of the purposes of this book is to trace the early history of what has become arguably the most powerful revolutionary force that Europe has unleashed on the rest of the world. But as Karl Marx, an early student of the historical implications of European business, has remarked, the revolution was not created "from whole cloth" but from materials found in the historical context of the period covered by this book.

The dynamics of the process of creation will be the particular focus of this introductory chapter. The reader may have already noticed that the authors believe the driving force for change in the medieval economy was created by the demands of the wealthy and powerful, the seigneurs of northwestern Europe. Clarifying the origins of this group and their needs and desires will cause us to range further in time from the strict confines of our delimited period and to concentrate our attention on economic and social developments to the north and west of the

Mediterranean basin. But the subject remains the same – the evolution of business in Europe as a whole.

Many languages have a variation on the well-worn cliché, "you are what you eat." While this expression is absurd literally, when applied to economic systems it contains a kernel of truth: what people put on their tables will have a great impact on the organization of their economy. In the Middle Ages, what people ate, and just as importantly, what they wanted to eat, played a marked role in defining the possibilities and limitations of business organization. Therefore to understand medieval business, one needs to appreciate the tremendous transformation of northern European eating habits and agricultural practices that occurred roughly between 700 and 1000.

ROME'S DIETARY LEGACY – BREAD ABOVE ALL

Some of the most arresting images of the Christian New Testament have to do with food. Jesus of Nazareth throughout his ministry sought to use images and objects that were readily comprehensible to his audience to express his teachings. His miracles reflect this: the first was the transformation of water into wine, his most famous the multiplication of loaves and fishes, and his most enduring, the ritual of breaking bread with his disciples at the Passover meal of Holy Thursday. And despite his famous phrase borrowed from a psalm, "Man does not live by bread alone," bread in fact dominated the diet of most of Christ's audience in common with that of most inhabitants of the first-century Roman Empire. Thus, as Christianity was a Mediterranean religion, it is not surprising that the dietary expectations of Mediterranean peoples were sacralized in Christian liturgy. Christianity's emphasis on bread, wine, and to a lesser extent olive oil, was to have a profound effect on the dietary and agricultural history of the vast non-Mediterranean territories of western Europe.

The Mediterranean as a region is not blessed with either great soil fertility or regular and ample rainfall. Arable land is widely scattered and abundant enough in only a few places, such as Sicily and North Africa, for large-scale grain cultivation during Roman and early Christian times. Rain is also often scarce and scattered, falling predominantly in winter months, leaving summers more or less arid. With an almost universal shortage of pasturage, significant stock-raising ventures were out of the question. Necessity dictated that the prototypical "Mediterranean diet" consisted almost exclusively of vegetable products, such as bread and other grain dishes, wine, and olive oil, supplemented with cheese, vegetables, and a scant quantity of meat. Only for a desert people like the ancient Hebrews could Mediterranean Palestine seem like a land of "milk and honey"; by modern standards the preindustrial Mediterranean was arid and famine-ridden.

Over time a strategy developed to cope with the inherent poverty of Mediterranean agriculture and its attendant crop failures and famines. The Pax Romana, the extensive free trade zone within Roman boundaries, both permitted the spread of the Mediterranean diet to the four quarters of the empire and remedied local shortages and inability to raise certain staple crops. The keys were crop specialization and shipping services: simply put, those regions endowed with natural advantages for the raising of a particular crop specialized in it and shipped the surplus in return for surpluses from other regions of specialized agriculture. Thus North Africa and Sicily raised considerable quantities of wheat on large farms worked by slave labor; by the first century A.D., North Africa alone was exporting 250,000 to 400,000 tons of grain per year to Rome. Other regions, such as Greece and Spain, specialized in viticulture and olive oil production, while Italy was known for its cheese among other products. In this way, as one historian has put it, a common dietary language was shaped, more widespread and persistent than even the Latin tongue spoken by the empire's rulers.

Common to all these staple foods is the need for a degree of processing – they are all to a certain extent manufactured. Not only is the production of wheat (the most popular bread grain of the Roman world), grapes, and olives time-consuming and expensive, but also the harvest of the crop is only the first step in the sometimes lengthy process of preparing it for the table. To speak only of wheat for the moment: after harvest it must be threshed to separate the edible wheat berries from the inedible chaff, then ground into flour, then mixed with water and some kind of wild yeast preparation, kneaded to develop a structure, allowed to rise, and lastly baked in a hot oven. The return for such labors is the capacity to be stored for a considerable period (properly kept, wheat berries remain edible for years) as well as a nutritious, portable, and slow-spoiling product – bread. No wonder then that daily bread was a given, and that the daily dietary question was what to have with bread, *cum panis*, the etymological root of the word "company" and its derivatives, which acquired great social and business significance over time.

What went with bread was more varied than suggested by Juvenal's jibe directed at ordinary Romans that they lived on "bread and circuses." The Roman diet even for the humble was never made up exclusively of cereal products. Garden crops such as onions, garlic, and green vegetables were always assumed to accompany bread as part of any meal.

Rations of meat were also commonly distributed by the emperor as part of the public dole, with pork being customary. Olive oil came in myriad varieties and was used for many purposes from culinary to cosmetic; wine was equally ubiquitous and diverse in kind and quality. Of course, for the rich of the Roman Empire, the choice of rare delicacies was endless. In the admittedly caricatured depiction of one Roman banquet, Trimalchio's feast found in Petronius' *Satyricon*, the courses numbered at least eight and ranged from simple black and green olives to roasted wild boar stuffed with live birds that were released when the roast was carved. Such variety and extravagant display of foodstuffs would only be equaled by the Burgundian dukes of the fifteenth century.

Even though the Roman Empire remained Mediterranean-centered throughout its history, its expansion under the first emperors had pushed its borders into a vast hinterland north, west, and east of the Mediterranean basin, from Britain to the Rhine and Danube river valleys. These were the vaguely conceived lands of "over there" across the Alps, whose peoples were barbarian both in speech and dietary habits, seemingly remote from the cultural norms of the empire. The names given these barbarians were as vague and imprecise as the Romans' geographical understanding of their homeland. Most were simply called *Germani*, Germans, and one of their chief identifying qualities was a preference for animal products – meat, both domestically raised and wild, milk and cheese, and beer, with butter and lard for cooking fats. To the mixed wonder and repugnance of Romans, this barbarian diet treated grain products from rye, wheat, and barley as distinctly second-class and in no way the principal object of food production. Indeed, much of the German grain crop must have been drunk in the form of ale, a product that the Roman historian Tacitus described as "a liquid distilled from barley and wheat, after fermentation has given it a certain resemblance to wine."[2]

From the second through fifth centuries of our era, the formerly distinct categories of "Roman" and "German" dissolved across increasingly broad areas of the western Roman Empire through intermarriage, settlement, and a mixture of Germanic conquest and Roman collapse. Nowhere was this merging of cultures more apparent than in diet: not only had the formerly rude barbarians acquired a taste for the bread and wine of Mediterranean provenance, but Romans also began to extol the strengthening qualities of meat and other animal products. The most important result of this shift in tastes, however, was in the lands of "over there," where the predilections and desires of the ruling class were translated into a new agrarian system whose formation would occupy the next several centuries and have consequences stretching across the next half-millennium.

Following the collapse of the western empire, the barbarian heirs of Rome still wished to retain the benefits of that civilization for themselves and their descendants; but numerous obstacles lay in their path. First among them was the geographical and climatological reality of northern Europe, which was a land of heavier soil, more constant rainfall, and ubiquitous forest – difficult conditions for large-scale wheat production. Second was a severe shortage of agricultural labor; where the Romans relied on slave gangs to farm the specialized crops of their agrarian system, German rulers could dominate only small settlements of peasants as their work force. Third was the absence of widespread, long-distance transport, due not only to political instability but also to the very different geography of the European north, where rivers, rather than a large inland sea, provided the transportation nexus.

Because specialization and transportation were out of the question, Germanic rulers and their peasantry forged a new economic relationship governed by the twin forces of compulsion and cooperation. Medieval peasants were unfree (their very name, *servi*, was derived from the Latin word for slave), but the essence of the serf–lord relationship was not the application of despotic force; rather, it was a remarkable meshing of interests. For the lord, the interest was provision of the elements of the "civilized" diet in sufficient quantities; for the peasant, it was to secure the survival of himself and his family through unfettered use of the land. Both sides came to agree on the purpose to which the productive potential of the land should be put: the realization of a diet based on bread.

Even though the goal and the social means to that goal were remarkably consistent across Europe, the reality of social and economic organization varied considerably. Village settlements were of many types depending on their location; the relationship of lord and peasant might vary in innumerable ways according to the evolution of custom; and the crop types raised also varied. The weather conditions of a region often determined that rye, spelt, and oats replaced wheat as the primary cereal crop, although wheat bread – the whiter the better – never ceased to be the ideal product of agriculture. Through all the bewildering diversity and local particularity, there remained continuous pressure for more and better bread grains, a pressure exerted both by the lords and, after ca. 750, by a growing population in the peasant community.

THE ROLE OF CHRISTIAN CULTURE

Christian culture played a crucial role in supplying the common vocabulary of diet in western Europe. As mentioned earlier, Christianity issued from a milieu foreign to many country dwellers, but through the assid-

uous encouragement of Germanic kings, notably the Carolingians
after 725, the full power of its message was brought to the countryside
of northern Europe before the year 1000. The first missionaries to these
Germanic peoples – Anglo-Saxons, Saxons, Alemanni, and many others
– borrowed copiously from the religious metaphors first fashioned by
the church fathers of the fourth and fifth centuries. Their greatest source
was Saint Augustine, who in a sermon addressed to a new Christian
drew a powerful analogy between bread and religion. "This bread retells
your history . . . You were brought to the threshing floor of the Lord
and were threshed. . . . While awaiting catechism, you were like grain
kept in the granary . . . [At the] baptismal font, you were kneaded into
a single dough. In the oven of the Holy Ghost you became the true
bread of God."[3]

All this merely complements the central ritual of Christianity introduced to the new converts, the reenactment of Christ's Last Supper,
which is itself a metaphor for Christ's presence among Christian believ-
ers. Even if the newly Christianized peasants rarely partook of the
Eucharist, the Christian invocation of bread, wine, and oil, but especially
bread, must have made a powerful impression among the European peasantry. Although we have no direct testimony as to its effect, we do have
the startling data that between the eighth and eleventh centuries, cereals
increased their share of the northern European peasant's diet from
approximately one-third to three-fourths or more of total consumed
calories.[4] Thereafter until the modern era, bread was the most significant item in the diet of the average European man, woman, and child,
and still today the price of bread is a politically sensitive subject in many
European countries.

Christian influence was also buttressed by the institutional example
of the monastery at the very heart of European agriculture. The founding father of western monasticism, Saint Benedict, had enshrined the
vegetarian diet as the ideal of the ascetic life. Though considered moderate in allowing monks comparatively abundant food in proportion to
the severity of their work, the Benedictine rule is uncompromising in
restricting meat consumption to the aged and infirm. The monks were
to be satisfied with a pound of bread a day and two cooked dishes, pre-
sumably gruel or porridge, and if any fruit or fresh vegetables were available, they could make up a third. Given the assumption that a monastery
should provide most of its own food, it is not surprising that monastic
institutions led the way in spreading cereal cultivation throughout
Europe.

We have already noted the variety and hierarchy of bread grains and
the pressure for more and better bread grains. For the elite, only white

loaves made of sifted wheat flour would do. Of course wheat was the most difficult of bread grains to produce under growing conditions prevalent in many areas of the European north. For the common people there were rye, barley, oats, spelt, millet, and a few others to make into their daily bread. These grains, especially rye, yielded more dependable and usually larger crops, but produced a darker, heavier bread without those qualities of whiteness and lightness esteemed in wheat bread. For centuries, the bread of the poor was understood to mean dark, heavy bread that was substantial and hard to digest.

Despite the cultural attraction of bread and other cooked grains, the consumption of other foods, especially meat, never lost its appeal for medieval Europeans. Domestically raised animals, especially pigs, cattle, and to a lesser extent sheep, as well as game, continued to supply the meat dishes demanded especially by the social elite. The Frankish king Charlemagne preferred roasted meat to all other foods and refused to give it up even upon the advice of his physicians. Somewhat surprisingly, there is evidence that ninth-century monasteries consumed large amounts of meat: the abbey of Corbie consumed 600 pigs in the year 822 alone. Pork remained the meat of choice for many, both for its flavor and for the relative ease of raising pigs, given their ability to forage for food. These preferences account for the fact that stock raising always remained an adjunct to farming in the medieval countryside and could become in some cases a specialization if sufficient demand were present for the meat, hides, or fibers.

The demands of religion also dictated a prominent place for fish in the European diet, especially after the seventh century, when meat consumption was prohibited for observant Christians on approximately 150 fast days per year. Much of the fish supply must have come from fresh water or coastal salt water, because deep-water fishing was not a significant activity until the later Middle Ages. Few data survive about fish consumption, but there are scattered mentions of fish ponds in sources predating 1000. In England, fish ponds are described in tenth-century charters, and the best documented case, the royal fishpond at Fosse, York, was constructed by William the Conqueror before 1086, supplying fish for the royal household and gifts for others until the thirteenth century. More sophisticated methods of farming fish began after the twelfth century with the development of specialized fish ponds, often linked with a system of pools by which supply could be tailored to fit the life cycle of the fish and to meet increased demand during Lent. Ingenious fish farmers also discovered that ponds could be drained every three to five years and planted with crops that profited from the enriched soil, then grazed over by stock and ultimately returned for use as fish ponds

[handwritten margin note: fish → New World → Grand Banks cod fishery → dominance in Catholic regions]

in a regular rotation. Large-scale commercial fishing seems to have begun in the twelfth century, when herring became the quarry of English and German fishing fleets that ranged across the North and Baltic Seas. But it was not until the thirteenth century, when Lübeck merchants both financed Baltic fishing fleets and provided vast quantities of salt needed to preserve the catch, that herring became the Lenten dish par excellence in northern Europe.

LORDSHIP, COOPERATION, AND TECHNOLOGY

Given this common dietary goal of grain supplemented with vegetables and some meat and fish, how did European agriculture organize itself to meet the demand and in the process lay the groundwork for the economic success that followed? The answer is what the French historian Georges Duby described as the exercise of banal lordship — that is, the productive tension of cooperation/compulsion between the lords and peasants of Europe. The institutional form of this relationship in northern Europe historians call manorialism, which is best understood as the sum of man-made productive forces brought to bear on the fields, forests, and pastures of that region. As in modern factories, the architecture of villages, field organization, and crop choice could differ, but the forces at work remained the same.

Compulsion was applied to medieval peasants in many ways. They were not allowed to leave the land; they owed their lord labor on his demesne and the land set aside for his crops; they owed various rents and payments; and they could not choose the kinds of crops they grew. Peasants also had to have their grain ground at the lord's mill and often had to bake their bread at the lord's oven, both for a payment in money or kind. On the other hand, a peasant household, unlike that of slaves, could not be broken up and sold by the lord; serfs had customary rights to remain on the land, and lords were also prevented by custom from outright confiscation of the agricultural surplus grown on their manors. These factors, taken together, meant that there was a basis of cooperation built into an otherwise exploitative relationship.

A fine example of the interaction of compulsion and cooperation between lords and peasants is the development and deployment of rural technology. In most places, it was the lords who provided the land, the animals, and that most basic farm implement, the plow. In the European north, this was a considerable investment, involving a stout iron plowshare, a mouldboard to turn over the heavy clay soils, and a team of two to four oxen, or more rarely horses. Such heavy, wheeled plows more than justified their expense and by the eleventh century were the standard tillers of the field across most of northern Europe.

A second implement provided by the lord but benefiting all was the watermill. Like the heavy plow, watermills had been known but little used by the ancient Romans. Some historians attribute this to a lack of fast-running streams around the Mediterranean, but there were plenty of exceptions, as in northern Italy, Spain, and southern France, where consistent flow was easily achievable with the construction of dams. Of probably greater importance, therefore, was the absence of a perceived need for a labor-saving device of this type. In the European north of the tenth through thirteenth centuries, however, there were perfect conditions for watermills and a real need to spare peasants the work of milling their grain so that their labor could be directed to more productive ends. This was especially true for women's work, which had traditionally included the hand milling of grain for domestic consumption. With the widespread construction and use of watermills, milling as women's work had practically disappeared by the eleventh century, "freeing" more of women's time for productive household and field work, tending animals, and brewing beer and ale.[5]

Mills and plowshares were just two of the many implements acquired and deployed across Europe, from England to the edges of European colonization in the east. Moreover, the effects of these and other tools and technologies rippled outward in their implications: for with the mill came the millwright; with the plow the blacksmith. In short, labor saved in the fields was redirected to more specialized pursuits, which aided but were distinct from work in the fields. Those who practised such pursuits are called artisans, and though they are often associated with urban crafts, the origin of artisanal labor lies very much in the countryside.

[margin, handwritten:] ✳ with technological advancement comes the artisans.

How the work of medieval artisans was organized is difficult to establish, but a useful approach is to examine the example of women artisans. From the earliest records of European manors, dating from the ninth and tenth centuries, there is evidence of the "women's workshop," a separate establishment given over to the production of cloth. Anglo-Saxon, Carolingian, and Saxon sources agree that cloth production occupied a special place in the rural economy, demanding separate investment in separate buildings and the tools necessary for spinning, weaving, dyeing, and otherwise finishing cloth. The laborers employed in this work were both female slaves and serfs together with free and even aristocratic women, all of whom had in common the expectation that women were the clothmakers. By the thirteenth century, however, mentions of such workshops disappear as does the apparent monopoly of women in the cloth trades. As the household became the locus of production, males came to share in the work of making cloth, so that by the thirteenth century, when more specialized cloth production was shifted to the towns, men and women worked side by side as weavers and dyers.

Technology, however, consists of more than tools; it includes strategies for production, in this case to create conditions for the enhancement of output of the prized cereal grains. The most significant brake on crop yields in all preindustrial agriculture was a chronic shortage of fertilizer, which in practice forced the farmer to "rest" or fallow a portion of land annually. Traditionally, half the arable fields were left unsown each year – the so-called two-field system – but beginning around the year 1000, a three-field system became increasingly deployed. This involved the entire village community in a compulsory pattern of dividing the arable land into three parts, employing a third for a winter crop, a third for a summer crop, and leaving the rest fallow. The fields were rotated annually, maintaining soil fertility while increasing production, often improving grain harvests by over fifty percent. With the gradual spread of the three-field system from the great grain growing regions of northern France to much of central Europe, the landscape of Europe was transformed.

The improvements in technologies of tools and land use nevertheless were not enough to satisfy the demands of lords and of an increasing population. Enhanced production of cereal crops demanded more lands beyond the settled islands of traditional village communities surrounded by tracts of forests, swamps, and waste. The conquest of the medieval frontier from the ninth to the thirteenth century is perhaps the best demonstration of the power inherent in the manorial social system. The dynamic was much the same: lords provided capital and incentives to peasants in order to capture their labor for the realization of a variety of objectives. Here, the lords – monasteries, princes, knights – offered peasants special privileges and power over newly won agricultural land. These "assarts" always gave peasants increased rights to the crops they produced, in the form of either reduced labor services owed or an increased share of the crop. Such incentives caused settled rural communities to chip away constantly at the surrounding forest, bringing more and more of it under the plow.

The gradual expansion of existing settlements was only one form taken by the opening of the medieval wilderness. Outright colonization was another, requiring the shift of peasants away from their native villages in order to found new ones some distance away. To secure these colonists, lords often drew up agreements with representatives of prospective settlers, offering terms far more favorable than those obtaining in the old population centers. In exchange for payment of a small tax per homestead, colonists in frontier areas usually received ownership of the land they reclaimed, the right to dispose of the property, and complete personal freedom. Moreover, groups of peasants were often organized into rural communes or *Landgemeinden*, which had legal standing and were invested with the power to govern their members and to exercise lower justice. The result, particularly in Germany and central Europe, was the creation of groups of free and equal peasants who largely exploited their own land without the intervention of the lord. This movement reached its height in the twelfth century and is perhaps the clearest example of the expansive forces unleashed by the collaboration of lord and peasant.

The activities of Wichmann, Archbishop of Magdeburg (1152–92), exemplify the inner workings of the movement of colonization across Europe. Twelfth-century Magdeburg lay on the easternmost edge of settlement of German-speaking peasants, and archbishop Wichmann was determined to to encourage colonization both to secure additional income for his see and to further the dispossession of the Slavic-speaking natives of the area. To this purpose, he hired *locatores*, men who would attract settlers from the west in return for grants of land. These land agents fanned out through relatively densely populated Flanders and Holland, extolling the advantages of moving to the east. The attractions were considerable: freedom from forced labor on castles or the lord's land, and possession of large amounts of fertile land in return for reasonable rent. The new villages thus realized the vision Wichmann had for his creation: "they (the locatores) will settle new colonists there, who will drain the marshy grasslands, which are presently good for nothing but grass and hay, and plow them and sow them and make them fruitful . . ." It is difficult to imagine a more succinct description of the colonizing mentality.

An even more remarkable form of creating new agricultural land occurred along the coast of the English Channel and North Sea shared by the modern countries of France, Belgium, and the Netherlands. Here, beginning in the tenth century and ending more than a millennium later with the vast Delta Project, submerged land was progressively diked, drained, and brought into use first for pasture and later, as the salt was leached from the soil, for crops. In this case, it was the great monasteries of the twelfth century, particularly the Cistercians, which organized and financed the largest projects along the Flemish coast. The most striking example was the monastery of Ter Duinen, "the Dunes," near Bruges, where the Cistercians supervised coastal reclamation work until the end of the eighteenth century, establishing villages complete with churches as every polder project reached completion. Ultimately, these monastic development projects were so successful that the abbot of "the Dunes" spent most of his time not at the monastery but in his opulent town house in cosmopolitan Bruges.

Analogous to the free villages of central European colonists were the so-called "water associations" that oversaw the maintenance and expansion of the reclamation projects along the Flemish and Dutch coasts. These organizations were composed of both peasants and representatives of monasteries or noble landholders who together apportioned the cost of construction and maintenance of dikes and canals among landholders, appointed the "Sluismeester" (manager of the drainage works), and even exercised some governing powers in the reclaimed areas. These became an institutional expression of the cooperation between lord and peasant in the drive to reclaim land from the sea and certainly contributed to the tradition of relative freedom of the peasantry in the coastal regions of Flanders. As institutions they survived for centuries, succumbing only to the near wholesale destruction of the French Revolution.

In north central Italy, the rural economy developed in yet another manner. The system of large estates left by the Roman Empire was inherited by the Lombard invaders in the latter half of the sixth century. They kept the estates intact, but, being pastoralists, they were more interested in animal husbandry than in agriculture. As a result, great stretches of the countryside gradually reverted to forest and marsh. The economic revival of the eleventh century reversed this process, although the origins and nature of the transformation are obscure and remained extremely localized. Whatever the causes, the big estates began to be broken into smaller and better exploited holdings, first by leasing and later also by purchase, with personal valuables of all kinds being used in addition to coin. In these circumstances, the great landlords tended to rely more on rental income and seigneurial rights than on direct exploitation of their demesne lands. Over the same period, much of the rural unfree population acquired free status, and although most remained tied to the land by poverty, many took advantage of the fact that there were no legal inhibitions upon seeking a better life in nearby towns.[6]

The evolution of Italian agriculture also differed from that of other parts of Europe because the old towns may have decayed but never entirely disappeared, thanks at least partly to the continuing moral, political, and economic power of the local bishops. As a result, there were always markets of a sort, and as the towns began to recover, they drew increasingly on the surrounding countryside for their sustenance, encouraging the cultivation of a wide range of produce in addition to cereal grains. Another source of difference is that the feudal practice of primogeniture never entirely took hold among the great comital families, some of whom were prepared to pass on their lands and rights to more than one heir. Moreover, lordly landholdings were rarely far from a town, where nobles tended to participate in political, social, and business activities and to own property. The result of all these influences was a connection between town and country encompassing all segments of society that was absent elsewhere in Europe.[7] And when the elite of the north later began to have the desire and the means to acquire exotic goods from the Mediterranean region, the inhabitants of those towns, especially of the seaports, were ideally situated to take on the role of middlemen.

MARKETS, MONEY, AND MERCHANTS

In one of the earliest and most famous books about medieval agriculture, the French historian Marc Bloch described the basic structures of the medieval agrarian system sketched above.[8] Bloch took his inspiration from the medieval field patterns still visible in aerial photographs of the French countryside, finding in them the beginnings of rural France. But just as the medieval landscape was altered to meet the demand for cereals, long-suppressed patterns of economic integration inherent in a grain economy began to reassert themselves in the course of the eleventh and twelfth centuries. For despite the similarity in patterns of demand — for the foods made from wheat, and wines made from grapes — the fact was that not all of Europe was equally suited to these crops. Diversification and specialization had been the ancient Roman response to the vagaries of crops and climate, and Europeans reacted in a similar if more limited way, with greater reliance on local markets and less on the large-scale specialization of Roman agriculture.

Markets were the key: they made possible the beginnings of agricultural and along with it artisanal specialization and the closely related return of cities to the European landscape. A market at its most basic is simply a meeting place of buyer and seller where the needs of one are satisfied by the surplus of another. In early medieval Europe, the move to a grain economy created regions of surplus production near or adjacent to regions of underproduction of grain which had potential surpluses in other commodities or manufactures. The fertile plains of Picardy by the twelfth century were supplying grain to help feed more populous Flanders; the productive southeast and east midlands of

England fed the population of London and provided exports as well; whereas in France the fertile country both upstream and downstream of Paris kept that city's people supplied with foodstuffs. Many of these patterns of interregional trade were to endure for centuries.

The beginnings of market structure across Europe are difficult to trace. The word itself has ancient Germanic roots and first occurs in a document from the mid-eleventh century as *gearmarket*, or "year-market," akin to the modern German *Jahrmarkt*, denoting an annual gathering of merchants. Even though all the Germanic forms of the word are ultimately derived from the Latin *mercatum*, it is clear that before the eleventh century words in many languages were being coined to describe a developing new reality. And *mercatum* was not the only root to be so used: *port*, *burh*, and *fair* all were created to convey a similar meaning.[9]

It is unlikely, however, that markets and merchants were ever entirely absent from western Europe, even in the darkest of the so-called Dark Ages. Jewish merchants maintained their trading networks, and archaeological evidence has long revealed the existence of emporia or *wike* in such places as Dorstad and Quentovic from the Merovingian period until well into the ninth century, when they were destroyed by Norse invaders. And recent historical and archaeological research suggests that early trading was being conducted from large estates. There is also evidence of market development in the heartland of the Carolingian empire, the region between the Seine and Rhine Rivers, in the mid ninth century. Here early monastic polyptychs show an organized procedure for gathering up surpluses from the monastic farms and disposing of them at local markets, where grain was exchanged for wine or other more distantly produced goods. In England, markets were reported in and around London by the eleventh century, and in such places as Norwich, York, Winchester, and Lincoln, local markets had achieved regional importance by the time of the Norman conquest. In the Mediterranean, active trade continued in Visigoth and Muslim Spain and also in Italy, despite a temporary interruption in the north following the Lombard conquest in the sixth century. Genoa and Pisa remained backwaters until the late tenth century, although inland towns such as Pavia boasted a successful merchant class by the early eighth century.[10] The ports of southern Italy, including Amalfi from the sixth century, maintained a profitable trade with the Byzantines and Saracens. And Venice, already engaged in local commerce by the ninth century, became a serious competitor in Constantinople before the end of the tenth.

By one means or another, therefore, a modest level of commerce persisted in most parts of Europe, but before the eleventh century there is an instability and vagueness about European market structure that reveals its essentially casual, ad hoc nature. Marketplaces and market times were rarely fixed or permanent; laws governing market conduct were imprecise or nonexistent; law and order on the roads and waterways was uncertain. Here again it was the intervention of the landlords and their assertion of privilege that established agreed-on terms, places, rules of procedure, and security for the buyers and sellers.[11] In England this jurisdiction was more often than not exercised by the king; in Flanders and elsewhere in the more decentralized dominions of the French kingdom, it was usually the duke or count who granted market rights and policed the market. In Germany the determining force could be wielded by a duke or count or by a bishop or archbishop in the role of secular lord. In Italy under the imperial system, the source of authority varied from city to city, residing in the office of the bishop or count or imperial agent or some combination thereof, but from the twelfth century onward, the commune assumed control in most towns.[12]

It should be stressed, however, that the seigneur was most often the organizing force or catalyst, not the original impetus for the development of markets beyond a local level. That came largely from the religious custom as the organizing stimulus for the cycle of fairs that spawned markets across Europe. Fair is often used synonymously with market, but actually it is derived etymologically from the Latin *feria* or festival and relates to the religious festivals that brought people together from various parts of Europe, often on the occasion of the feast of a particular local saint. Crowds of pilgrims provided both customers and merchants for trade, and as different localities had different local saints whose feast days encompassed the calendar, a progression or cycle of fairs could develop.

Originally, fairs were regional in their reach, as in Flanders, where with the encouragement of the count a cycle of fairs came into existence around the mid eleventh to early twelfth century. These were eventually five in number, shared among Ypres, Lille, Mesen, Torhout, and later Bruges, each lasting thirty days in a staggered cycle from late February through the beginning of November, with two to four weeks between them to allow for travel. In England there is evidence of a less organized cycle of fairs that becomes clear in the thirteenth century. Fair structure analogous to that in Flanders appears primarily in the fairs of Stamford, Saint Ives, Boston, Winchester, King's Lynn, and Northampton in the northeast of the island. Also in the thirteenth century the most important of the fair cycles, the Champagne fairs, evolved into their final form. These were the first to transcend the regional to become truly international in scope and significance.

By the thirteenth century all fairs were markets, but not all markets were fairs. What distinguished the former was their annual and extraordinary nature, recognized through explicit license from king or prince granting special conditions for trade and security for merchants en route. Thus in the hierarchy of markets, fairs became the outlets for more specialized, rarer commodities whose customers came from proportionately greater distances. The regional web of weekly and smaller markets remained, however; the great medieval fair rose like a cathedral tower anchored to a foundation of local and regional markets.

The renaissance of markets and trade in Europe from the tenth through the thirteenth century naturally brings the triple question of what was traded, by what means, and who were the traders. We have argued that inherent in the grain economy is a dynamic of frequent scarcity that encouraged exchange of agricultural commodities at least on the local level. In successive centuries, market networks grew to embrace regional and international areas, but more distant market relations brought greater problems of transport and payment, making the direct exchange of one commodity for another increasingly difficult. The incentive for traders to adopt coins as the medium of exchange thus became more and more compelling, until in truth it can be said, "no mint, no market."

The triumph of coins must be kept in perspective, however. Mints and markets tended to go together even in early medieval times. A glance at a map of Carolingian mints from 730 to 849 shows a preponderance of coinage activity precisely in the area of greatest economic expansion, that bounded by the Loire and the Rhine. Almost twice as many mints existed there as in the rest of the Carolingian empire combined, suggesting that even in the infancy of medieval economic expansion, money was greasing the wheels of growth. The coincidence of mint and market is equally true in Germany, where at the beginning of the tenth century there were virtually no mints east of the Rhine. Thereafter, under the Ottonian emperors dozens of new mints were created, many of them east of the Rhine. By the year 1000 these formed a chain linking the easternmost mint at Magdeburg to the western trade emporium of Cologne, itself perched on the eastern edge of the most densely developed minting network of the Carolingian heartland.[13]

To the phrase "no mint, no market," however, must be added another: "no metal, no mint." The surge of mint creation across Germany did not happen by accident; mints are only established when there is a critical mass of raw material to work with, and that appeared in plenty with the discovery of silver in the Rammelsberg above the town of Goslar in the Harz Mountains late in the tenth century. These supplies were augmented shortly afterward by further discoveries in the southern Black Forest. The increased quantities of silver, promptly coined in the new mints, rapidly "irrigated" – in Peter Spufford's elegant term – both countryside and city, greatly increasing the use of coin throughout western Europe.

Tracing the origins of markets and coins used for trade is analogous to describing the set and props of a play but leaving out the actors. Just who the actors were in the revival of markets in western Europe and where they came from is a subject of some debate among historians. Henri Pirenne's classic argument was that the origins of medieval "marketers" (from the Latin *mercatores*) lay in the peasantry, specifically those who for one reason or another had been uprooted from the land, becoming vagabonds and wayfarers first and evolving into merchants in the course of their travels. Pirenne's favorite example was the eleventh-century English merchant Saint Godric of Finchale, who began as a beachcomber collecting merchandise from shipwrecks, then became a merchant in his own right travelling with his wares from England to Flanders, Scotland, and Denmark. Godric ultimately made his fortune but turned his back on business in favor of voluntary poverty as a hermit.

Historians since Pirenne have disputed the idea that the origins of the medieval merchant class can be traced exclusively to the poor and dispossessed peasantry. Many have cited evidence from the north that merchants included the well-to-do peasantry with capital to invest, as well as younger sons in aristocratic families given money or other movables as their patrimony in lieu of land. And in Italy we have already seen that the nobility cheerfully entered into the trading life of cities. Given the fact that markets never really disappeared in most parts of Europe, it is somewhat futile to seek the "origins" of a prototype medieval merchant. Saint Godric was just one of many classes of individuals who ventured into trade.

Monetary stability and with it market expansion could only be guaranteed when mints and markets were anchored in the context of a new or revived social institution, the city. Only sheltered within the walls of an urban area could the kind of stability, market demand, and a modicum of law and order come about that in turn could lead to increased manufacture and trade. The history of urban origins is extremely complex, differing in detail from one part of Europe to another. In Italy, for example, cities enjoyed a measure of continuity after the collapse of the western Roman Empire that was lacking in many parts of the north. In Flanders, which became the most densely urbanized region of Europe, nearly every city was created during the tenth or eleventh century. But despite this complexity, urban history itself is a model of the interaction of seigneurial power and merchant self-interest, the continuum of cooperation/compulsion in another arena.

The narrowest definition of the medieval city had little to do with economic fundamentals. The city was a creation in law, according its residents special rights of property holding, limited self-government, and jurisdiction. Such rights could be granted by the sovereign in a foundation charter ceded in most cases after prolonged struggle and negotiation. In Bruges and many other Flemish cities, for example, the first urban charters were granted in 1127 in the midst of a civil war between two rival claimants to the comital throne. The people of Bruges took advantage of the situation to extort what the chronicler Galbert of Bruges called a "little charter of agreement." Typically, the charter contained clauses guaranteeing freedom from comital tolls, security of urban property, and election of members to a governing council for the city.

It is obvious in the chronicle description, however, that Bruges already possessed the character and functions of a city well before the granting of urban privileges. It was already a market town with a populace made up of merchants and artisans. Galbert even gives us evidence of long-distance trade links when he states that merchants were so terrified by the news of the assassination of Count Charles the Good that they fled the fair of Ypres, which was then in full swing. This underlines the fact that in most cases the economic origins of cities lay more in their role as collection and trade points for regional and interregional commerce than as creations of kings or princes. The awarding of urban privileges thus fits neatly into the context of the steady seigneurial drive for greater profits. Recognizing cities was akin to encouraging peasant colonization of waste lands, investing in mills and ovens, and using the proceeds to obtain the trappings of noble life. This demand for luxuries thus both began and completed the circle, for if peasants supplied the surplus, it was the merchants who converted it into money, traded that money for the desired luxury good, sold the item to the lord, and profited from the role of entrepreneur. The first great age of European business history was nothing more than a nearly infinite number of variations on this simple theme.

THE CHAMPAGNE FAIRS

Just how far the linkages of local, regional, and extra-regional markets could extend is apparent in the Champagne fairs, which reached their apogee in the thirteenth century. Champagne, at that time a semi-autonomous region in north central France, lay across the most impor-

tant overland routes connecting the Flanders/England axis in the north
with the Italian/Mediterranean trading network of the south. As part of
the agricultural hinterland of Paris, the region had developed a significant agrarian economy before the twelfth century, generating urban
markets, notably those in Troyes, Provins, Lagny, and Bar-sur-Aube. These
became the venues for fairs, which were originally religious festivals, but
through the assiduous attentions of the counts of Champagne, who
granted special privileges and safe conducts to foreign merchants, the
Champagne fairs became the favored meeting place of southern and
northern merchants and merchandise. At intervals from January to
October, the six Champagne fairs (Provins and Troyes hosted two)
offered the regularity and security necessary for conveying merchandise,
displaying it for sale, and arranging shipment and payment.

All these long-distance merchants from the north and south were
obviously not trading grain and wine, but more exotic, high value, and
easily portable wares. The southerners brought with them a range of
articles from the western and eastern Mediterranean prized by the
increasingly affluent elite of the north. In return, the northern merchants
offered an array of woolen textiles, from ordinary to luxury, finished and
unfinished; but their total value was inadequate to balance the demand
for southern goods. That balance was largely made up by silver, both
bullion and coin, made available in ample quantities from the new and
exceptionally rich mines at Freiberg. Thus began what was to become
a fixture of medieval long-distance trade, a large and persistent shortfall
of merchandise movement from north to south, made up by quantities
of silver and, to a lesser extent, of gold.

Although the net flow of specie was inevitably from north to south,
there were myriad transactions among the participating merchants
entailing flows in many directions. In this connection the international
fairs transcended themselves as merchants developed a payment system
based on credit instruments called *lettres de foire*, or fair letters. These
documents recognized sales of merchandise, but often specified payment
at a later fair, when the total of debits and credits for a season would
be computed and a final reckoning made between buyers and sellers.
Letters were not endorsable, but could be transferred from one party to
another. Sometimes payment could be specified in a different coinage
than the original transaction, and all in all the fair letter obviated the
need for large shipments of specie. Thus the Champagne fairs increasingly came to play the role of financial clearinghouses for long-distance
trade between north and south.

The Champagne fairs are significant for many reasons, but above all
they symbolize the true dawning of the age of the international busi-

nessman in their integration of regional and long-distance trade through urban centers following the established pattern of annual fairs. And in true medieval fashion, they succeeded in becoming something new in the guise of something old, conforming to the role of a rendezvous of merchants while at the same time becoming a bridge between the great European economic zones of north and Mediterranean south.

We have seen that medieval business grew in the interstices of the dominant institutional forms of lordship and peasant-based agriculture. It is incorrect to think of the growth of merchant Europe as superseding either; rather, as entrepreneurs medieval merchants succeeded in completing what were simply potential trading and commercial systems, driven by the wealth and power of the seigneurial elite. Like grass growing in the cracks of a sidewalk, medieval business adapted to conditions not of its own making, yet ultimately succeeded in transforming them. Medieval fairs, cities, money, law – none of them were made-to-order for the growth of business. Yet they all became part of the essential infrastructure leading to the remarkable economic takeoff of the High Middle Ages.

2

TOOLS OF TRADE: BUSINESS ORGANIZATION

•

A tool extends human ability, either literally, as with the familiar hand implements of hammer, saw, and spade, or figuratively, as embodied in human organizations and institutions.[1] All are means to the realization of individual and societal goals by overcoming the limitations of the individual. In the medieval European context, business made use of a vast array of tools. Some, like looms and spinning wheels, were essential to industrial processes; others, like accounting and credit instruments, proved invaluable to the solution of business problems; still others, like the company branch networks and guilds, provided superior organization. But all medieval business tools were shaped by the twin realities of opportunity and constraint and in particular by the need to mitigate constraints on the opportunities to trade. For it was exchange in all its forms that was both the goal and the lifeblood of medieval business enterprise.

What constrained trade? We have seen that medieval business developed in the narrow space between dominant lordship and peasant-based agriculture and that, as the junior partner, business had to accommodate itself to the devices and desires of the others. Senior partners, of course, were the lords, both secular and ecclesiastical, who sought to fulfill divinely ordained roles as fighters or worshipers with scant regard for the pursuit of wealth as an end in itself. And though the lords created a great deal of wealth (largely through the efforts of their peasants), they were often indifferent to the economic effects of their actions. Not surprisingly then, medieval businessmen had to contend with frequently unreliable coinage, seizure of trade goods, forced loans, imposed monopolies, and a host of other evils inflicted on them by their social betters.

In the countryside, moreover, there was the obstacle of a largely tradition-bound agriculture limited by shortcomings in technology and capital. All these left their mark on business tools.

Opportunities, on the other hand, were vast. Despite an indifference to trade per se, neither lords nor peasants were immune to the allure of wealth, as they had proved this with their remarkable expansion of agriculture sketched in the previous chapter. That expansion brought increased possibilities for travel and trade across Latin Christendom. Then, in the late eleventh century, the Latin tide of conquest and colonization made an extraordinary leap to the Middle East in the form of the First Crusade, transporting thousands of warriors and pilgrims to the edge of the then-known world and back again. No one returned unchanged by the experience, nor were their tastes in food, clothing, and other consumer goods unaffected. However, the dazzling initial success of the crusades should not obscure the longer-lasting colonial successes that were achieved over the same period in Britain and Ireland, on the German-Slav frontier, and on the Iberian peninsula.

If opportunity and constraint formed the poles between which medieval business took shape, the expanding borders of western Christendom were its context. Several centuries of intense experimentation and improvisation in search of effective business tools resulted in a host of techniques and forms of organization across Europe and beyond. Traditionally, historians investigating medieval business have oversimplified this profusion by focusing on limited aspects of it and searching out "modern" precursors while largely ignoring the rest. We have departed from this approach by examining, however briefly, a very broad range of business activities, along with a representative sample of the tools of business, all in the historical context out of which they emerged. By so doing, we are able to reveal that medieval business was more unstable, more complex, and more foreign than modern historians have led us to believe.

Paradoxically, however, medieval and modern business are similar in their reliance on the family as the basic business unit. Even today, family businesses account for upwards of 75 percent of all business enterprises in the industrialized countries of western Europe and America;[2] in the Middle Ages the percentages were probably even higher. But this fact obviously understates the complexity of today's business environment, just as it fails to describe commercial reality in the Middle Ages. Already in the thirteenth century, the organization of business varied by trade and was evolving into more complex forms, as producers began to hire labor and forge associations to satisfy expanding markets and meet competition. And in the large trading centers, the resort to written contracts was becoming commonplace and the services of notaries eagerly sought.

The intense family orientation of medieval business shows up most clearly in the intermingling of the affairs of a business and the extended family of its owners that so often appears in the surviving accounts and letters of medieval businessmen. The books of even the largest and most complex companies of the early fourteenth century, such as the Peruzzi Company of Florence, are replete with entries dealing with food, cloth-ing, medical bills, real estate, and dowries of family members and employees. And as late as 1494, Luca Paciolo's famous treatise on book-keeping enjoined readers to include in their records of business assets all their personal possessions, including house, jewelry, clothing, and fur-niture. Modern scholars have sometimes found this attitude difficult to grasp; accounting historians even of the stature of Federigo Melis have described some early bookkeeping systems as "lame," because they jumbled business and household transactions. But like it or not, the separation of business and personal affairs, a feature of today's economic life so encouraged by our legal and tax systems, was alien to medieval thinking at all levels, from royalty on down.

Medieval enterprise encompassed a wide range of activities, each of which developed a distinctive system of organization in response to the opportunities presented by a growing and more sophisticated clientele and to the constraints on trade that had to be overcome. This and the following chapter will review the various kinds of business organization, both urban and rural, that evolved in different parts of Europe from roughly the twelfth to the mid fourteenth century. Our survey will include the artisanal crafts, the industries of textiles, construction, mining, metallurgy, minting, and transportation, and the businesses of trading, international merchant-banking, and tourism. And it will discuss the devices created by businessmen to finesse the constraints imposed on them by their physical and cultural environments.

THE ARTISANS — EVOLUTION OF WAGE LABOR AND GUILDS[3]

The artisanal trades described here are the occupations of specialists who provide goods and services primarily for local consumption — bakers, butchers, blacksmiths, tailors, and cobblers, to name a few. At the sim-plest level, the artisans were self-employed individuals, masters of a trade, drawing on family members for additional labor as needed and training at least one of their offspring to take over the business in due course. When offspring failed to materialize or were untrainable, or business needs expanded beyond the resources of the family, masters sought outside help from two sources.

The first was to find a trainee to fill the family void for the long term. The master entered an apprenticeship contract with the parents or guardian of a minor, agreeing to teach, and usually to feed, clothe, and house the apprentice, who consented to work and learn. Such contracts varied greatly by trade and by location. In some cases, the employer paid a small wage to attract the candidate; in others, the guardian paid a fee to get the appointment. The term was for several years, the exact length of time depending upon location, training needed to acquire the necessary skill, economic conditions, and relationship to the owner. During that time, the master assumed a parental role, with responsibility for the apprentice's morals as well as his education. At the end of the period, the apprentice might be given a small sum or, in certain crafts such as turners and masons, a set of tools. He might then become a master in his own business or go out to work for a wage.

The second source of help was a more immediate and transitory solution to the master's production problem. This was the hiring of wage labor, a practice that had fallen out of use for centuries after the collapse of the Roman Empire. Its revival in the eleventh and twelfth centuries reflected the economic expansion that had begun to take place in western Europe. Hired labor most often was arranged through an oral or written contract with a mature trained person, called a journeyman (literally a day-worker), for a period of several months or even years. Wages, at a daily rate usually paid weekly, depended on the skills of the journeyman and the importance of the work. In some trades, ranging from humble wool carders to skilled armorers, pay was at piece rates. A master could also hire casual labor for specific, usually less skilled jobs, for a few days.

In another important development of the High Middle Ages, masters of the same trade began to form combinations that became known as guilds. Private associations of this type (*collegia*) were common in imperial Rome, but died out by the end of the fifth century. New affiliations of laymen arose in the early Middle Ages, but these were confraternities, formed by people not necessarily of the same occupation, to advance religious or social objectives. The earliest documented case of a craft guild in medieval Europe dates from the twelfth century, but the introduction – or rather the reintroduction – of trade associations probably occurred during the eleventh century. By the thirteenth century, such organizations were well established in cities and towns throughout western Europe, covering not only the artisanal trades discussed here, but also the "industrial" crafts and merchants described later in this chapter. There were great variations from place to place, but no regional patterns differentiated one area from another, even though guilds in northern and southern Europe developed independently.

Broadly speaking, craft guilds arose out of the need for tradesmen to band together to meet the pressure of increasing local and import competition. The guilds were associations of masters, and although they tended toward monopoly, they sought to regulate competition rather than to abolish it. They evolved statutes setting standards and terms of apprenticeship and qualifications for admission as members. They also established criteria for employment of journeymen and their pay scales, determined the observance of no-work feast days, and set quality standards. But usually the crafts and their guilds were also subject to the overriding laws and regulations of the municipality, especially in the foodstuffs trades, where strict rules concerning quality, sanitation, and sometimes pricing were enforced.[4]

Wage rates, daily or piece, varied according to three main criteria – the skill or risk involved in the work, the age and experience of the employee, and the time of year (highest in periods of peak demand for agricultural or seafaring labor, lowest in winter, when competition for labor was least intense and days were shortest). Note that there were no hourly wage rates. Aside from the fact that the low daily wages (3d to 5d, for example, for carpenters in thirteenth-century London) would have made hourly rates ludicrously low, business was not measured in terms of subdivisions of days until the late Middle Ages. The first documentation of time any more precise than a day appeared in a Genoese notary's account of a transaction in 1201 that took place "after compline." Notaries thereafter used the canonical divisions of the day, rather than hours, but interest in hourly time is evidenced by the appearance of outdoor mechanical clocks in several cities in the mid fourteenth century (see also Chapter 7, page 152). Such clocks, however, were incapable of providing reliable time measurement until the fifteenth century, so until then the length of the workday normally ran from dawn until the ringing of the vespers bell. Nonetheless, some recognition of hourly pay is evident in the fact that daily wages were at least partially affected, as noted above, by the seasonal differences in daylight. Night work was uncommon and was often forbidden in trades such as metalworking or weaving, where working in poor light would be dangerous or detrimental to quality.

The artisanal trades of medieval towns were dominated by free Christian males. Slaves did not form part of the labor market, except to an

insignificant extent in some Mediterranean cities; and Jews were largely
barred from all but unpopular or unrewarding trades. The status of
women, however, was less than clear-cut.[5] Adolescent females in English
(less so in Italian) towns commonly left home for service in other
households, usually for their upkeep, occasionally supplemented by a
small wage. But rarely were they apprenticed in skilled trades, and few
became recognized as masters, the silk and brewing industries being
notable exceptions. For the most part, women were confined to occupations requiring little capital, such as spinning, needlework, petty retail-
ing, and laundry work, or as day laborers at wages significantly lower
than those for men. Even where apprenticed, they were likely to spend
much of their time performing household duties, and when married
their occupation was normally determined by that of their husband.
Nevertheless, Christian women were not entirely excluded, and the
daughter of a master could undergo apprenticeship and aspire to succeed
him, especially in occupations with a tradition of female participation,
such as weaving and brewing. Moreover, a master's wife often partnered
him in workshop and trade, and if she became his widow, she typically
had the right to continue to run the business. And, of course, women
played a part in some of the social and religious aspects of guild
activity.

The practice of imposing quality standards differed considerably across
Europe. Mainly they were designed to ensure competence, but often
uniform standards stifled competition and, where overly rigid, even
curbed advances in technology. On the positive side, the standards for
nonfood items applied only to finished product, not to process. Thus
manufacturers remained free to work toward reducing costs through
improved methods. The establishment of recognized yardsticks had
decided commercial advantages, enabling product characteristics to be
identified by the name of the material and the city of origin. Thus "rays
of Ypres," for example, would be known to a buyer as cloth of a
specific length with specific characteristics and quality. Standards were
especially useful in the case of internationally traded products such
as textiles, whose market values were affected by the city of production.
The commercial value of product standards was further buttressed by
the use of trademarks registered with the guild to identify the shop of
origin. In this connection, it must be remembered that many of the craft
trades sold their output directly to the public, so that such craftsmen
were also merchants. But generally speaking, such tradesmen organized
themselves along craft lines and did not belong to the powerful merchant guilds, which were composed mainly of long-distance traders. The
merchant guilds will be discussed in the following chapter.

As associations of mutual support, the guilds were almost invariably also religious confraternities. They followed the teachings of the church and promoted rules of honesty and fair dealing. And although the guilds emphasized aid to their members, they also worked through the church in dispensing charity to the poor in general. Moreover, many guilds had no meeting halls of their own and assembled in parish churches. This practice saved money, added respectability, and reinforced the religious objectives of the guild. And most churches were happy to oblige, as the meetings included prayers as well as business and the relationship brought substantial donations. Each guild had its own patron saint, often that of the church where it met, but sometimes one directly connected with the trade. Examples of the latter included Saint Martin as patron saint of the fullers, Saint Leonard of the coopers, Saint Joseph of the carpenters, and Saint Catherine of the wheelwrights (as she had been martyred by being broken on the wheel).

The guilds thus had a very powerful social component that helped generate solidarity and a strong sense of identity among their members. These attributes were enhanced by celebrating with public display the feast day of the guild's patron saint and honoring with other guilds the many holy days authorized by the church. And such opportunities for public identification were numerous: by the end of the thirteenth century, the church had codified thirty-seven holy days to which Sunday rules applied, in addition to those for local saints.

Overall, the guilds, being by nature exclusive, fostered trust and mutual support within, but hostility toward outsiders, other peoples, other towns. The importance and prestige of guilds varied considerably within each town, depending upon whether their trades were considered "noble" or "base." The criteria affecting this determination included the value of the raw materials, the skills needed to convert them, the wealth of the masters, and the social standing of the customers. The ranking of the guilds was politically significant because in most cities guild officers had a hand in municipal government and could influence public policy. Conversely, urban politics could, and increasingly did, dominate the corporate politics of the guilds. As usual, there was great variety in the ranking and potency of guilds from town to town. In London, for example, the most influential guilds became those involved in the local distribution trade, whereas in Florence those engaged in the textile industry and long-distance trade and finance predominated. But in Paris, the monarchy kept a firm grip on the guilds, forcing them to deal subserviently with its bureaucracy. There participants in vital trades gained royal favor, but had no form of self-rule or lasting political influence.[6]

THE TEXTILE INDUSTRY

At the end of the twelfth century, most textile production in western Europe was still accomplished by rural or urban family-based crafts for domestic or local consumption. But we have already seen in the previous chapter that the growing appetite for competitively priced ready-made goods in the burgeoning cities and the increasing export demand for fine-quality cloth had given rise to the industrialization of the process in certain regions. And this industrialization affected not just the manufacture of cloth in the towns of the Low Countries, southern France, northern Italy, and England. It included the entire process of securing the necessary raw materials from various sources, transporting them to the manufacturing sites, and disposing of the finished goods in markets throughout western Europe and the Mediterranean. The length and complexity of this process required the initiative and resources of well-capitalized merchant adventurers at each stage. By the late thirteenth century, several Italian merchant-bankers had grown large enough to manage and finance this flow of commerce from beginning to end. Much more will be said about them later, but at this point, the discussion will be confined to the urban manufacturing phase.

The organization of the production and marketing of textiles was broadly similar in north and south. The central player in both areas was the small entrepreneur, the master weaver-draper, who managed a "putting-out" system involving several distinct crafts in the town and surrounding countryside. He bought his wool locally or from a wool merchant, and after having cleaned it, put it out to combers and carders and then to spinners. Most of this work was done by women with their own tools in their homes in the nearby rural district, for which they were paid piece rates. The yarn then went to contract weavers, or to employees in the entrepreneur's own shop if he was also a master weaver, and was converted into cloth, again at piece rates. True woolens and certain semiwoolens would again be put out, this time for fulling by contractors who were paid a combination of piece rates and daily wages. The fullers scoured, cleansed, and vigorously stomped upon the cloth in vats of hot water, with the object of compressing and felting it. The fulled cloth, or unfulled lower-grade cloth, finally passed out of the hands of the weaver-draper to finishers or cloth merchants for dyeing and finishing. The compensation of the weaver-drapers came in the form of profit – the difference between the selling price of the unfinished cloth ("grey goods") and the cost of the raw materials and conversion services. Profits were small in spite of the fact that the weaver-drapers organized themselves in potent guilds. Their operations were small-scale, capital investment was modest, risks were low, competition was plentiful, and their end product was for the most part a commodity, not a consumer good.

The professional craftsmen, dyers and shearers, who completed the conversion were highly skilled and well rewarded, earning set fees for their work. At certain places and times, they enjoyed independence and owned their raw materials; at others, they were employees or partners of cloth merchants. In Florence, finisher-merchants of imported grey goods from northern Europe formed the powerful and wealthy Calimala Guild, while finishers of locally manufactured cloth became subsumed into the equally powerful guild of the master weaver-drapers, the *Lana* (Wool) Guild. The final stage of the process, the marketing of the finished product, was controlled by the merchants who operated for profit.

This final stage illustrates one important difference between Italian and northern cloth producers. Whereas in Italy cloth was sold along with other trade goods by merchants who acted as entrepreneurs, in France and Flanders the marketing of cloth was far more specialized. There, production of the cheaper grades of cloth woven from indigenous wool seems to have been in the hands of ordinary weaver-drapers, who operated with little capital, owned at most three or four looms, and sold their product in the town cloth hall. By the early thirteenth century, however, the production of luxury cloth attracted another class of businessman, the so-called merchant-entrepreneur, who purchased the raw materials, hired the labor necessary to process the wool and weave and finish the cloth, and sold the cloth himself. This type of merchant was common only in the cloth centers that featured a luxury product, probably because of the capital requirements inherent in purchasing English wool and paying for the more complex process necessary to produce fine cloth.

There were other differences in textile industry organization from location to location, both north and south, the most significant being that of guild structure. At one end of the spectrum, as in Florence, membership in the woolen and finishing guilds was restricted to master drapers, while the specialized artisans remained unorganized, but subject to guild regulations and discipline. At the other end, as in Verona, specialists such as weavers, dyers, and fullers organized themselves into guilds, whereas the guild of master drapers filled a coordinating role. In between, in localities around Europe, the variety of arrangements seems infinite, although two patterns were emerging. First, in Flanders, the wealthy and influential weaver-drapers never formed a distinct guild, choosing rather to dominate the weavers guild and the other minor cloth guilds. This weaver dominance of the cloth guilds was opposed in Ghent, and to a lesser extent elsewhere, by the fullers, leading at times to riots and near revolution. A second pattern was an increasing tendency of the specialist artisans to form guilds of their own in order to improve their bargaining power with the master drapers. Conversely, in some places the master drapers were determined to keep their guilds distinct from and superior to those of the specialists. The most striking manifestation of this tension was Florence's famous Ciompi Revolt of 1378, as discussed briefly on page 145.

Three technological advances played a significant part in the industrialization of woolen textiles. One was the introduction of the spinning wheel into western Europe in the twelfth and thirteenth centuries. The spinning wheel increased the productivity of wool spinning over the traditional drop-spindle by at least three times, but its use was limited mainly to weft yarns and was banned in many places for spinning warp yarns. A second great advance was the spread of the treadle-operated horizontal loom during the twelfth century, which permitted efficient manufacture of cloths of much greater length and tighter, more uniform weave than the old vertical loom. This was followed in the thirteenth century by the horizontal broadloom, which not only had the desired effect of producing cloth of double width, but also eventually brought weaving productivity to a level not exceeded until the late eighteenth century. The treadle looms, especially the broadloom, which involved two weavers sitting side-by-side operating expensive equipment, effectively transformed much of industrial weaving into an urbanized male-dominated occupation. The reason for this change was not the physical demands of the broadloom, which women could and did master, but rather the substantial investment that drew men into taking a leading role. Women continued to play a part, however, not only where the vertical loom was in use, but also in broadloom weaving, often paired with their husbands.

Both of these great improvements were adaptations of technology originating in the Orient centuries earlier. The third innovation was a true European invention, the mechanization of the fulling process by means of a water-driven fulling mill. Here, the cloth was beaten with great force by heavy trip-hammers operated by a rotating drum. Introduced in northern Italy in the late tenth century, the fulling mill spread gradually into Flanders and other major textile-producing areas of northern Europe by the twelfth and thirteenth centuries. Its primary attraction was significant cost saving. It was a controversial contrivance, however, as the process was believed to produce an inferior product and even to injure fine woolens. Foot fulling therefore continued to be used throughout the Middle Ages for the luxury cloth trade, especially in Flanders, where the fulling mills eventually disappeared.

The discussion of textiles here has focused entirely on woolens, and certainly woolens dominated the trade in medieval Europe. But other cloths were manufactured and marketed in significant volume for a variety of purposes, especially to cater to the need for lighter weight garments in the warmer parts of the continent. Cotton from the Levant and Islamic Africa made significant inroads into Italy, Spain, and southern Germany as a popular material in its own right, as well as in combination with linen or wool. Its uses ranged from candle wicks to ready-to-wear underclothes, to padded doublets, to sailcloth. These were all rapidly growing markets: wax candles provided better light than oil lamps; the aristocracy, and then the common folk, began to appreciate the hygienic attributes of underwear and the comfort and fashion appeal of the doublet. Cotton replaced linen as sailcloth in the Mediterranean not only because it was cheaper, but also because it was more adaptable to the rigging requirements of an increasingly specialized range of ship designs. The manufacture of cotton goods was concentrated in the towns of northern Italy, and its organization was similar to that of woolen textiles, except that the specialist artisans enjoyed greater autonomy, participating more directly in the councils of the overarching cotton or cotton/linen guilds. Those guilds stressed quality control at least as rigorously as did their woolen industry counterparts. Despite the inroads of cotton, linen remained the lightweight cloth of choice in northern Europe throughout the Middle Ages. The production of linen was more like that of woolens, moving from rural to urban centers and becoming organized in a similar manner under small operators. And again, distribution was in the hands of merchant capitalists. Unlike woolens, however, this industry was concentrated mainly in southern Germany and Switzerland.

Finally, two other textiles at opposite ends of the spectrum deserve brief comment. The first is hemp, from which coarse cloth was manufactured mainly in the country for the very poor or for sacking. The notable exception was in Venice, where a lively urban industry produced ropes and rigging under close government control for its great fleets.[7] The second is silk, the luxury fabric, the European manufacture of which was concentrated almost entirely in Florence and Lucca, especially the latter, until the mid fourteenth century. Both of these businesses were very small segments of the textile industry in the thirteenth century, but the production and uses of silk greatly increased in the fifteenth, as will become evident in Part II.

THE CONSTRUCTION INDUSTRY

The High Middle Ages was a period of considerable building activity throughout western Europe in town and country, some of it on a monumental scale. Between 1050 and 1350, some eighty cathedrals, 500 large churches, and 10,000 parish churches were built in France alone. The rapidly expanding towns repeatedly encircled themselves with walls of increasing extent; for example, Florence's third set of walls, completed in the early fourteenth century, enclosed five times the area of its second set, built in the late twelfth century. The second walling of Bruges in 1297 increased that city's extent by six times. Monarchs with increasing resources mobilized large forces of men and materials to project their power into newly-acquired parts of their kingdoms, as in the cases of the construction of the port of Aigues-Mortes by Louis IX in the 1240s, and erection of the numerous Welsh castle-towns by Edward I in the late thirteenth century. And the population boom by itself, especially in the towns, ensured plenty of continuous small-scale building.

All this activity, although impressive by the standards of the early Middle Ages, did not give rise to a coherent, well-capitalized industry; construction remained essentially artisanal in nature. To be sure, there were significant advances in the design and engineering of those monumental structures for defense and worship, but there was little change in the technology of the manufacture and preparation of materials or in the organization of labor. Aside from urgent projects for military purposes, most building proceeded at a leisurely pace. Edward I was able to enforce the mobilization of over 3,000 workers during the peak two or three years of construction of his Welsh castles in the 1280s, but most other projects, even for the great cathedrals, involved work forces of only 100 to 300 artisans and laborers.

The principal building materials were wood and stone. Wood was widely used throughout the north for rural and urban structures, both as the main material and also for supports, roofing, and templates for stone buildings. Over time, wood became less favored for construction, partly because of the hazard of fire in closely packed communities and partly because of its increasing price and scarcity caused by the demand of so many other uses in a rapidly growing population – furniture, ships, carts, and above all fuel. Brick became popular, especially in the later Middle Ages, in regions such as the Low Countries, eastern England, and southern France, where stone was not available locally. Northern Italy, in particular, had a long tradition of building in brick and developed a distinctive brick architecture. And the brick developed in the

Middle Ages was twice as thick as the one-inch Roman brick, making it much sturdier and easier to lay, a forerunner of the type in use today.

Stone was the material of choice for structures requiring attributes of great strength, durability, and prestige. Its main drawback was the high cost of transporting it from quarry to building site. To mitigate this cost, it was common practice to work and dress the stone at the quarry to minimize the size of the piece to be moved. And wherever possible, the stone was moved by water. In one extreme case, a sluice was made to enable the marble from Lake Maggiore to be shipped directly to the moat alongside a new cathedral under construction in Milan.

Small-scale construction was usually contracted by an independent mason or waller who had a wide range of skills and led a small crew of assistants and laborers. Sometimes he supplied labor and materials for an all-in fee for the job, sometimes labor only for a fee that amounted to little more than wage labor or more often just for his own wages. The reason for the frequent resort to a simple wage was a deficiency in the small contractor's ability to make estimates and discipline labor.[8] In effect, these entrepreneurs were little different in function and organization from the artisans discussed earlier in this chapter.

Large-scale and long-lasting projects were different qualitatively as well as quantitatively. They required cooperative effort from several different trades working together under the leadership of an individual qualified to design the building and plan and supervise the construction. They also required large-scale funding and budgetary control under the supervision of an administrator. This man was responsible to the patrons or owners of these projects, who were determined to exercise their influence over design and their control over costs.

The technical manager was usually described as a master mason or master engineer, but in today's terms he would be regarded as an architect with some of the responsibilities of a general contractor or, as Jean Gimpel puts it, an architect-engineer.[9] He was normally responsible for selecting his team, not only of masons but also of the other disciplines, such as carpenters, quarrymen, blacksmiths, mortarmakers, and plasterers. In very large projects, such as the Welsh castle-towns, he also had to see to the timely provision and transport of materials and equipment to the site, and often had quarrying, brickmaking, and timber cutting under his management. But his contract was that of a salaried employee, not a capitalist entrepreneur. The terms were usually generous, often including housing and clothing, with appointment for several years, sometimes for life. The best-known of the early thirteenth-century architects, Villard de Honnecourt, left evidence of his great skill in cathedral design in the form of his fascinating sketchbook. This is especially valuable as no cathedral plans survive. Parchment, being very expensive, was used many times, and the equivalent of blueprints were often drawn on plaster on the floor of a "tracing house."

The administrative manager was a combination works accountant and site director, usually appointed for one year, at the end of which he would submit an account and explanation of expenditures to the owners. In cathedral projects, he was usually a knowledgeable canon, reporting to the canons of the cathedral chapter, who maintained a separate "fabric fund" for the project. His responsibilities often overlapped those of the architect. Robert Clavel, overseer of the accounts of the Church (later Cathedral) of Saint Lazaire in Autun for the year 1294–95, had to arrange the provision and transport of materials for the site and to organize the workmen. He was also required to ensure that religious services could continue without interruption.

The fabric fund was financed from a variety of sources – gifts from regional and local aristocrats and wealthy merchants, contributions of the faithful obtained through bequests, annual subscriptions, fines, and diocesan fund drives, to name a few. Gifts were in kind as well as cash, including labor, timber, stone, and occasionally even entire quarries. Fund drives included tours of the district and even abroad, with cathedral relics and methods of persuasion that would be regarded even today as aggressive. Some were merely enterprising, such as exacting a fee for ringing church bells in Strasbourg during the great funding drives of the mid to late thirteenth century. But others deployed the full spiritual power of the church. These included the highly productive granting of indulgences for relief from required observances, such as abstinence from eating meat during Lent, or reduction of time to be spent in purgatory. A preacher at Amiens in 1260 proclaimed that benefactors would be "twenty-seven days nearer to Paradise than you were yesterday." The fund-raising effort had to be continuous, with the objective of ensuring the steady inflow of money and materials sufficient to keep the work force intact and the construction on schedule. Simply piling up money would not necessarily speed up the project, because the normal optimum size of the total team was about 300 in summer and 100 in winter, when work was limited by short days and adverse climatic conditions.

The craft status of masons was quite different from that of other medieval tradesmen in two significant ways. First, they were of necessity more mobile, obliged to go with their easily portable tools to where the jobs were available, be that in towns or countryside. Second, they were accustomed to the discipline of working in teams, rather than in isolation. As a result, they were slow to form guilds locally, being more interested in developing ties to their brethren around Europe through their lodge organizations. Each major job site would have contained a masons' lodge, which was a combination of workshop and lunchroom where masons gathered to gossip and discuss working conditions, standards, and employment opportunities. Such contacts promoted a sense of solidarity and a uniformity of customs of the craft, and even led to the formation of regional assemblies. But the authority of these associations was vague and, curiously, did not extend to regulating rates of pay. Building records reveal a surprisingly wide range of wages paid to different masons for apparently similar work. Nevertheless, masons who were able to live more or less continuously in one location eventually formed guilds; in larger cities they did so on their own, and in smaller towns they sometimes combined with other crafts of the construction industry.

MINING, METALLURGY, AND MINTING

Europe is generously endowed with widespread deposits of a variety of minerals, many of which have been exploited for centuries, some since antiquity. Stone was quarried in enormous quantities throughout Europe to feed the building boom of the High Middle Ages. Of the major base metals, iron was mined in west central Europe, Italy, Spain, and Sweden, lead in England and Germany, tin in west England, and copper in central Europe and Scandinavia.[10] Coal was available near the surface in many parts of Britain and western Europe. But the precious metals, especially silver, attracted most attention, given the insatiable demand for this commodity in trade with the Levant and the instant rewards to its owners. A succession of silver discoveries between the late twelfth and late thirteenth centuries – Freiberg in Saxony, Friesach in Austria, Montieri in Tuscany, Iglau in Bohemia, Iglesias in Sardinia, and Kutná Hora in Bohemia – was crucial in maintaining Europe's money supply and trade balance with the East until late in the fourteenth century.

Mining in the High Middle Ages was very much a cottage industry, with small scattered operations, little capital, and primitive technology. Mineral rights were the property of the rulers of the territory, overriding the claims of private owners of the land surface. These "regalian rights" over mineral deposits and the system of concessions were broadly similar throughout Europe, whether the rulers were princes, bishops, or towns. A prospector had to request a concession from the officer of the ruler, promising in return to mine the deposit continuously and pay stipulated royalties. In the case of important deposits, the scores of miners and smelters involved formed privileged communities, distinct from the local villages or towns, with their own customs and laws and exemption from ordinary taxation. Overall, miners and smelters enjoyed a degree of independence that attracted the envy of nearby serfs, more than making up for the often disagreeable nature of their occupation.

Extraction of most minerals was close to the surface, by quarrying or digging shallow caves. Shaft mining for silver became general in central Europe only by the end of the thirteenth century and was severely limited by flooding. This problem was partially but inadequately addressed in Bohemia by experimentally digging long adits and developing horse- or water-driven pumps. Smelting too was primitive, characterized by large numbers of small hearths and forges in woodlands near the deposit seams. Larger iron bloomeries began to appear in the fourteenth century, especially in central Europe, but did not become widespread until the end of that century. Silver smelting was more complex and sophisticated, employing by the early thirteenth century water-powered bellows and also water-driven hammers to crush the stone.

Because technological backwardness was the main constraint against exploiting Europe's abundant mineral wealth, the industry ran into hard times in the fourteenth century, as the the more easily accessible discoveries began to play out. But the insistent demand for minerals, especially precious metals, fueled the interest of owner and miner alike in continued prospecting and in promotion of technological improvements, leading to the startling advances of the late Middle Ages.

Minting was, unlike mining, largely urban in character, and was one of the rare medieval "factory" situations where workers were concentrated in a single workshop headed by a licensed moneyer. Formerly these had been small and scattered operations controlled by regional princes or local communities. But as the thirteenth century wore on, minting became increasingly centralized under the close control of more powerful governments. In England all mints were subordinated to the Royal Mint under the supervision of a highly skilled master moneyer in 1279, a consolidation that was completed in 1300 when the Royal Mint moved to the Tower of London. In France, the kings from Philip II to Louis IX gradually standardized coinage into two main types, the denier of Paris, called the *parisis*, and that of Tours, the *tournois*, with a specific relationship between the two. Barons in France continued to mint coins, but the kings increasingly interfered, and in 1263 Louis IX established the principle that royal money be acceptable as legal tender throughout the kingdom. In the larger cities of Italy, where gold coins began to be produced in quantity from the 1250s onward, minting operations were substantial. The largest of all, in Venice, employed at least 100 people, including several moneyers. The objective of putting all these people together in one place, however, was not improved productivity, but rather to safeguard the materials and to control the product standards.

Although numerical evidence is elusive, it is probable that the transportation industry was the largest employer of hired labor in medieval Europe. Many thousands found employment as overland carters, riverboat crewmen, porters, and saltwater seamen, and many thousands more built the vehicles and vessels and provided ancillary services. Transportation of goods and people was indeed a distinct industry, as in most cases the providers of the services owned the facilities and rented them to the users. But because of its scattered nature, the industry was not easily discernible as such, except in the great seaports such as Venice and Genoa.

The business of overland transport was relatively simple and largely local. The main capital investment took the form of horses, wagons, and their accoutrements, and of barges for river traffic. Wheeled commercial cartage was performed by individual wagoners who moved bulk goods such as grain and wine for a fee based on a standard rate per unit carried or a daily rate per vehicle hired. For hauling grain they employed a team of four horses pulling a load of four quarters, but two-horse teams were also used. According to a recently published study, unit cartage costs for grain transport were surprisingly low, but were nonetheless twice as high as river transport for similar goods.[11] Hence, wagoners generally operated over relatively short distances across areas not served by river or canal barges. The movement overland of less bulky, more valuable goods, including textiles, was normally accomplished by trains of pack animals. This was also expensive, entailing the hiring and victualling of horses, attendants, and where necessary armed escorts. And all forms of overland travel attracted tolls from the rulers of the lands through which the goods passed.

Overland transport was nonetheless an important part of the long-distance trade network. The variety of transportation services employed is well illustrated in Francesco Pegolotti's description of the normal routing of wool shipments from London to Florence in the early fourteenth century.[12] After clearing customs and tipping and wining the officials, the merchants' agents had the wool loaded onto a ship destined to Libourne in Gascony. There an innkeeper took charge and arranged payment of carriage and turnpike fees for the overland journey to Montpellier, where another innkeeper saw to the onward transfer to the port of Aigues-Mortes. The wool was again loaded onto a ship for Pisa, where it was placed in rented carts for the journey to Signa, where it was unloaded and reloaded onto carts or barges (depending on the water level of the Arno) for the final lap to Florence. Tolls were levied at various points – no less than three between Pisa and Signa. The innkeepers, known as *osti*, played an important part in this distribution network, providing not only lodging, victualling, and forwarding services, but also assistance in financing and dealing with local officialdom.

Maritime transportation was normally the cheapest means of moving goods and could be big business, especially in the Mediterranean, involving considerable capital outlay and sophisticated organization. This industry divides into three constituent elements – shipbuilders, ship owners, and ship users – despite much overlapping, especially between the latter two. Here, the construction aspect is similar in many ways to the building industry already discussed. It required intelligent design oversight, a variety of specialized tools, and skilled craftsmen working as a team. And here too, construction was subject to sudden surges of demand from princes for war needs and, most notably, for the great crusades. The Fourth Crusade generated frantic activity in the Venetian shipyards at the beginning of the thirteenth century; and Louis IX's ill-fated crusades did the same for Genoa in 1246 and 1268.

For the most part, however, ship construction differed from the building industry in that it was driven almost exclusively by economic forces. Whereas great stone edifices were often erected for reasons of defense, worship, or prestige, ships, even those built for war, were designed to balance the economic objectives of their users – carrying capacity, speed, security, and cost effectiveness. Most design improvements during this period occurred in the north, driven by the need for bulk-carrying round ships (cogs) of increasing size to accommodate the growing trade in wine between Gascony and England and in grain and timber between Poland and western Europe. The builders, mostly private small-scale operators, did their work on beaches near the ports or in small shipyards. The notable exception was, of course, the Arsenal of Venice, owned and operated by the republic, but this facility was initially a storehouse and repair shop and did not undertake construction of the great galleys until its fourfold expansion in the early fourteenth century. And even then, private yards accounted for a considerable share of Venetian shipbuilding.

A large proportion of all vessels built were destined for fishing along the seacoasts and rivermouths of western Europe and the Mediterranean. Most were small boats, literally tens of thousands of them, carrying crews of up to eight men engaged in fishing for local markets. But already in the thirteenth century, some fishermen had become "industrial," catching herring in great quantities along the Scania coast for Hanse merchants who cured the fish, packed them in casks, and shipped them in large cogs to towns throughout western Europe. These shippers found convenient and appropriate return bulk cargo in the form of salt from southern Brittany. More will be said about the great northern fishing trade in the second part of this book.

The owners of most ships other than fishing vessels focused on sailing and managing them for profit as an end in itself, rather than as a means of profitable commerce. To be sure, some owners, or more often part owners, were merchants, but even these regarded the shipping activity as a distinct profit center. In Genoa during the first half of the thirteenth century, ships were financed by issuing shares (*loca*) that were bought, sold, or pledged by individuals from all sectors of society. This system later faded as individuals became wealthy enough to buy entire ships by themselves or in consortia. Some owners bought ships for special purposes such as transporting pilgrims or crusaders, from which they expected a quick return. Profit, of course, was no object for a royal crusader. King Louis IX's bureaucrats set detailed specifications for his ships and paid the price – more than £7,000 Genoese, compared to £2,000 for a normal ship of comparable design and size. (The $150 toilet seat of Pentagon fame has a long history!)

Genoese shippers employed an innovative system to set rates for long-distance journeys. Because they expected to earn their profits on rich return cargoes, shipowners allowed merchants free outbound freight on all but very heavy or bulky products, if they guaranteed return cargoes of specified amounts. And those who carried a stipulated minimum cargo could enjoy free passage for their persons. On long trips involving many ports and wintering over, the contracts were extraordinarily complex, covering rates, terms of the voyage, ports to visit, and return cargo guarantees. The need for so many carefully drawn contracts had much to do with Genoa's unusually large and prosperous notarial profession. And monitoring contractual performance necessitated at least one scribe-accountant as part of the ship's crew on most long-distance voyages in the Mediterranean. He recorded in the voyage book the contracts with the merchants and the crew, weights and values of goods loaded and unloaded, receipts, disbursements, allocations of costs among the participating merchants, and settlement of claims.

On short trips, or in relatively safe waters, most ships sailed alone, especially if their cargoes were of low value, with voyages timed to suit their owners or clients. Ships with rich cargoes and distant destinations, however, were often organized in convoys to achieve better protection at reasonable cost. The Venetians developed a highly sophisticated convoy system for their great galleys trading in the East. Timetables were stipulated by the Senate in coordination with the movements of other fleets, and ship's masters were obliged to obey the orders of the flotilla commander, a salaried official of the commune. And in areas or times of exceptional risk, the commune would deploy its own ships manned by its own personnel and collect the profit from the venture.

The ability to make such complex dispositions of shipping owed much to the increasing use of the technological innovations of the latter half of the thirteenth century, described by Frederic Lane as the "medieval nautical revolution."[13] These improvements, which included the construction of marine charts and the development of the box compass and traverse table, all contributed to the new art of dead reckoning. By providing better knowledge of position and direction, dead reckoning permitted more deepwater sailing and extended the sailing season into the late winter months. The gradual spread of these innovations significantly broadened the scope and reduced the cost of marine transportation at a time when the demand for this service was reaching its peak.

It may be worthwhile at this point to add a word about the literacy of medieval businessmen. Sophisticated literacy and numeracy are two essential tools in modern business, but precisely when they became widely available in the Middle Ages is uncertain. One complicating factor is that the custodians of the written word throughout the Middle Ages were members of the clergy, whose definition of literacy demanded the ability to read, write, and speak Latin, a skill that required years of intense study. As for the disciplines of measuring and counting – geometry and arithmetic – these occupied a relatively minor place, along with astronomy and music, among the seven subjects of the traditional clerical curriculum of the medieval grammar school and university. Thus according to the clergy, nearly all medieval merchants and artisans – not to mention most aristocrats – were illiterate, as the German economic historian Werner Sombart argued seventy years ago.

Most of the artisans and "industrial" workers described so far were indeed illiterate by any standard, but medieval merchants rapidly recognized the value of literacy in their businesses, a point emphasized by the historians Henri Pirenne and Armando Sapori. Merchants, however, did not require mastery of a dead language or the subtleties of dialectical argument, but rather the ability to read and write vernacular languages and to grasp the basic elements of mathematical calculation. As a result, in most European cities of the twelfth century, schools were established to teach the basics of a merchant education – a movement that did not go uncontested by the clergy, who felt their monopoly on education to be threatened. Eventually compromises were reached that allowed either school attendance or home tutoring for children bound for careers in trade. But city accounts and many business documents continued to be kept in Latin until the mid thirteenth century, a fact that required either employment of clerically trained scribes or training in Latin for at least some merchants. In southern Europe this need for Latin documents was largely met by civic notaries or notaries public, who in twelfth-century Genoa and elsewhere became essential drafters of business documents of all kinds. In the north, notaries never fulfilled this role, except in places with colonies of foreign merchants such as Bruges; and even there demand for written documents was not very great before 1250. Thereafter, most records were kept in the vernacular, and it is safe to say by the fourteenth and fifteenth centuries, the majority of men and women of the merchant class in Europe could read and write, often in more than one language. We will be discussing this group in some detail in the following chapter.

3

TRADERS AND THEIR TOOLS

·

Most of the business occupations described in Chapter 2 are suscepti-
ble to easy isolation and identification. But the people who made many
of those occupations possible, the merchants, are more difficult to define.
They can readily be described as mainly urban-dwelling, profit-seeking
traders of goods; but this assessment, although broadly accurate, fails to
do justice to the great range of endeavor and status encompassed by this
profession. At the local level, some merchants were among the artisans
discussed earlier who sold their produce to the public. Others were professional middlemen, buying goods, often at local and regional fairs, for
resale; and still others carried merchandise on their backs as peddlers to
customers in the countryside. Then there were the long-distance merchants, some of whom shepherded products back and forth along the
overland trade routes, while others embraced the extreme financial and
physical hazards of maritime ventures; and finally, there were the sedentary merchant-bankers who masterminded a complex flow of goods and
money from their headquarters. These various kinds of endeavor entailed
differing levels of intelligence, capital investment, and risk management.

THE MERCHANT "CLASSES"

The wealth and status of merchants varied according to these categories
and to the status of the products in which they dealt ("noble" or "base").
The international traders in luxury goods were generally at the top of
the heap, and the itinerant peddlers of household goods at the bottom.
But the culture of the towns in which they lived also mattered. The
successful merchants of the great Mediterranean trading ports enjoyed

great prestige and formed the governing elite. In inland Italy and in Flanders the landed nobility initially were somewhat contemptuous of trade, but before long overcame their distaste and participated success-fully in it. In the feudal societies of northern Europe, however, the mer-chant class was held by both the nobility and the church to be clearly inferior. Indeed, the idea that being "in trade" is undignified has per-sisted in northern Europe into the twentieth century.

These cultural attitudes are important, because they influenced the continuity of family businesses at least as much as did the competence of the members of succeeding generations. In northern Europe, the suc-cessful merchant was likely to invest his wealth in land, leave his busi-ness, and marry his offspring into the landed gentry. In one of the more striking examples, the de la Poles of Hull cheerfully deserted their great enterprise for the earldom of Suffolk. Merchants in Italy and Flanders retained their urban connections but tended to lapse into a landhold-ing rentier status. As a result, a family business would typically die with its founder, and the name might only reappear a generation or two later when a new entrepreneur in the family established a completely differ-ent company. The same phenomenon of disappearance and reappearance occurred also among the long-lasting firms of famous families, such as the Frescobaldi and Peruzzi. But the wealthy merchants of Venice and Genoa proudly continued their involvement in the commerce of their cities, generation after generation.

By the thirteenth century, merchants of all kinds had proliferated in the growing market towns throughout northern Europe and the western Mediterranean, and some of them dominated the port cities of Venice, Pisa, and Genoa. The latter three had become large and powerful towns trading aggressively throughout the western Mediterranean, North Africa, the Levant, and the Black Sea. They were joined by other con-tenders, such as Barcelona, Palermo, Marseilles, and later the inland towns of north central Italy. All of these participated in the develop-ment of the famous Champagne "fairs" of the thirteenth century that was traced at the end of Chapter 1. Meanwhile, in the far north, mer-chants from the towns of northern Germany, led by Lübeck, began to dominate Baltic Sea commerce, including the lucrative trade route between Novgorod and Bruges, overshadowing the Swedish town of Visby, which had been the leading Baltic commercial center in the twelfth century.

So far, the discussion has dealt with merchants in general, albeit with greater emphasis on the long-distance traders. In fact, little more needs to be said about the organization of local-level merchants, even though they outnumbered the international traders in most cities by a wide margin. For the most part, they were either artisans, already discussed, or petty traders organized in much the same way. And like the artisans, they were mainly individuals or family firms associated with similar units in a guild. Also, not much is known about itinerant peddlers, who by their nature were independent operators in the countryside. But one important group of local merchants does deserve attention, the distributors in the food industry – butchers, millers, fishmongers, and grain merchants.

These distributors operated at both wholesale and retail levels. In small market towns, landowning peasants or stewards from nearby manors often engaged in informal trading, and women also participated as retailers of poultry, dairy products, and ale. But in the larger towns, professionals predominated. The mid thirteenth century was marked by a sharp increase in municipal regulation of these merchants, necessitated partly by the fact that many towns had outgrown their local food resources, and partly by the extreme sensitivity of the population to the availability of quality food supplies at an acceptable price. The food-distribution guilds were held to be inadequate to this task. In France, for example, municipalities channeled the distribution of fresh fish through public brokers to ensure a fair allocation of supplies. In the larger towns of England, controls were enforced by royal ordinances or charters, whereas in Italy the municipal authorities endowed special commissions with the responsibility for managing food supply and overseeing the relevant trades. The *Biadaiolo* that governed the grain markets of Florence even employed spies to check on the traders. And failure of the commissioners to perform could be hazardous; during the famine of 1329 in Siena, mobs rioted, killed four officials, and made off with the grain stores.

ORGANIZATION OF INTERNATIONAL TRADE

The long-distance trade of medieval Europe was essentially demand-driven. The prime objective of merchants engaged in this activity was to seek imports that they knew would be attractive to their local customers. Initially they did not look for outlets for exports of local produce to foreign markets, but as they gained experience, they began to see opportunities for two-way trade. As has been noted in the section on transportation, traders such as the Genoese expected that the bulk of their trade and profit would be in imports, but they did encourage exports by offering free or reduced passage outbound.

We have already seen that the producers of trade goods, such as textiles, essentially worked for a wage or a modest profit. The merchants

who furnished the raw materials, supplied most of the capital, and marketed the product gained profits commensurate with the risks. For local
sales the risks were manageable, mainly those inherent in anticipating
consumer preferences and judging the state of the market. But the added
risks of foreign sales – losses due to transportation mishaps, currency
exchange fluctuations, and political uncertainties, in addition to the
problem of discerning consumer preferences in the foreign locations –
warranted more attractive rewards. Moreover, most merchandise in international trade moved on consignment, so that the eventual selling price
could never be known in advance. The risks were such that for most of
the thirteenth century, merchants felt obliged to accompany their goods,
facing the danger not only of robbery, but also of physical assault on
their persons. But the rewards were well worth the hazards, and the
merchants became increasingly prosperous as the century wore on. And
prosperity quickly converted into power. The merchants became the
towns' capitalists, financing industry and acting as money changers as
well as lenders. The power of the merchants' guilds grew with the wealth
of their members and eventually enabled the merchants to dominate the
town councils. Florence provides an excellent example in the 1290s,
when the wealthy merchant class, the *popolo grasso* (fat people), effectively disbarred the old nobility from municipal office and assumed
control of the city government for several decades.

Much has been written about the transition from the itinerant to the
sedentary merchants in connection with the decline of the Champagne
fairs around the end of the thirteenth century. This metamorphosis
involved the establishment of permanent agencies or branches in the
northern cities of Bruges, Paris, and London by Italian merchants from
Tuscany and Lombardy, enabling them to conduct business from their
headquarters instead of accompanying their merchandise on trips north.
Raymond de Roover attributed this change to superior business organization, made possible by new long-term partnership agreements,
new techniques of accounting and control, and new instruments of
exchange.[1]

De Roover aptly pointed out that the transition was gradual, evolving over the latter half of the thirteenth century. But he and others seem
to have put the cart before the horse in attributing the change to superior business organization and new techniques. Evidence from the Italian
cities strongly suggests that the superior organization and techniques
were a response to another problem – the compelling need for the
owners of the businesses to be in their home cities to protect their interests and to influence the political decisions affecting their enterprises.
From the middle of the thirteenth century onward, the inland Italian

cities were in turmoil, divided by local and papal-imperial struggles into Guelf and Ghibelline factions. Florence, in particular, suffered from this tumultuous ebb and flow of events, as first one faction, then another predominated. These events are all well known to medieval historians, as is the fact that businessmen were principal actors on both sides of these dramas, and that members of the same families often served opposing camps. But economic historians seem to have overlooked the obvious conclusion that this was no time for successful merchants to be on the road protecting their merchandise, when a higher priority was the defense of their homes and businesses. Then, during the reconciliations of the 1280s, the important merchants became deeply involved in city politics, requiring their continued presence at home. Over the succeeding sixty years, the top businessmen were preoccupied with government affairs and with ensuring that government policy, both internal and foreign, advanced their commercial interests. It was therefore essential that throughout this entire period they remain in their home cities, not tucked away in their counting houses (as is often cited) but moving about in the city, maintaining close contact with their colleagues in business and government. And that, for the most part, is what they did.

The first order of business in making this "sedentary" system effective was to find and train competent and above all trustworthy personnel to represent the firm in the foreign locations. Because of the importance of trust, the appointees were often family members or, if none were available of adequate quality, more distant relatives by blood or marriage, or close associates of the family. In many cities, such representations expanded into full-fledged branches managed by experienced partners or subordinates. Initially, personnel were also selected to accompany the merchandise until satisfactory transport networks and reliable innkeepers at appropriate intervals could be organized. And even well into the fourteenth century, young trainees, such as the chronicler Giovanni Villani, or factors (i.e., salaried employees) being transferred to a branch, would accompany cargoes of high value.

Once the right people were in place, the new techniques followed. The most obvious and immediate need was for a more elaborate scheme of accounting to keep control over multiple transactions executed in multiple locations, so that the owners at the head office could understand the business as a whole. But the key innovation was the bill of exchange, which permitted the transfer of money from place to place without the high cost and hazard of shipping actual specie. Both of these changes will be discussed more fully later in the chapter.

Merchant reputation and trust were the foundation of the commercial revolution of western Europe.[2] The use of a paper transfer rests upon the confidence of all parties to a transaction that the others will honor their commitments. Reinforcing this confidence was the fact that virtually all of the agents of the Italian companies residing abroad were Italians, usually from the same city and often from the same "extended family" as the principal. Such representatives had much more to lose than a local person from a breach of trust. And the new accounting techniques provided additional security against malfeasance: one of the main advantages of double-entry bookkeeping is that it makes cheating more difficult.

The new system suited the large inland Italian firms very well, and they extended its use to their operations throughout the Mediterranean, where they also set up branches. But because their organization and techniques are more like our own, historians have tended to describe them as "advanced" and those of northern Europeans as "archaic" and inferior. In making such judgments, we should take care to remember that the Hanse, Flemish, and English merchants were intelligent and resourceful and conducted their business in a way that made sense to them. It is inconceivable that these men could have remained unaware of the Italians' operating concepts through centuries of dealings with them.[3] In particular, the Hanse merchants' "backward" way of doing business – accompanying their merchandise and avoiding bills of exchange – seems to have helped keep foreigners from breaking into their trade. It is also worth noting that the merchants of Genoa and Venice, who helped pioneer double-entry accounting and sophisticated financial techniques, did not adopt the Tuscan form of organization but continued to achieve excellent results with single-venture partnerships, described later in this chapter.

The organization of business in international trade was in many ways similar to that described for artisans, with individuals or immediate families as the typical business unit. This pattern of numerous small entrepreneurs was a persistent feature throughout the Middle Ages; even in early fourteenth-century Florence, where the mighty super-companies flourished, there were hundreds of small merchant enterprises. The merchants of course formed their own guilds, many of which became extremely powerful and dominated municipal politics. But these individual units were often also part of a more informal but highly effective "extended family" of interests. The extended family could be narrowly defined by kinship, but was often expanded to include distant family relations by blood or marriage, as well as associates and mere fringe hangers-on. This latter description applies to Genoa's Guercio clan, which was in effect a power bloc that attempted to manipulate political forces for the benefit of the group.[4] Venice had similar extended family blocs, but these tended to work together for an equitable distribution of political favors and to keep any one group from securing a dominant position.

The extended family blocs described here were essentially business-oriented. The Guercio clan actually had a specific business agenda, the promotion of trade with Byzantium, which other groups regarded as too risky. And such blocs were valuable in providing their members a source of men of proven skill and loyalty to undertake overseas business ventures. These blocs, however, should not be confused with the widespread political factions, such as the Guelfs and Ghibellines of Italy and the Blacks and Whites of Florence. Such factions were complex, frequently changing mixes of participants, motivated by papal/imperial and local politics along with inter- and intrafamily vendettas. But although businessmen usually acted in concert with other members of their lineage in such matters involving family prestige and power, they tended to choose their partners in commerce on the basis of resources, trust, and talent, rather than kinship. The larger firms formalized their extended families by creating companies, in which capable kinfolk and associates became shareholders or employees.

What did the international merchants do? The answer is "just about anything that would turn a profit." To illustrate this point, there appears in Pegolotti's *pratica* under the rubric "spices" imported from the East no fewer than 288 items, including threads, waxes, rock candy, glue, elephant tusks, tin sheets, and asphalt, in addition to the seasonings, dyestuffs, perfumes, and medicinals that one would expect.[5] The most important of these by far were pepper and ginger. Other typical imports from the East were silks and other luxury cloths, and jewelry; and one must not overlook the large shipments of alum, important to the textile industry as a fixative for dyes. And it should be remembered that "international" in medieval Europe would have meant any trade outside a town's immediate vicinity. Thus Milan, Siena, and Pisa, for example, would have been "foreign" to Florence – and, indeed, each had its own currency. Many towns had to import basic foodstuffs – grains, meats, dairy products, and fish – from near and far, as their populations outgrew the local resources. Wool, linen, cotton, and hemp were also imported into the textile manufacturing towns mentioned earlier. As for exports, merchants shipped considerable tonnage of grains, wine, wool, fish, salt, base metals, military equipment, and timber within western Europe. But their exports to the great markets of the eastern Mediterranean and beyond in the thirteenth century were unimpressive. Sales consisted of small quantities of fine woollen and linen cloths, saffron, northern furs, minerals, metals, and timber. These minor shipments were vastly out-matched in value by the imports, producing a deficit that was made up largely by silver bullion and coin.

There is no doubt that this imbalance in normal trade goods between West and East was both significant and persistent throughout the Middle Ages. Macroeconomic data are very scarce in the thirteenth and four-teenth centuries, but all surviving documents point unambiguously to continuing deficits of very large amounts. For example, Genoese customs figures for 1376–7 on trade with the Levant show total imports and exports in Genoese pounds of 626,200 and 248,500 respectively. But economic historians have seized on these undeniable facts and applied to them modern macroeconomic terminology, such as "balance of payments deficits," which are inappropriate and confusing. In modern economies, such deficits are carefully monitored and result in future claims on the resources of the deficit country – executed by means of purchases of goods and services, or investments in real estate and busi-nesses – and in IOUs in the form of government securities. No such "balances" were recorded or even considered in European trade with the East. Each trading venture was complete and discrete in itself. In fact, as John Day has perceptively noted, most trade with the East was essentially an exercise in barter. But the term "barter," which is a direct exchange of goods for goods, is inadequate to describe this kind of commerce.

The kind of business conducted in the Mediterranean is much better defined as "countertrade," in which exchange is indirect, the money value of goods is understood, and markets exist. In countertrade, the parties are prepared to engage in a series of exchanges, each one of which may or may not be profitable, as long as the venture as a whole is successful. This approach was commonly used by modern Western firms in dealing with communist countries in the 1960s and 1970s. In the medieval version, each venture involved a series of exchanges that included cash transactions, direct trades, and indirect trades. Western merchants carried with them goods, including precious metals, which they expected to trade for other goods, moving from port to port until they had a cargo that would yield a handsome profit when sold back in western Europe. Voyages from Genoa usually included many stops along the way, especially in western North Africa, where, in exchange for European manufactured goods, wine, olive oil, and imitation silver half-dirhem coins, merchants obtained cheap Sudanese gold. This metal, in both unminted and minted forms, was then carried to eastern Mediterranean ports, where it was traded for the luxury goods and raw materials much desired in the West. In the case of Venice, merchants exchanged merchandise of all kinds for bullion and other metals from central Europe specifically for reexport to the East.

In contrast to the quasi-barter nature of commerce between western Europe and the East, trade within western Europe was decidedly on a monetary basis, with purchases and sales carried out in the currency of the polities concerned. This situation gave considerable scope for bankers and money changers to deal with the risks of exchange-rate fluctuations, a role usually filled by international merchants. It also permitted the use of bills of exchange and paper transfer instruments to avoid the costs and risks of moving specie from place to place. Such instruments had limited use in trade with the East, where the precious metals involved were to a large extent merchandise.

TOOLS FOR MANAGING RISK

The financial and administrative tools used by thirteenth-century businessmen varied from nonexistent to sophisticated, according to the size of the business and the needs of each trade. At the artisanal and small trading firm level, such tools were rudimentary at best, as most businesses in these categories ran on a day-to-day cash basis, routinely mixing personal and operational transactions. The industrial entrepreneurs, despite having to buy materials, pay for labor, and sell their products on a larger and more complex scale, used few financial techniques other than the minimum needed to permit a reasonable grasp of income and expense for each batch of product. Construction costing was also mostly rudimentary, except for large projects where we have already noted the careful recording of income and expenses and the discipline of annual budgets. But these were primarily reporting and control devices not unlike those employed by rural estates and governments.

Although international trade constituted a relatively small portion of total commercial activity in thirteenth-century Europe, it was the international merchants who spearheaded the development of the techniques that transformed medieval commerce. They had perceived rich opportunities for profit in long-distance trade and constantly sought new means to overcome constraints and turn opportunity into reality. To this end, they developed a range of devices designed to increase the availability of capital by spreading risk and improving deployment. The earliest techniques appeared in Genoa and Venice during or even before the twelfth century and focused on risk dispersal. We have already seen how the hazards of ship ownership were diluted through shareholdings or consortia. Another way in which the merchants shared risk was by means of maritime partnership and loan contracts.

The typical partnership contracts are likely to have been adapted from those long in use among Islamic traders in North Africa (the word "risk" is believed to be derived from the Arabic *rizq*). They appeared under a variety of names, the best known of which were the *commenda* and the *societas maris*. Both were single-venture agreements between an investing partner who stayed at home and a traveling partner who accepted the personal challenge of the sea venture. In the *commenda*, the investor put up all the money and received three quarters of the profit; in the *societas maris*, he invested two thirds of the money and the traveler one third, with profits (or losses) split fifty-fifty. Such partnerships, with liability limited to the sums invested, proved to be excellent vehicles for attracting both capital and ambitious young men into long-distance commerce. A different kind of contract was the sea loan, whereby the investor lent funds to a venture merchant, charging a high premium, but with repayment of principal and premium contingent on the safe arrival of the cargo. Here, the traveler took the normal commercial risks of the venture, while the investor accepted the hazards of shipwreck or piracy for a set fee. In effect, the contract was a combination loan (usually secured by a lien on the traveler's property) and insurance policy. These examples are simple "plain vanilla" versions to illustrate the contract structures. In practice, both partnerships and loan contracts took a bewildering variety of forms, carefully drawn up by notaries, attesting to a remarkable degree of flexibility and ingenuity on the part of all concerned. Moreover, a traveler might deal simultaneously with both types of contract on the same voyage, and both investor and traveler could be involved in opposite roles in different contracts at the same time![16]

Marine insurance, in the normal sense involving underwriters, developed much more slowly. In Venice, the need for insurance was mitigated by the fact that most goods of high value were carried in fast, well-defended galleys; insurance contracts, mainly for round ships and their cargoes, did not become common until well into the fourteenth century. Genoa was the acknowledged center in insurance underwriting, but most of the early examples were in the form of disguised loans. On rare occasions, the large merchant companies of inland Italian cities might insure special cargoes for others, but the port cities dominated this line of business. After all, they were in the best position to control the risks that they covered, at least with regard to war and piracy. Insurance of overland cargoes was even slower to develop. Most of the larger international merchant companies assumed the risk for their own merchandise in overland shipments, but occasionally insured others for a fee. These firms, with their innkeeper networks, political connections, and trading experience, were best able to assess and manage such risks.

The thirteenth century saw not only a surge in the growth of long-distance trade, but also a significant enlargement of the areas participating in it. Most notable were the towns of north central Italy, whose merchants developed a number of new risk-management and capital deployment systems. The first of these was the long-term business partnership or company, which would run not for a single venture but for several years, the length of time determined by the partners or shareholders. This form of organization was a partnership in the sense that each partner was subject to unlimited personal liability in case of bankruptcy. It was a recognizably modern company in that it was based on share ownership, with each owner contributing a specific amount of money and sharing in profit or loss pro rata. It had corporate by-laws, a company seal, and a set of accounts. It was sometimes strictly a family firm, and sometimes included nonfamily shareholders, but always bore the name of the founding family. There were literally hundreds of such firms in each of the towns of thirteenth-century Italy; most were small, but several were of significant size, and some became very large indeed. All helped expand international trade by offering their expertise and by mobilizing substantial cash from investors and minor traders, in addition to their own contributions.

Probably the best known management device used by almost all organizations of substance was bookkeeping, and the system most commonly employed was single-entry accounting, also known as charge and discharge or stewardship accounting. Feudal manors and governments recorded income, expense, and the settlement of obligations, sometimes in narrative form with figure references, sometimes in separate lines for each category, and sometimes in separate lines with figures in columns. Merchants everywhere used single-entry throughout most of the thirteenth century and well beyond for controlling individual ventures. This form of bookkeeping had the advantage of providing at low cost a rational basis for decision making. It had the disadvantages, however, of not providing profit measurement automatically and not distinguishing between capital and revenue. Most important, it made concealment of fraud easy, creating the need for frequent audits and other antifraud devices.

In the late thirteenth century, as the international merchants of the port and inland cities of Italy faced increasingly complex transactions in more and more locations, they found they needed a system that would improve control. The concept of double-entry bookkeeping evolved when accountants noticed that the receipt of cash involved two entries, a discharge in the account of the debtor and a charge in the record of the cashier, permitting the establishment of cross-references. By 1300, the use of the prefixes *dove avere* and *dove dare* distinguished positive entries (cash receipts) from negative entries (cash payments). The new system spread rapidly among the Italian firms and by the early fourteenth century had reached a sophisticated level of development in the larger companies. Scholars have debated whether or not this was "true" double-entry accounting as we define it today, but the important point is that it satisfied to a large extent the pressing needs of the international businesses. It demanded greater care and accuracy by the clerks, providing arithmetic checks from periodic balancing, and it permitted the division of labor among several clerks of varying qualifications. It provided balance-sheet data, separated capital from revenue accounting, and introduced useful concepts such as accruals and depreciation. Above all, it gave the owners of the enterprise a much-improved system of control. But it is important to note that double-entry bookkeeping was far too ponderous to play the revolutionary role often attributed to it in *managing* the business. It had no advantage then, as now, over single-entry in assessing the merits of a business proposition.

TOOLS FOR LUBRICATING TRADE: MERCHANT-BANKING AND THE BILL OF EXCHANGE

One of the most pervasive problems besetting medieval business was the rigidity of the money supply, and some of the most creative innovations in medieval business were directed at alleviating that problem. In the thirteenth century, money in circulation was overwhelmingly in the form of minted coins. Lower-value coins might be regarded as at least partially fiduciary in character, as they were struck from base metals or from alloys (billon) containing small amounts of silver. Although the quantity of such coins was significant, their total value as a proportion of all coins in circulation was modest. In effect, most of the money in use was represented by coins of intrinsic value, made primarily of silver and also, from the middle of the thirteenth century, of gold. The money supply was therefore profoundly affected by physical phenomena associated with precious metals – the production of mines, losses from wear and hoarding, diversion into objects of art, and constant exports to the East. The economies of western Europe could afford the syphoning off of the great quantities of specie as long as mining production was sustained at a high level. In fact, these forces not only stimulated trade, but also reduced inflationary pressures. But when mining production

declined while heavy exports continued, Europe experienced the defla-
tionary effects of the repeated "bullion famines" of the fourteenth and
fifteenth centuries that will be discussed in Part II.

Businessmen were happy to move precious metals from place to place
as export commodities or as materials for minting, because these were
profitable transactions. Moving coins as money, however, was a business
cost that added no value to the transaction. The cost of transport, armed
guards, and tolls was significant; for example, the charge for moving
specie from Naples to Rome could range between eight and twelve
percent of the value of the bullion being moved. Even transferring
money within a town was tiresome and wasteful, given the need to
verify the worth of each coin. The earliest financial inventions were
therefore designed to avoid this need by arranging paper transfers.

It is generally agreed among historians that medieval banking owed
its origins not to moneylenders and pawnbrokers, but to money changers. And most money changing was actually performed by certain
merchants as a natural subspecialty of their main line of business. These
people possessed the equipment and skills to assess the weight and fineness and hence the values of a daunting variety of coins of differing
quality. In this capacity, they performed the useful service of bringing
some sort of order into a coin-dominated economy. They also provided
profitable service to governments as the main suppliers of bullion and
used coins to the mints. Their superior knowledge of bullion prices and
exchange rates of foreign currencies gave them commercial advantage
over their fellows, but also imposed an obligation for fair dealing. The
money changers who acquired the requisite reputation began to attract
deposits of specie for safekeeping, recording the assessed value in their
books in terms of a standard unit of account. As the number of accounts
multiplied, the depositors began to use them to settle payments.

In this manner, merchant money changers gradually became merchant-bankers, executing payments not by issuing checks, but by transferring charges and credits in the accounts of their clients. This was the
so-called giro system (from the Italian *girare*, to rotate) still in use in
Europe today. The system worked smoothly because the bankers and
their merchant clients knew each other and gave their instructions orally
at the banker's table, so that the entries could be made on the spot.
The personal nature of the business and the fact that the banks also
took deposits for safekeeping inevitably led to the extension of credit
by means of overdrafts. But creation of credit in this manner, that is, by
a bank's use of fractional reserves, appears to have been limited to close
associates of the bank. Fractional reserves were illegal in most towns,
being regarded as an abuse of public trust. Recent data indicate that,

relative to the scale of total commercial activity, the availability of bank deposits as credit was modest in Venice and miniscule in Florence, and did little to expand the money supply until the late Middle Ages.[7]

The most important financial innovation of the High Middle Ages was the bill of exchange, which combined three attributes of great value to international merchants who traded within western Europe. It avoided the cost of transporting specie, it provided a practical mechanism for international credit and currency exchange, and it finessed the church's prohibition against usury (to be discussed later in this chapter). In addition, it facilitated the one-way trade of merchants specializing in certain commodities such as textiles. The earliest version of this new device is believed to be a notarized exchange instrument that made its appearance in Genoa late in the twelfth century. Stated in its simplest terms, medieval bills of exchange made it possible for one party to receive a sum of money in one currency in one place on one date and repay it in another currency at another place at a later date. The transaction involved four parties, the borrower and lender in the town of issue and the borrower's correspondent (the payor) and the lender's representative (the payee) in the town of repayment. The difference in dates, called "usance," normally reflected the generally accepted time required to move goods between the two locations, such as sixty days between Venice and Bruges and ninety days between Venice and London; or it could also be a negotiated figure. The bills themselves, however, could move much more quickly. Also negotiated were the exchange rates, with the objective of giving the issuer a reasonable profit on the deal. The lender's representative might be instructed to use the foreign exchange to buy merchandise, or to convert it into the lender's own currency by raising a new bill in the opposite direction. During this entire process, the lender was vulnerable to exchange-rate fluctuations, so that his final profit might be considerably more or less than predicted.

The bill of exchange is essentially a European invention, notwithstanding claims that it has an Islamic antecedent in the *suftaja*. This latter instrument is sometimes referred to as a bill of exchange, but is much closer to a letter of credit, as payment and redemption are in the same currency.[8] Bills of exchange attained widespread use during the thirteenth century and evolved into a variety of versions of increasing complexity. Their original stimulus came from the Champagne fairs, but their use continued to increase after the decline of the fairs in the late thirteenth century. Although merchants of cities throughout western Europe (excluding Germany and Scandinavia) participated in the exchange network, the Italians dominated it. By establishing branch offices in many of the cities, they effectively reduced the number of parties per transaction from four to two. But the use of bills did not actually create credit or increase the supply of money, because the bills were not discountable. They did, however, make much more efficient use of the existing supply of coin by advancing the dates on which business transactions could be accomplished and by avoiding the cost and potential wastage of specie in transit. And although the bill of exchange was primarily an invention by merchants for merchants, it was not a merchandise but rather a currency transaction, secured by the assets of the drawer. And its advantages were enjoyed not only by merchants but also by the great institutions of church and government.[9]

The letter of credit was another instrument of finance that flourished in the Middle Ages. Banks sold them to pilgrims, traveling businessmen, students, churchmen, and diplomats, who paid for them in advance like modern traveler's checks. They could be issued redeemable by the issuer, or by a named beneficiary, or to order. This was another device that did not add to the money supply, as the advance paid by the purchaser was a short-term deposit that had to be available on demand.

No treatment of business tools of medieval Europe would be complete without mention of those ubiquitous devices, the abacus and the tally. Both have their roots in antiquity; indeed, evidence of the tally dates back to prehistoric times. The medieval version of the abacus was a counting checkerboard that came in a variety of forms with counters of varying sizes, shapes, and colors representing different items and quantities. The abacus was simply a calculating machine – and a very efficient one, in the hands of a skilled operator – about which nothing more need be said here. The tally, although merely a recording device, acquired some complex characteristics that deserve special attention.

In its simplest form, the tally is a stick with notches scored on it to indicate quantities of goods, money, or time. The more sophisticated version widely used in medieval Europe was the split tally, usually made of hazel or willow rods that split easily. They were notched and often written upon, then split into unequal lengths, with the longer piece (the stock) kept as a receipt by the donor of money or goods and the shorter (the foil) kept by the receiver. The genuineness of the transaction was easily established by joining the two parts together for a perfect fit.

Tallies were popular among estates, monasteries, and private persons and were familiar to international businessmen. But their real importance stemmed from their intensive use – and misuse – by governments. Because their income and expenses rarely matched, despite the elaborate systems to improve the balance, governments routinely paid creditors by tally instead of cash.[10] The tally authorized the bearer to draw the moneys due from specific revenue sources, not always conveniently located, and frequently out of funds. Collection, especially by minor creditors, could be difficult and time-consuming, so that tally owners in need of cash were prepared to discount them, especially to persons with greater influence on the authorities dispensing the cash. Or they might try to improve their chances by settling with the treasury for a lesser amount. In effect, governments were often able to operate from day to day by forcing businessmen to provide them with extensive credit and even gifts.

The great Italian financiers were also caught up in the tally system. To be sure, their very large loans to King Edward III of England during the 1330s and 1340s were formalized by paper documents, such as indentures, letters obligatory, and assignments of revenue, but their recoveries and much of their regular commerce with the crown involved them in a vast number of tally transactions. The private use of tallies apparently declined sharply among merchants (although not among artisans) in the fourteenth century, but governments used them liberally throughout the Middle Ages and beyond. Thus, to the extent that they served governments, businessmen continued to be embroiled in the tally system as reluctant lenders.[11]

BUSINESS AND THE CHURCH

Tourism

Tourism is often overlooked as a significant industry in medieval Europe, because it was almost entirely motivated by religion. But a business it was. Virtually all "pleasure travel" took the form of pilgrimages to visit one or more holy shrines, the three most holy of which, and thus the most desirable destinations, involved long, slow, and dangerous travel by land and sea. They were Jerusalem and the Holy Land, Rome, and Santiago de Compostela near the northwest coast of Spain. The spending of the floods of pilgrims affected much more than the sites and their immediate environs. It generated commerce of all kinds along the routes, adding an extra dimension of trade to otherwise backwater market towns, such as those on the long and winding "way of Saint James." The pilgrimage business required not only the provision of food, lodging, clothing, and souvenirs, but also the construction of transport equipment and the arrangement of financial instruments including letters of credit for the travelers. And because most pilgrims preferred to travel in groups for company and safety, there was a lively business in tour organization, the most prestigious of which was that run by the Abbey of Cluny. The crusades, of course, were vast pilgrimages consisting of armies

of devout and not-so-devout hangers-on, as well as the fighting "soldiers of Christ."

Pilgrimages of much more modest length were available all over
Europe, but even these entailed considerable time, expense, and preparation. A pilgrimage was often the highlight of the lives of the travelers, so that they were prepared to proceed at a leisurely pace, indulging
in stopovers and detours, and to spend a meaningful amount of time at
their destinations. For example, the journey from Southwark to Can-
terbury undertaken by Chaucer's pilgrims was not very lengthy, but the
total absence from home of, say, the widow from Bath would have been
substantial. Aside from the sites of special significance, virtually every
town worthy of the name boasted a large church or cathedral containing one or more precious relics, most of which had been brought back
from the Holy Land and Constantinople, along with tales of the miracles wrought by them. The possession of important relics assured that
the building that housed them must be appropriately magnificent.
Although the great cathedral-building boom of the thirteenth century
owed much to civic pride, construction in many cases was likely also
justified as a tourist attraction, beneficial to the local economy, much as
great sports stadia are justified today. Indeed, the economic beneficiaries
– artisans, construction workers, and merchants – were many, and represented a cross section of the community. And yet, it was the importance of the relic rather than the grandeur of the building that drew
the pilgrims. To illustrate, the elegant abbey church of Vézelay in north-
eastern France was so renowned an attraction that it was chosen as the
site from which Saint Bernard launched the Second Crusade in 1146.
It was one of the four points of departure for pilgrimages to Compostela, and notables such as Thomas à Becket, Philip Augustus, Richard
the Lion Hearted, and Louis IX (the devout Saint Louis) stopped there
to pray. But after 1279, when the authenticity of its prized relics associated with Mary Magdelene began to be questioned, the site and its
stunning church rapidly sank into obscurity.

The term "industry" may seem inappropriate for an enterprise as dis-
persed and diverse as medieval tourism, but it did enjoy a considerable
degree of coherence, thanks to the church. That institution was a consistent source of advertising and direction and even a kind of infrastructure in the form of its network of monasteries and hostels made
available to the wayfarers. The movement of pious pilgrims strengthened
the church in every way, reinforcing the faith of its adherents and their
perception of its universality, and conferring significant economic advantage. Rome itself was one of the great beneficiaries of tourism. There
was always a steady stream of genuine pilgrims, augmented by the

regular flow of church officials, aristocrats, and businessmen seeking favors and judgments from the Curia on all kinds of matters. The ranks of such visitors were further swollen by throngs attracted by the rituals of the great holy days of the year, or by special inducements of the papacy. Probably the most successful pilgrimage promotion of the Middle Ages, aside from the crusades, was the Jubilee Year of 1300. To encourage travel to Rome, Pope Boniface VIII declared that any of the faithful who visited the churches of the Blessed Apostles of Saint Peter and Saint Paul for fifteen to thirty days during that year would be granted full remission of punishment for their sins. The result was a flood of visitors bringing with them rich offerings for the church and much profitable business for the Roman merchants and innkeepers.

Pervasiveness of Christian morality and church authority

The relationship between business and the medieval church was close, complex, and uneasy. The church, as administrator of western Europe's largest single enterprise, recognized the contribution of businessmen to society, understood money and commerce, and frequently engaged in it, as exemplified by its promotion of the tourist industry. But the church also saw business activity as morally suspect and felt impelled to impose its authority. The tale of Saint Godric of Finchale is illuminating in this respect. Whereas Godric's entrepreneurial spirit is seen as praiseworthy, the moral of the story is that he becomes a model for all businessmen only when he gives his wealth to the poor and spends his final years as a hermit seeking salvation.

Christian teaching and church authority affected day-to-day business activity in other practical and profound ways, given the fact that business and personal values were so closely intermingled. Evidence of the pervasiveness of religious attitudes appears in the most mundane of commercial documents. A company's books normally opened with a prayer for the success of the business and the health and safety of its personnel. Italian accounting journals were peppered with the phrase *al nomen di Dio, amen*, and bills of exchange between sophisticated merchants routinely concluded with phrases such as *Cristo vi guardi*. Flemish bankers introduced their statements with "to the glory of God." These were not mere pious invocations, but were given seriously, adding moral sanction and enhanced legal enforceability to otherwise informal documents. And there is a vast pool of bequests to church and charity from businessmen who did follow Saint Godric's example toward the end of their careers.

Christian scriptures and canon law were more than merely intrusive; they constituted a vital part of the fabric of business life. The medieval concept of "just price," formalized in the thirteenth century by the scholastic theologians Albertus Magnus and Saint Thomas Aquinas, had its foundation in the Golden Rule and Christ's injunction in Matthew 7:12, "so whatever you wish that men would do to you, do so to them; for this is the law and the prophets." This message was especially relevant to the agrarian and small-town cultures of western Europe, where life was seen as a zero-sum game in which one person's gain was inevitably at the expense of others. Thus, although vague and subject to myriad variations, the concept of just price had practical application among artisans and local traders, whose close connection to church, guilds, and municipal government and involvement in price regulation we have already noted. Because costs of local products were well known, it was not difficult for the guilds to establish controlled prices that would ensure recovery of costs, plus a reasonable reward for labor. And because the price agreements were broad-based and sanctioned by church and government, they allowed little room for price gouging, especially in the case of processed foodstuffs. But the principles of just price were also interpreted to recognize utility value and demand rather than cost alone, and the pronouncements of scholastics and jurists increasingly reflected a realistic acknowledgment that the market must be allowed to establish prices. These views fit especially well with mining and international trade, where the market forces of supply and demand largely determined price, and costs were not readily discernible.[12]

The theologians and lawyers of the church, concerning themselves with all aspects of human behavior, closely examined all kinds of economic transactions and pronounced on their morality and legality. During the exuberant economic expansion of the twelfth and thirteenth centuries, the number and diversity of such exchanges multiplied. The church faced rising internal tension, as its administrators were significant beneficiaries of the growing commerce and favored a flexible approach, while its theologians viewed the rising tide of business as a threat to morality deserving greater, not less, control.

The doctrine of usury and business adaptations to it

The issue most affecting this tension and of greatest importance to businessmen was the treatment of usury. The medieval doctrine of usury, with roots in both the Old and New Testaments, regarded any interest, not just excessive interest, as a mortal sin. The New Testament source, Jesus's admonition that when lending, "expect nothing in return" (Luke 6:35), was confirmed by the Council of Nicaea in 325. The denial of interest was also embodied in secular law when Charlemagne, citing tradition, prohibited usury by both clerics and laymen, defining it broadly in 806 as occurring when "more is demanded back than what is given." And in the lengthy restatements of usury doctrine in the thirteenth century, the scholastic theologians drew upon the views of the ancient Greek philosophers who regarded lending money at interest as contrary to natural law, in that it required money to "breed."

At the time that the usury doctrine took hold in western Europe, the economy was largely agrarian and most loans were of a "consumption" type. The borrowers were often people living close to the margin who needed short-term funds to recover from misfortune and then became trapped by interest into a downward spiral of misery. Interest rates were high, partly because of the lender's risk and partly because of the paucity of alternatives; interest was charged weekly at a rate compounding to about fifty percent per annum. The moneylenders and pawnbrokers who participated in this business found it attractive enough to bear public opprobrium and the risk of eternal damnation. Many of them were Christians from northern Italy and southern France, contemptuously referred to as lombards and cahorsins. But a large number of them were Jews, unconcerned with Christian doctrine, although forbidden to lend at interest to fellow Israelites. As important sources of finance for the wealthy as well as the poor, Jewish merchants enjoyed the protection of princes in most of western Europe until they were expelled from England in the 1290s and from France in the early 1300s. And small loans, whether from Jews or Christians, were not destined only to the penurious or the profligate. Entrepreneurs and merchants of all stripes frequently availed themselves of modest short-term advances to cover gaps in their cash flow and found it profitable to do so. Many were successful businessmen who borrowed repeatedly and repaid promptly.

Here we see the main problem of the usury doctrine for medieval businessmen; it did not distinguish between loans for consumption and loans for productive purposes. The latter were becoming increasingly necessary to fuel the commercial expansion from the eleventh century onward. The pressure to attract capital drove businessmen to seek ways around the usury obstacle, creating tension with the church over what merchants felt were legitimate needs of enterprise. Tension arose also within the church, as its more urbane administrators struggled with its doctrinaire theologians over where to draw the line between sinful advantage and justifiable profit. And despite the economic dynamics and the revival of Roman law that tolerated moderate interest, the restrictive views of the doctors appeared to have the upper hand throughout most of the thirteenth century. The Second Lateran Council in 1139 explicitly declared usury a sin; Pope Alexander III condemned mortgage interest in 1180; and the Fourth Lateran Council in 1215 decreed that the tolerance of Roman law for usury could be pleaded only by Jews. And still later, notwithstanding the papacy's pressing need for the good will of merchants in its titanic conflict with Frederick II, Gregory IX in 1236 condemned the sea loan as usury. But during this period and later, fertile minds among the clergy and laity gradually worked out acceptable borderlines between licit and illicit practice.

The principle involved in the condemnation of usury was that the lender sinfully exacted from the borrower the promise of a predetermined extra payment at the time of granting the loan. To avoid the charge of usury, the lender must justify the added compensation on grounds other than the loan itself. Moreover, and most important, the amount of the compensation must not be predictable. Thus, the *commenda* contract and other forms of partnerships were deemed acceptable, because the providers of the cash could not predict what eventual profit, if any, they would earn. Conversely, the sea loan was invalidated because the lender specified his reward in advance, notwithstanding the insurance risk that he assumed. The church doctors apparently saw the "insurance" as a smoke screen for interest and merely an addition to other risks of default inherent in any loan.

By far the most successful invention to escape the usury ban was the bill of exchange referred to earlier. Here, the amount to be reimbursed by the borrower was clearly stated, but in another currency in another location, so that the lender could not predict what gain, if any, he would make on the transaction. Although the lenders normally made a profit on the exchange and regarded it as a return on the use of the money advanced, the church authorities ruled the device to be legitimate. Because the odds were stacked in the lenders' favor, historians such as Raymond de Roover have accused the theologians of inconsistency with their basic premises, prompted by expediency. This is probably an unfair judgment, given the unpredictability of the gain on any specific transaction, a fact supported by the wide range of profit and loss uncovered by de Roover's own investigations.[13] Moreover, the church doctors scrutinized the practice carefully and condemned the use of mechanisms such as the fictitious or "dry" exchange, whereby final settlement did not take place abroad, assuring the lender of a known profit in his home currency.

Another important approach to usury shifted the focus from the lender's gain to compensation for the loss of his use of the money. Failure to repay the debt on the date stipulated in the contract could justify recompense to the lender for the damage inflicted on him by the delay. The idea of loss was taken further and applied more widely through the notion of *lucrum cessans*, the potential trading profit the lender has foregone by lending to a borrower who is able to trade profitably instead. Merchants in Genoa and Venice apparently felt justified in charging fees easily identifiable as interest on commercial loans from their earliest ventures, as did those in the inland Italian cities. Rates, however, were well below those for consumption loans, around twenty percent in the early twelfth century and declining to as low as seven percent a century later. In this "back door" recognition of time value of money, the merchants were evenhanded. They awarded the same rates for deposits as they did for loans, recording the interest credited or debited euphemistically as money "they gave us" or "we gave them for profit of the accounting period."

Other methods of circumventing the usury proscription entailed the collusion of borrower and lender. In some cases, the parties simply set the amount in the contract higher than that actually advanced. In others, especially those involving princes, the borrower would make an elaborate show of awarding "gifts" to the lender. A third popular procedure was to set the repayment date deliberately earlier than actually planned in order to assess a charge for "damages."

Overall, the actions and doctrines of the church affected business in a multitude of ways, many of them constructive. The challenge they presented provoked responses that shaped the unique character of European business. As will be elaborated in Chapter 5, the church was a large and valued customer, an important participant in the movement of funds around Europe, and a powerful generator of business. Its political initiatives – crusades, conflicts with the Holy Roman Empire, prohibitions of trade with Islam – all impinged on business decisions, for better or for worse. And the desires and demands of the church will play an important part in the role of politics in business, to be discussed in the following chapter.

In this brief two-chapter survey of the "nuts and bolts" of business organization and practice during Europe's High Middle Ages, we have caught a glimpse of the enormous variety and vitality of responses to the opportunities and constraints cited at the beginning of Chapter 2. Two important conclusions can be drawn from the material presented in this review. The first is that while business units at the beginning of our period in 1200 were small, simple, and particularistic, business itself was extremely complex, requiring multiple transactions among numerous business units to transform raw materials into finished goods and to move products from place to place. This business complexity was costly and inhibiting to trade. The second conclusion is that there was an unmistakable trend throughout the 150-year period toward larger and more complex units coincident with a move toward simpler business processes. This evolution was most obvious in the textile industry, where single entrepreneurs were extending their control over an increasing span of the product transformation operation, but was also evident in most other areas of business activity, especially in international marketing. The trend was substantially aided by the broad-scale application of improved technology and new financial instruments that simplified processes and significantly reduced costs. For some products, such as mass-market woolens, the lower costs translated into lower prices and expanded markets, permitting the large-scale export of such items, at least until 1300, from Flanders to destinations as distant as Sicily. For luxury goods, the savings likely translated into increased profits. Because of the mixing of household and business affairs cited earlier, profits are difficult to identify, even where records of dividends have survived. But the vast increase in numbers of entrepreneurs willing to undergo the financial and even physical hazards of regional and long-distance trade suggests rewards that compensated for the risks.

4

THE POLITICS OF BUSINESS

·

Possibly the greatest single difference in business practice between medieval western Europe and today's advanced economies is the role of politics. Today, businessmen and governments try to influence each other's behavior at all levels in an enormous variety of ways. For example, businessmen try to persuade politicians through contributions to political parties, the efforts of armies of articulate lobbyists, appeals from their employees, and occasionally through direct bribes. Governments, for their part, employ selective taxation, antitrust legislation, and product regulation to nudge businesses in desired directions. Although these are but a few of the many devices used by each side to put pressure on the other, they are applied in the context of an elaborate set of ground rules that have developed over time and that are subject to only limited political tampering. Most advanced economies enjoy widely accepted company laws, banking regulations, statutes for fraud and bankruptcy, rules for the protection of property rights, and conventions for settling disputes on a national and international level. To be sure, today's governments are constantly having to respond to complaints of unfair practices, tilted playing fields, and the like, but underlying all domestic and international trade is a bedrock of generally accepted law.

Medieval businessmen, on the other hand, could not escape the fact that in no European legal jurisdiction was there such a concept as "inalienable rights": there were only legal privileges. Because privilege in essence means "private law," one's legal standing depended on either the customary privileges attached to one's status as a noble, peasant, or burgher, or prerogatives granted by charter or other agreement by a king or other sovereign power. Outside his native city, a merchant typically

had no legal standing beyond that granted those of his nation or city.
Because that depended on the vagaries of diplomacy and the whims of
kings and emperors, venturing abroad was never without risks and
uncertainties for a merchant even when he carried a royal safe-conduct.
Parallel and complementary to the relations of merchants and kings were
the legal customs that governed trade among merchants themselves,
particularly the means of legal recourse open to a merchant in cases of
fraud, breach of contract, or other malfeasance. Here businessmen had
particular needs quite distinct from those of ordinary justice. In short,
business required a stable and predictable legal environment in which
property was protected, fraud and dishonest dealing punished, and
speedy justice made available to all.

EVOLVING RELATIONSHIPS OF GOVERNMENT AND BUSINESS

We have already seen that with the revival of trade, small settlements
began to expand into commercial centers, bringing about new sets of
relationships. Some of the residents of these centers broke free of their
feudal landlords through payment of ground rents. Others, especially in
Italy, were themselves landholding aristocrats who saw opportunities in
trade as a means of enhancing their income. All banded together to form
sworn associations, often known as communes. These negotiated with
their overlords for charters establishing collective privileges for the
communities as a whole. The chief negotiators, irrespective of their
social class, were almost always businessmen, who had already taken the
responsibility for drawing up rules of conduct within the communities,
now become communes or towns. Politics, then, for early medieval businessmen, became the first order of business. And the townsmen were
not reluctant to resort to force to defend their newly established interests, as attested by the well-known incident at Laon in 1112. There, the
bishop levied taxes on the merchants, overriding the privileges previously granted by the king. The merchants succeeded in getting their
privileges confirmed but only after they rioted, stormed the cathedral,
and slew the bishop.

Violence may have been necessary on occasion, but it needed to be
tempered by the development of an acceptable framework of coexis-
tence. Because businessmen of western Europe had few examples to
follow in the early twelfth century, they were obliged to create new
legal systems of their own. Here, the dynamics were cooperation/com-
petition rather than the cooperation/compulsion that characterized the
earlier rural economy. Cooperation was essential both to establish sound

internal working relationships and to present a united front against feudal princes or competing communes. At the same time, competition inevitably arose among the free citizens for power and pride of place, generating divisions into a hierarchy of classes, with landowning patriciates and prosperous merchants at the top, artisans in the lower middle, and the working poor at the bottom.

The twin forces of cooperation and competition created patterns of similarities, but also differences in the organizational structures of towns throughout western Europe. The similarities arose because the objectives that inspired citizens to cooperate – the achievement of an orderly, commercially oriented society – were broadly the same everywhere. All had to organize collective services such as police, firefighting, sanitation, food supply, and defence, and design the taxes to pay for them. The differences stemmed from the fact that the challenges, cultures, and personalities involved were unique to each case, so that the responses all bore a distinctively local stamp. But by the opening of the thirteenth century it is possible to discern amid this bewildering variety four broadly representative types of towns and their budding legal systems that can illustrate the reciprocal relationship of politics and business.

First, in the small market towns throughout most of Europe the leading entrepreneurs enjoyed a modicum of self-government but exercised little control of affairs beyond their immediate environs. Second, merchants and artisans in the royal cities of Paris and Barcelona retained a limited degree of independence but were directly subject to the sovereign and his officials. Third were the self-governing commercial-industrial towns such as Ghent and Bruges in the Low Countries and Lübeck in northern Germany. Businessmen there essentially controlled local politics and had the authority to deal with their comital overlords, but were subservient to them. Finally, there were the truly independent city-states. In these, businessmen managed not only local politics, but also foreign policy, which they directed to further their interests, projecting their power by force or cash or some combination of both. The most obvious examples occurred in north central Italy and in two distinctive types – the powerful maritime cities of Venice and Genoa and the commercial-industrial centers of Florence and Siena.

In all these situations, urban businessmen were in effect the political leaders as far as local matters were concerned. Only in the truly independent city-states of Italy did they also fully control the conduct of foreign policy. But ambitious merchants from all locations were gaining increasing influence with regional potentates, especially in the developing nation-states of northern France, England, and southern Italy. Between the twelfth and fourteenth centuries, a kind of symbiosis was evolving, as rulers and businessmen began to recognize a community of interests, despite their differing objectives. Sovereigns saw that trade could be managed to produce tolls, taxes, and tariffs for a steady flow of cash to buy military resources, rewards for followers, and symbols of prestige. The flow of money also provided the means for rulers to build the administrative structures, often manned by businessmen, that enabled them to tighten control and enhance their power over their subjects. Businessmen, for their part, saw in the sovereigns the means to the secure environment they needed to carry on predictable and profitable operations.

As daunting as were the problems faced by businessmen in their hometowns, they paled alongside those confronting resident foreigners (denizens). In addition to capricious rulers, these merchants faced the constant ambivalence and occasional violence of the locals among whom they lived and worked. To strengthen their influence and security in foreign locations, merchants engaging in long-distance trade found it useful to congregate in colonies or "nations" along with their fellows from the same city or region. In most significant trading towns, especially seaports, such merchants established compounds, complete with docks, warehouses, offices, churches, and living and recreation areas, sometimes surrounded by a wall but often physically integrated within the host city. Within the compound, known as the *fondaco* among the Italians and the *kontor* among the Germans, the merchants enjoyed certain freedoms, such as the use of their own weights and measures, coinage, and laws for settling internal disputes. Otherwise, they were subject to the laws, taxes, and regulations of the host state, unless they were able to obtain privileges from its overlord.

In such colonies, the relationship between merchant and monarch took on another dimension. As Gerald Day has noted, medieval trade took place on two distinct levels.[1] At the lower level, merchants paid the regular exactions of the local governments and suffered the arbitrary delays and bribes imposed by their officials. Considerable trade occurred on this basis, especially with the Muslim cities along the Mediterranean. At the upper level was privileged trade, whereby the favored merchants might enjoy reduction or even elimination of tolls, special access to materials, markets, and warehousing, and the cooperation of bureaucrats. Herein lay much of the politics of medieval business. Privileges were gained by means of astute diplomacy backed by the ability to provide the ruler concerned with something he needed, usually cash or military assistance or both. The privileged status won by an Italian city-state in the Mediterranean by these means, and sometimes also by brute force, was conferred upon all of its merchants, giving them an advantage over their competitors from other cities. The struggle for commercial superiority was joined by most cities with varying degrees of success, resulting in a bewildering variety of tolls and regulations, constantly changing with the relative influence of each city.

In northern Europe, Italian trading cities lacked the power to negotiate privileges on behalf of their businessmen, Here, some of their companies became large enough to do so on their own, securing special rights and exemptions usually by advances of cash. Powerful indigenous merchants, such as William de la Pole in early fourteenth-century England, and foreign merchant associations such as the Hanse in London and Bruges, were also able to acquire privileged status. But the relationship of merchants and monarchs was not a partnership of equals; rather, it was a cohabitation of convenience between unequal actors, one that could be disrupted whenever the arrangement ceased to be convenient to the dominant party, the monarch. There was little respect and no trust between the two, so that each took elaborate precautions to thwart potential trickery from the other. And the merchants did hold good cards: despite the arbitrary power at the disposal of the sovereign, his actions were constrained by his increasing need for the goods, services, and cash that only international businessmen could furnish.

This chapter will deal with all these relationships, citing examples of the interaction of business and civil authority in the evolution of political structures at local and international levels in the four types of town cited earlier. It will also cover the politics of business with the papacy and other arms of the Latin Christian church, and will conclude with a brief discussion of legal structures as they developed in the different parts of Europe.

MARKETS AND TOWNS − ENGLAND

Politics and business had a curious arm's-length relationship in this strongly governed but for the most part not very centralized kingdom. The power of the English monarchy after 1066 was unquestionably among the most extensive in Europe at the time; but the crown played little direct role either in granting urban liberties or in building economic infrastructure, unlike the Flemish counts. English cities on the whole enjoyed less independence than those in France and far less than in Flanders or Italy. But English kings, despite their faults, did preserve and guarantee a considerable period of peace and order along the internal trade routes of the kingdom. The unceasing search for royal tax revenue also made the king's government amenable to negotiation with town authorities, resulting in considerable freedom in English cities by the late twelfth century to apportion and collect taxes themselves. Along with tax privileges came the right to choose their own mayor, first by 1191 in London, whose example was soon followed by other cities. All in all, the development of urban freedom from erratic and unreasonable royal demands was rather more gradualist and uncontentious in England than elsewhere in Europe. On the other hand, English merchants played little or no role in royal politics in this era.

Royal power was quite apparent in the rigorous application of the king's right to license new markets and fairs. However, it required more than a century after the Norman conquest for such royal rights to be clearly defined and regularly exercised. There are, for example, no surviving market charters from William the Conqueror's reign, although the Domesday Book clearly proves the existence of markets before 1086. This suggests that there was a thriving undercurrent of local markets without royal authorization by the mid eleventh century at the latest. It was not until roughly 1200 that fairs and markets became a preoccupation of royal government, leading to what Britnell calls the "triumph of legal formality," with the crown successfully monopolizing the licensing of markets and fairs.[2]

It was also during the period 1180–1270 that the English royal government embarked on a campaign to dictate and regulate weights and measures, as well as to establish quality standards for bread, wine, and ale. Although such attempts to guarantee consistency and fairness in the marketplace were typical in European cities, England was practically alone in attempting such uniformity on a kingdom-wide basis. Henry II's Assize of Measures of 1196 attempted to standardize the measures used for cereals, liquids, weights, and the measurement of woolen cloth. Henry II also issued an assize of wine, and his son John issued an assize of bread, to which an assize of ale was added in 1202, underlining the close relationship of the latter two foodstuffs. Although these standards were widely disseminated and policed, it is difficult to assess their overall effectiveness in controlling trading practices. Ultimately, cities and local jurisdictions took over the regulation of weights, measures, and quality standards for comestibles.

If the royal record as a guarantor of measure and quality was a mixed one, the reputation of English coinage was impeccable. This was largely due to the very tight royal control over both the circulation of coins in the kingdom and the bullion content of English coins. Unlike many governments on the continent, the English monarchy allowed no foreign coins to circulate, so that all silver, either ingots or coins, had to be taken to the royal mint for recoinage. Until the thirteenth century, there was only one kind of coin, the silver penny, whose weight and fineness remained remarkably stable. This system has been criticized for its lack of utility – the silver penny was too large a denomination to be used for the small transactions of daily life – but the stability and reliability of the English currency was undoubtedly a boon to larger scale business.

ROYAL CITIES – FRANCE, SPAIN, AND ARAGON

France

The Capetian kings of France had directly ruled Paris as part of the Isle de France from the inception of the dynasty in 987. And as the monarchy began to acquire significant new territories at the opening of the thirteenth century, it continued to maintain control through a centralized bureaucracy. Following his conquests of Normandy and of John of England's other possessions in northern France, Philip Augustus divided his enlarged kingdom into bailiwicks, each headed by a salaried, royally appointed bailiff who administered justice, collected taxes, and maintained order in the king's name. The positions of *prevôt* and other lower offices of the bailiwick continued to be farmed by auction, with the officeholders expecting to recover their payments and much more through profits on the administration of justice. Such a system was prone to abuse, and when Louis IX returned from his long absence during the Seventh Crusade, he determined to tighten his administration. His Ordinance of 1254 did not change the system, but made it more responsible by rotating the bailiffs and by appointing investigators (*enquêteurs*) empowered to ferret out and correct wrongdoing, while affirming the rights of the king. Previous kings had also exercised direct control of the major cities (*bonnes villes*) of their realms, taxing them heavily and regarding their mayors, even though elected, as responsible to the king for administering part of the kingdom. Louis IX extended this control even further; in 1262, he required the cities to nominate three candidates from which he would choose the mayor. At the same time, he imposed on them the obligation to submit their accounts to the king's auditors. Thereafter, Capetian cities enjoyed little independence.

Paris, as the first city in western Europe to become the fixed capital of a kingdom, presented special problems. It had become the locus of the organs of political and administrative power of France, while at the same time developing as a thriving center of commerce. Initially, the responsibility of governing Paris had been split between two officials of middling rank with middling success, until Louis IX created a new position with the rank and status of a provincial bailiff. To this highly paid post, he appointed a series of superb administrators who systematized royal controls over the business community through a semiautonomous creation, the "prevost of the merchants." The *prevôt* and his magistrates oversaw the judging of commercial matters and the assessments for urban expenditures, such as roads and police. Regarding the latter, Louis also appointed a highly competent knight as chief of police, supported by paid sergeants to establish order in the streets. These innovations made Paris a much more attractive place to do business, so much so that the chronicler Joinville was moved to write that the city experienced a veritable economic boom during Louis's reign. This civic organizational structure persisted in Paris for several centuries, and although its effectiveness and fairness varied over time, its domination by the royal bureaucracy remained intact, leaving little political power in the hands of businessmen.

Businessmen prospered in this environment, as stability and the richness of the market more than made up for their lack of political influence. But their comfort in this situation began to fade starting in the last decade of the thirteenth century, when King Philip IV became increasingly autocratic, subordinating all other interests to the concentration of his own power and the furtherance of his territorial ambitions. To these ends, he tightened control over the management of his finances, milking, and then expelling the Jews, crushing the Knights Templars, and marginalizing the Italians. Worse, to help finance his costly war with Edward I of England he resorted to a deceptively easy, but economically destructive, tactic – debasing the coinage. His example was mimicked by subsequent French monarchs during the 1330s and 1340s, and although some merchants profited from the currency fluctuations, business per se was severely constrained by them. Coinage manipulation became a much more widespread practice in Europe in the late fourteenth and fifteenth centuries and will be discussed more fully in Part II of this book.

Spain and Aragon

Throughout the High Middle Ages, the direction of business and trade in most of the Iberian peninsula was dominated by political forces. Initially the commerce and culture of al Andaluz – the name given to Muslim Spain – was almost entirely integrated into the Muslim Mediterranean world of North Africa and the Near East. The Christian victories of the thirteenth century that eventually reduced Muslim holdings to Granada in the southeast of the peninsula completely changed the structure of industry and trade. Spain's east-west commerce with the

Muslim world rapidly declined, its role as entrepôt between Europe and North Africa diminished, and certain exports, such as silk and Christian slaves, dried up completely. This business was only gradually and partially replaced by increased regional activity and trade with northern Europe.

This change was a wrenching experience. From a producer of olive oil, silks, leather goods, and a range of manufactures for Islamic destinations, Spain became a source of raw and semiprocessed materials (wool, iron, and olive oil) for local and northern European markets. Moreover, the effect of the *Reconquista* was to divide Christian Iberia into three distinct trading zones, each with its own special interests and orientation. One was north Castile and Portugal, which competed in the Bay of Biscay and northwestern Europe. The second was Andalusia and the southwest coast, including Seville, whose ports served as way stations and transfer points for foreign commerce in all directions and were controlled largely by foreigners, especially the Genoese.

The third was Aragon/Catalonia, which had come into the trading orbit of Christian Europe at a relatively early date and deserves special attention here. Its main port, Barcelona, although a smaller and somewhat later arrival on the international business scene than its larger Italian rivals, was nonetheless an important player in the commerce of the Mediterranean and southern Europe, able to compete confidently in this arena. As part of the domain of Aragon, whose kings were also counts of Barcelona, the port enjoyed the advantages of a large fertile hinterland and a muscular monarchy that understood the political benefits of promoting business. In its early days, Barcelona traded mainly agricultural goods, as well as iron, salt, and fish; but in the thirteenth century, in particular after King James I's conquest of Majorca in 1229, it became a significant competitor in the general commerce of the Mediterranean. It was an especially potent one in the western half of that sea, fanning out to busy markets in southern Spain, North Africa, Sicily, Italy, and Provence.

The international merchants of Barcelona, unlike those of the Italian port cities, did not take charge of their own political destiny, but they did play a vital part in furthering the expansionist plans of their benevolent overlords, the count-kings of Aragon. At the same time, they were not handicapped by the rivalries of the local landowning families. In the words of Stephen Bensch, "aristocratic clans played only a marginal role in the Catalan capital; as a result, the city's political life was not dominated by the factional struggles that overwhelmed many Italian towns."[3] Businessmen worked cooperatively with the monarchy in framing the municipal institutions. Thus, James I, during his long rule in the mid thirteenth century, issued a series of charters that granted the merchants increasing autonomy. Further, he codified their commercial law and in 1257 organized the maritime sector of Barcelona as a city within the city. He and his successors also took the lead in negotiating favorable conditions for Barcelona's businessmen in North Africa's Muslim cities as far east as Alexandria. And of course the merchants profited from the Aragonese territorial gains of the thirteenth century that included Provence, the Balearic Islands, and Sicily. At first this symbiotic relationship between crown and commerce appears to have been an unmitigated blessing to Barcelona's businessmen, but it became less so when the internal politics of Aragon began to deteriorate seriously in the fifteenth century.

COMMERCIAL-INDUSTRIAL TOWNS – FLANDERS AND GERMANY

Flanders

The political evolution of the county of Flanders could hardly be more different from that of the French monarchy, offering a fascinating and complex picture of how the interaction of rulers and merchants could unfold. A series of exceptionally able warriors and administrators as counts succeeded during the eleventh and twelfth centuries in unifying an extensive and diverse group of territories wedged into the unpromising far north of France and far west of the German empire. Despite losing some of this territory to the growing power of the French king in the twelfth century, the count of Flanders remained a powerful prince and head of an efficient bureaucracy.

A ruler's intervention in the economy is often a good indicator of his power, and here the Flemish counts clearly distinguished themselves before the thirteenth century. Land reclamation, an important interest because much of coastal Flanders was marshy and flood-prone in the eleventh century, owed much to a comital policy of diking and drainage. The resulting property, called in Flemish a polder, remained subject to the regalian rights of the count, even that which passed into the possession of a monastery. Thus the count derived income and power from these new lands, while depriving local nobles of additional lands. This pattern also established an important comital presence in the economic development of coastal Flanders.

The task of land reclamation was complemented by the creation of waterways linking the developing urban centers. Canals could serve both to drain polders and to allow boats access to the interior, which, together with the Scheldt, Ijser, and Leie rivers, made virtually all of western Flanders navigable by the early twelfth century. This area of comital initiative was capped by Philip of Alsace, who from 1160 to 1180 directly participated in implementing a master plan to link interior towns such as Bruges, Ypres, and Saint-Omer with coastal ports where docking facilities for large boats could be provided. And in 1180 a monumental dam was built ten kilometers northeast of Bruges, allowing access to the North Sea via the new port city of Damme. But to many foreigners, the chief marvel of Flanders were its dikes, worthy of mention even in Dante's *Inferno*.[4]

Comital policies also affected the development of urban communities and local fairs in the county. Many of the great medieval cities of Flanders owed their beginnings at least in part to a count's fort built at a significant crossroad. Another important stimulant to urbanization was the establishment of the five fairs of West Flanders around the beginning of the twelfth century, as described in Chapter 1. This was the earliest cycle of fairs in any northern European region, and each enjoyed the count's peace, which granted safe passage on Flemish roads and waterways and also apparently gave special privileges to foreign merchants. Although confined to five communities all west of the Scheldt River, this February-November cycle of fairs stimulated trade and growth in the rest of Flanders as well. Merchants from other Flemish communities could travel to the fairs and were either exempt from tolls on their goods or subject to much reduced rates.

In the mid to late twelfth century, the balance of power between the count and the growing urban entities of his county began to change. This was most clearly apparent in the series of privileges won by cities during the civil war following the assassination of Count Charles the Good in 1127. These grants by protagonists for the comital succession show that the support of townsmen had become crucial. By the thirteenth century, businessmen of the wealthiest and most powerful families of the towns took over much of the economic initiative in the county, assuming considerable control over land reclamation, waterway construction, and investment in agriculture. By the mid fourteenth century, Bruges, Ghent, and Ypres, the "three cities," as they called themselves – were able to challenge the power of both the count and the king of France when a conflict developed between comital politics and the economic interests of urban Flanders. Thus Flanders became a significant example of how cooperation ultimately became confrontation between the count and the cities.

Germany

Politics and business at first glance seem the most removed in the complicated disunity of the German empire. Unlike the rulers of Flanders or England, the German emperors usually had relatively little direct power in many parts of their realm and when they did, they usually made common cause with local lords in opposing grants of urban freedom. Interaction between the forces of lordship and commerce took place mostly at the local level, and was often marked by conflict. This in turn has traditionally caused historians to view the growth of German cities as essentially violent, like the movement of land masses grinding against each other and over time and leading to intermittent earthquakes.

The example of the Rhine city of Cologne is often adduced to support this view. Cologne was ruled by its bishops, one of whom sparked a riot in 1074 by requisitioning a ship owned by a wealthy merchant. Urban historians have concluded that this incident foreshadowed the communal movement of the early twelfth century, in which security of property was always a central goal. But the weakness in this model of essentially turbulent interaction is that many German towns won independence from their lords in the twelfth century without recourse to violence. Moreover, many sworn associations of townsmen, traditionally regarded as a precondition for revolt, were actually encouraged and used by their lords. This contrary view is well expressed by historian Susan Reynolds: "The independence which some German towns won in the twelfth century was achieved by the piecemeal accumulation of local government functions, and this was a process, as it was in Italy, to which slow encroachment in periods of relative harmony contributed as much as did either victories in open conflict or the formal concession of charters."[5]

Freed from the "earthquake" analogy of urban development, we can more clearly see the forces of cooperation between lords and merchants across the German empire. East of the core of ancient Rhineland cities, the development of markets and fairs went hand in hand with the establishment of cities that punctuated the eastern wave of German colonization. The most impressive example of the cooperation and interdependence of lord, town, and market is Lübeck, founded on the site of a destroyed Slavic settlement in 1143. Count Adolph II of Holstein supervised the construction of harbor facilities, town walls, and churches resulting in his nearly immediate popularity with merchants intent on pursuing trade in the Baltic Sea area. Ironically, Lübeck was able to thrive even after Count Adolph was forced to surrender the city to a more powerful rival, Duke Henry the Lion, in 1159. After Henry took possession of the city, a chronicler noted, "At his bidding the merchants at once returned with joy and . . . started to rebuild the churches and walls of the city."[6]

The most familiar medieval German merchant organization, the German Hanse (often misleadingly called the Hanseatic League), owes its beginnings to a number of by-now familiar factors: newly created cities in the Baltic, increased autonomy in the Rhineland and in other German cities, and common goals among these cities of opening up new trading territories and excluding non-German competitors. By the late thirteenth century, there emerged an incipient transurban network, to which the majority of German cities from the lower Rhine to the Baltic would eventually belong. At first this Hanse was simply a loose association of merchants from various cities who traded in one or another of the northern trading outposts, especially Novgorod and Bergen. These merchants affiliated in order to defend and promote their common interests against foreign rulers. The concrete form of this association was the "German quarters" created in these foreign cities as a neighborhood or a particular set of buildings. By 1300, these *kontors*, as they came to be called, had been established not only in the north and east, but also in two major trading cities of the west, Bruges and London. By this time the chief articles of this trade were furs, timber, and other forest products, and the important food commodities, fish and wheat. But the Hanse remained a merchants' cooperative; it was only after 1350 that it acquired any semblance of the state or bureaucratic organization that will be discussed in Chapter 7.

CITY-STATES OF ITALY: GENOA, VENICE, AND FLORENCE

The medieval expression, "a Genoese, therefore a merchant," may have been an exaggeration, but not by much, given the fact that aside from shipbuilding and small-scale textile manufacturing, there was little industry other than trading in this seaport city. But to say, "a Genoese, therefore a businessman," would involve no hyperbole at all. Virtually everyone, from the highest of the nobility to shopkeepers, artisans, and even women, participated in Genoa's business as merchants, sailors, chandlers, notaries, financiers, investors, bureaucrats, and frequently warriors. Throughout all of north central Italy, business families were ubiquitous and predominant, so much so that their number necessarily included many of the famous figures of high medieval culture – Dante and his divine Beatrice, Boccaccio, and Saint Francis, to name a few. The manner in which such families conducted their affairs and organized their political structures differed in each community, but before discussing the differences in the representative cities, it is useful to touch on the similarities in their early political history.

The evolution of the communes in Italy began in the second half of the eleventh century when the imperial system, with its delegation of local rule to bishops or lay aristocrats, was breaking down. As the old regime collapsed, there was a need to end the ensuing anarchy by finding compromise among the conflicting local forces. The solution most widely adopted in north central Italy was the commune, which was a private personal association established by oath whereby members swore to help each other in peace and war, obey the orders of a governing council and its appointed consuls, and attend assemblies when summoned. Communes did not issue a ringing declaration of sovereignty, but in practice simply usurped authority in the power vacuum of the time. They thus did not overthrow imperial and comital rights but merely bypassed them, often co-opting feudal aristocrats into positions of leadership. And they were able to persuade most of the bishops to play the role of impartial president and figurehead, maintaining the city's connection with the church and the special identity attaching to its patron saint. Communes appeared not just in the major cities and bishoprics, but anywhere down to groups of villages that faced similar challenges of creating order out of chaos.[7] Many of these cities became large and some very important, but it will be possible to examine the political structure and characteristics of leadership of only the three that are the most relevant to our survey – Genoa, Venice, and Florence.

In Genoa, broad participation in the commune was encouraged by the rule that prohibited members from including in a venture individuals who had refused to take the oath. Despite the appearance of democracy suggested by the all-inclusive membership, the consuls appointed by the council were usually drawn from a small group of powerful landowning families, and the assemblies of the membership were called to ratify decisions rather than to debate them. It was these feudal patricians, using capital generated by their estates and by privateering expeditions, who directed their energies toward financing international trade. Although active merchants began to share power by the early thirteenth century, there was no merchant guild; the commune performed its functions, including the minutiae of regulating trade at home and abroad.

Throughout the Middle Ages, Genoa's internal politics and external policies suffered from the factional rivalry of the great clans and their clients. And yet the city's power owed much to the ability of these businessmen to rise above their short-term personal and commercial priorities to promote ventures in the interest of the commune as a whole. By volunteering the city's fleets to support the First Crusade, for example, the Genoese obtained trading quarters in Jerusalem and all the Latin coastal cities, including Antioch, where Bohemond granted them a church and a street for helping him defend the city. Later, they acquired exclusive use of the outports of Saint Gilles and Montpellier in southern France in return for the use of their fleets against the local count's enemies. Adventures such as these and the repeated attempts to establish colonies in or near Constantinople, although beneficial in the long run, were also costly and entailed considerable sacrifice in taxes and borrowing on the part of the whole community.

Although the commune usually, but not always, directed the original foundation of the foreign trading quarters, the relationship between Genoa and these colonies was loose and became progressively looser. For example, the enclaves along the Black Sea coast formed their own self-governing communes, establishing direct diplomatic relations with eastern potentates. And Genoese military ventures and diplomatic initiatives were often carried out by individuals or groups of merchants who acted independently, not as representatives of the republic.[8] Large-scale raids in the many wars against Venice were often the work of free-booters acting on their own initiative for their own profit, not unlike the Elizabethan adventurers of a later age. And on an even grander scale, Genoa's greatest admirals were prepared to contract the services of their fleets to the highest bidder, as in the case of Admiral Doria, who made his squadron available to the French during 1338 and 1339 to harass the English and plunder their coastal towns.[9]

Venice was at least as dedicated to commerce and seafaring as Genoa, but its approach to these endeavors could hardly have been more different. Where competition and buccaneering enterprise were the norm in Genoa, cooperation and control dominated in Venice. We have already seen evidence of these Venetian characteristics in Chapter 2 in the manner in which the state authorities managed the city's merchant fleet, and later its shipbuilding facilities. Such sophisticated management systems, unique to medieval western Europe, developed out of Venice's political structure, which, in turn, was a product of its geography and history.

Venetians took pride in their independence from the great powers that struggled for primacy in Italy, being subservient neither to the Holy Roman Empire nor to the papacy. The city's location in a series of defensible lagoons gave its residents centuries of freedom from invaders, along with a pragmatic appreciation of the virtues of cooperating for the common good. Cooperation and self-imposed regulation were essential for the maintenance and proper use of limited space and constantly clogged waterways. History's contribution was a longstanding connection with Constantinople, a nominal outpost of the Byzantine Empire, which provided a tradition of authoritarian government headed by a *dux* or doge appointed by the emperor. This office continued after the disappearance of Byzantine jurisdiction but became elective for life, rotating among a small group of early patrician families. The Venetian commune did not form until the middle of the twelfth century because there was no collapsing old regime to replace. Nonetheless, like the other cities, it transferred power to a collective executive, the ducal council, while retaining the doge as a powerful, albeit controllable, head of state.

The political center of Venice, the doge's palace, was distinct from the commercial center on the Rialto, but the great wealth of the city and its leading inhabitants derived from the skillful interplay of the two. In effect, Venice became governed by an oligarchy of businessmen who had extensive landed and commercial interests. This executive group was supported, not by a permanent bureaucracy, but by several hundred elected officials who rotated through administrative positions of varying importance. These men all came from a larger group of select families who made up the Great Council, membership of which was made hereditary at the end of the thirteenth century. This reform assured a place in Venetian politics to so many families that it mitigated, as intended, the kind of fierce clannish rivalry that plagued other Italian cities of this period. This system left little room for other forms of political organization. There were no guilds of international merchants, mariners, or legal professionals; all their activities were regulated by the commune. Artisanal guilds were permitted, and many developed a considerable measure of self-government, but they were forbidden to establish rules or take actions deemed contrary to the public interest or the honor of the commune.

Venice ran its colonial empire in a manner very different from that of the Genoese. It adopted a strictly mercantilist policy, discouraging local industry and ensuring that trade with the colonies was entirely in Venetian ships carrying raw materials to Venice and finished products to the outposts. Each controlled port or territory was governed by a salaried Venetian aristocrat who served for two years, during which time he was forbidden to engage in private business. He was kept under close surveillance and required to account for his stewardship at the end of the assignment.

One of the special characteristics of Venice, and a source of its lasting power, was its role as entrepôt and staple. Politics played a key part in creating and maintaining this profitable situation. Sea power ensured that after the Fourth Crusade in 1204, all commerce from the East became channeled up the Adriatic to Venice, bypassing potential competitors such as Zara, Ancona, and Ferrara. The next step was to direct the overland trade from northern Europe into Venice and away from Ferrara, the traditional transshipment point for merchandise moving down the eastern Alpine passes. First, the Venetians provided lodgings and warehouses (*fondaci*) for visiting merchants, requiring them to make all their transactions there and not to ship their wares over-seas.[10] Then, in 1240, in alliance with the papacy against Frederick II, the Venetians defeated Ferrara and obtained a treaty giving them control of the latter's Adriatic trade.

By these means, Venice effectively became the staple city for the northern Adriatic, whereby all goods being exchanged within and outside the region had to be brought there for unloading and payment of taxes. This happy arrangement did not exclude foreign traders; on the contrary, it drew them into Venice and made sure that all their transactions were executed and controlled there. The "goods" of particular importance included German silver and, later, Hungarian gold. The channeling of those precious metals through Venice assured the city a leading position in the rich Eastern trade. Much of Venice's subsequent history, including its territorial acquisitions in north-east Italy in the fifteenth century, reflects a continuing effort to preserve and extend this extremely lucrative entrepôt business.

In Florence, the institutions of the commune were relatively fragile and did not come to dominate urban life until late in the thirteenth century. This weakness stemmed from the fact that many of the people who gravitated to the towns did not leave the country behind. The landowning aristocracy, in particular, maintained their rural estates and brought with them to the city their lineage ideals, customs, and vendettas, constructing fortified urban towers of increasing heights to project their power and prestige. Then to protect themselves against the lineage towers, groups of unrelated families formed tower societies to erect towers of their own. Under these circumstances, violence was endemic, and the commune had great difficulty exercising control over the sectional interests. But despite such antagonisms, all concerned entered enthusiastically into the commercial life of the city.

During the thirteenth century, the internal factional disputes became externalized as the contestants took sides in the overarching struggle between the supporters of the papacy, known as the Guelfs, and those of the empire of Frederick II, known as the Ghibellines. After Frederick's death in 1250, the cleavage in cities such as Florence became complete, even within families, as the papacy determined to destroy the Hohenstaufen dynasty root and branch. In 1260, the Ghibellines triumphed at the Battle of Montaperti, took control of Florence, and drove the Guelfs from the city. But in 1266, the papal forces of Charles of Anjou, including a contingent of Florentine Guelf exiles, defeated the Hohenstaufens in southern Italy and in 1268 finally crushed them. The victorious Guelfs seized Florence and dominated its politics even after a general reconciliation with the exiled Ghibelline families was achieved in 1280 with papal help.

Throughout this tumultuous period, business, industry, and the Florentine population expanded vigorously. The main participants in and beneficiaries of this explosive growth were the urbanized landed aristocracy and the successful merchants of humbler origins, who became known as the *popolo grasso*. In particular, the Guelf businessmen, having brought to their Angevin allies desperately needed funds as well as military prowess, reaped commercial rewards. The success of the Hohenstaufen campaign resulted in increased business opportunities with the church and access to the raw material resources, especially grain, and lucrative markets of southern Italy. This latter advantage became enormously important to Florentine businessmen as the Angevin monarchy in Naples gave them preference not only over their Ghibelline competitors from Pisa and Siena, but also over local merchants.

Political life in Florence was further complicated by the fact that the guilds were not prepared to accept the subordinate role allotted them in Genoa and Venice. Here, leading businessmen held high positions in the most powerful of these guilds – the international merchants' and cloth finishers' guild (Calimala), the guild of money changers and bankers (Cambio), and the wool manufacturers' guild (Lana) – often combining to influence the policies of the commune and to resist the commune's efforts to regulate them. With so many forces competing for control, it is not surprising that the governance of commune was at times chaotic. But whatever faction was in power, the government of Florence was, with the possible exception of the brief Ciompi interlude, always unabashedly pro-business throughout the Middle Ages.

ITALIAN BUSINESSMEN IN WESTERN EUROPE

We saw earlier in this book how companies from the cities of north central Italy established branches in southern Italy, France, England, and Flanders in the thirteenth century. Their activities quickly involved politics, because they usually had to obtain the protection of the sovereigns in order to do business at all. In southern Italy, this came about naturally because of a long history of close economic control by the sovereigns dating back to the Normans. Those kings treated the products of the earth and sea as their God-given property, the export of which was subject to their control and thus a privilege to be taxed. They regarded local merchants with suspicion and contempt, preferring to deal with foreigners whom they could control and eject at will. The conquering Angevins held much the same view; moreover, the new King Charles was accustomed to recruit the administrators of his possessions in southern France from outside the area to make sure that they were beholden to his regime. Here was a situation made to order for the Sienese and Florentine merchant-bankers as a consequence of their having helped bankroll the Angevins to power.[11] However, despite Charles's favorable inclinations, the Italians enjoyed little advantage initially, being outdone by Provençal merchants. But during the wars following the Sicilian revolt of 1282, the Angevins again desperately needed help. By the time the war officially ended in 1302, the Italians were firmly entrenched. Then three of the largest Florentine companies, the Bardi, Peruzzi, and Acciaiuoli, provided a steady stream of loans in return for the privilege of exporting huge quantities of grain. Their managers established banks, managed tax farms, and served as high government officials, literally dominating the economy of the kingdom. But this is a story that will unfold in more detail in the next chapter's discussion of the supercompanies of Florence.

In France, Italian businessmen were active throughout most of the thirteenth century, providing services to the government as lenders, managers of mints, and tax collectors. Some became bankers to the crown, and two men, Albizzo and Musciatto Guidi, better known as "Biche" and "Mouche," were directly employed by Philip IV for many years as receivers, treasurers, financial consultants, and ambassadors. But, as noted earlier, Philip was extremely distrustful of foreign financiers of any kind and determined to eliminate all external influences over his financial control. After the deaths of the Guidis in 1306–7, he excluded all Italians except the Peruzzi from governmental activity, expelled the Jews, and forced the dissolution of the Knights Templars and their important banking function. Italians continued to do business in Paris and other parts of France, but they had no government influence even after Philip's death and were often subjected to arbitrary and harsh treatment.

The first wave of Italian merchants to land in England arrived after the Third Crusade, when foreign financing was needed to help meet Richard I's huge expenses abroad, including the staggering ransom for his release from captivity in Germany. But Italians were not very impor-

tant in the coveted wool trade, which for most of the reign of Henry
III had been dominated by Flemish merchants. Then, after the accession
of Edward I in 1272, the Flemish lost their primacy, unfortunate casu-
alties of the political antagonism between England and Flanders. Edward
I first learned of the usefulness of Italian financiers while on his leisurely
journey home from the Holy Land to claim his throne. Soon afterward,
in 1275, he succeeded in establishing a substantial customs duty on virtually all exports of wool. With this assured source of income for his
ambitious projects, Edward turned to a consortium of merchants, the
Ricciardi of Lucca, to provide him with advances on the security of the
customs revenue. His problem was that the flow of his revenues and
taxes and even the new customs duties was uneven and often delayed,
whereas the expenses of his ambitious foreign policy were immediate
and urgent. The Ricciardi system, designed to match the king's income
and expenses more closely, expanded to include most sources of royal
revenue and to provide an array of financial services.

The prize to the Ricciardi for all this management effort was not
interest charges or fees, but the capture of a large share of the immensely
profitable English wool trade. In the late thirteenth century, most of this
trade was still destined for the textile industries of the Low Countries,
and the Italian role was that of middleman in control of a much desired
product. But kings can be capricious partners, and when Edward grew
dissatisfied with the arrangement in 1294, he revoked it and imprisoned
members of the firm. Several years later, the system was reinstated, this
time with the Frescobaldi Company of Florence at the helm, but this
firm too was ejected and its personnel forced to flee as a result of the
Ordainers' revolt of 1310 against Edward's successor, Edward II. For all
his faults, Edward II was a saver rather than a spender and rarely called
on the services of outside financiers during his reign. His successor,
Edward III, an extraordinarily ambitious and extravagant monarch,
utilized every source of funds he could lay his hands on, borrowing
prodigiously from numerous Italian, Flemish, German, and indigenous
merchants. His favorite Italian financiers until their collapse in the 1340s
were the Bardi Company of Florence, and later the Peruzzi.

In order to retain the privilege of exporting wool, the larger Italian
companies became increasingly enmeshed in the day-to-day affairs of
the monarchy. They contracted to provide the royal household with
fixed monthly stipends. They were expected to provide services of all
kinds, from acquiring rare baubles and delicacies for royal family
members or favorites to carrying out espionage. In one instance, the
Bardi Company was able to ingratiate itself by tracking down a rene-
gade in Sicily and returning him to justice in England. Securing repay-

ment of their loans was an extremely complex and laborious process, often taking the form of receipts from tax levies, which were elusive and had to be pursued diligently. Their multifarious transactions with the government were often subjected to detailed audits, which brought them into close and uncomfortable contact with the bureaucracy. And they were bitterly resented by the English merchants, who, envious of the Italians' privileges, did everything in their power to undermine their position, with the enthusiastic support of the populace at large.

The large Italian colonies in Bruges and other Flemish towns were important to the local communities for the services they were able to perform for the vital textile industry. Italian companies imported many of the raw materials, provided considerable financing and creative financial instruments, and found markets for a large share of the finished product. But the relationship was delicate, and not only because Italians had supplanted Flemish merchants in the English wool trade. From the early fourteenth century, Flanders frequently erupted in bloody revolt against its French masters, which found the Italians in the middle as agents of the French crown. The Peruzzi Company, for example, collected indemnities for Philip IV after the defeat of the 1302 revolt, and later, during the 1320s, its branch manager in Bruges was named receiver-general for the Count of Flanders. The Peruzzi then helped the count crush yet another revolt in 1328 by granting a large loan, repayment of which was assigned to the city of Bruges over a five-year period. Finally that same company, along with the Bardi, became committed after 1337 to King Edward III in his war with France, helping him promote Flanders' entry into the war on the English side. And yet, throughout all these twists and turns, the Italians continued to enjoy a robust business in the Low Countries.

Finally, the political connections of Italian businessmen with the church were longstanding and complex. We have already seen how Florentine merchants ingratiated themselves with the papacy by supporting the latter's struggle against the empire, and in particular the Hohenstaufens. By this action, the firms won enormous economic advantage in the territories of southern Italy held by the Angevin monarch as a vassal of the pope. They also assumed responsibility for collecting and remitting the king's annual tribute to the Curia. Business with the princes of the church was important and lucrative, but was a privilege that often had to be earned by political services. And the favor of the Holy See was necessary to enable companies to participate in the business of transferring church funds around Europe, an activity not very profitable in itself, but immensely prestigious and useful in constructing a financial network. The papal bureaucracy could also be invaluable in intervening on behalf of favored companies to apply pressure to high-ranking problem debtors, both lay and ecclesiastical.

The converse was true for those who directly opposed the papacy, as evidenced by the lack of consideration given the merchants of Ghibelline cities in southern Italy. But the relationship of any town and its businessmen with the church cannot be described in straightforward terms. The pontifical organization was at least as faction ridden as the towns, and given the relatively short tenure of most popes between 1250 and 1350, papal policy zigged and zagged with the shifting dominant factions. Even in loyal Florence, the machinations of Pope Boniface VIII so exacerbated an intramural struggle that the most famous of the embittered losers, Dante Alighieri, made highly uncomplimentary references to that pope in two cantos (XIX and XXVII) of his *Inferno*. And at times, the relationship between the Florentine leadership and its archbishop grew so hostile that the city was placed under interdict. An interdiction was a serious matter for businessmen. By closing the churches and stopping the ringing of the bells, it upset the normal rhythm of business activity. And of potentially great importance to international merchant-bankers, an interdict released outsiders from the moral obligation to honor contracts with businessmen of the afflicted city.

EVOLUTION OF LAW

We have seen that kings and other sovereigns, driven by the desire to profit from trade, offered remedies for the legal insecurities of business life. The basis for these appeared in the charters granted to towns, which always contained provisions guaranteeing the inviolability of a burgher's personal property besides specifying customary tolls and other taxes. Charters establishing fairs also offered legal boons such as safe conduct for all merchants journeying to the fair, as well as security for their property, and special courts intended to resolve mercantile disputes expeditiously. The permanent foreign merchant communities that we have frequently described obtained special courts attached either to the city or a merchant guild, where *lex mercatoria* – merchant law – held sway. This law was a mélange of custom and special privilege that varied from region to region but always held fast to the need for speedy justice according to principles instituted and accepted by the merchants themselves. These emphasized equity, contract, and commonly accepted notions of fair business practice.

In the broader legal environment, four important developments had taken place by the opening of the thirteenth century. First, the *Corpus iuris civilis* of Emperor Justinian had been rediscovered toward the end of the eleventh century and gradually clarified during the twelfth century. Second, as we have seen, sovereigns of regions and governments of city-states began to initiate and codify legislation, often specifying that the enactment had the consent of the populace. Third was the formation of the law schools, beginning at Bologna, where masters and students studied, interpreted, and disseminated the texts of both canon law and civil law, compiling many of the civil codes. And finally, canonical and civilian lawyers were radically revising their attitudes toward private property, making it a sacrosanct principle deriving from natural law.[12]

The Italian city-states were unsurprisingly among the first polities to make practical use of the new flow of jurisprudence. As early as 1156, the commune of Pisa convened a commission of "wise men" learned in the law to compile a new code drawing upon Roman principles, the collected legislation of the Lombard kings, and customary local practice. The code, promulgated in 1160, was issued in two parts, one dealing in civil procedure, including marriage and inheritance, and the other primarily concerning merchant, sea, and feudal law. Within the next century or so, virtually all major Italian city-states had followed suit with their own adaptations. The need for the codes arose from the fact that laws and regulations had accumulated over time, scattered in a number of volumes, and were often confusing and contradictory. Moreover, laws had to be codified coherently to deal with rapidly changing conditions, to accommodate relationships with the numerous guilds (which had their own statutes), and to provide for corporate structures of business partnerships.

Roman law had only limited penetration outside of Italy. It revived fairly readily in southern France and the Christianized territories of Spain, where the teaching of Roman law was able to build upon an old linkage to Roman tradition. In northern France, the influence of Roman law was slow to develop, except in church courts, as law books were based on custom and the registered statutes promulgated by kings. Its effect, nevertheless, was significant in establishing principles. For example, the law faculty of the university at Orléans cited the judicial power that Roman law accorded to the emperor in support of Louis IX's claim to be the supreme repository and dispenser of justice in his kingdom. In England, however, the early headway made by Roman law was thwarted by activist kings, starting with Henry II, who laid the foundations of a robust common law system out of customary usages and the king's writ. And those English kings also permitted foreign merchants to make up half of the jury in the law-merchant courts, ensuring the primacy of mercantile interests and creating a true international body of legal practice and precedent.[13]

The existence of an expanding body of law afforded international businessmen at least a degree of protection against arbitrary abuse by sovereigns and their officials. But the superabundance of laws and the inconsistency of their application created problems, notwithstanding the welcome relief of the legal concessions provided in the commercial colonies and periodic fairs at certain foreign locations. And laws, even just ones, could be inequitably administered, ignored, or ruthlessly overridden whenever it suited the local authorities. The adroit use of political pressure therefore continued to be essential to successful business in most parts of medieval Europe.

We have seen in this chapter the vital importance of politics to business and the great variety of forms that political involvement took at different times and in different parts of Europe during the Middle Ages. The simple overriding motivation of political interventions, however, was always the narrow self-interest of the rulers, even where the rulers happened to be businessmen. The effect on business was sometimes clearly constructive, as in the case of the infrastructure projects of the counts of Flanders and Holstein, and sometimes clearly harmful, as in the excessive tolls, taxes, and mercantilist practices of many sovereigns. For the most part, the growing community of interests between rulers and businessmen drove the former toward actions and policies that proved mainly favorable to business. Beginning in the early fourteenth century, however, costly expansionist activities drove certain rulers, especially in England and France, to resort to rapacious financing tactics that were extremely deleterious to business. In England, the most noteworthy of such actions took the form of milking the wool trade; in France, the manipulation of coinage values. Similar demonstrations of royal indifference to business interests continued to occur throughout the late Middle Ages, but we shall also find in Part II that sovereigns were becoming increasingly sensitive to the usefulness of business in advancing their own interests.

5

BUSINESS GETS BIGGER: THE SUPER-COMPANY PHENOMENON

•

A new business phenomenon emerged in western Europe in the latter half of the thirteenth century, reaching its apogee in the first quarter of the fourteenth century. This was the very large international company headquartered in the inland towns of north central Italy, such as Lucca, Siena, Piacenza, Asti, and, above all, Florence. This type of enterprise, often misidentified as a bank, was primarily a large-scale merchanting operation that included international banking activities as an important segment of its business, and thus is better described as a merchant-bank.

It is not surprising that this new type of business organization should appear in Italy, given that territory's strategic location athwart the trade routes of northern Europe and the Mediterranean. Venice and Genoa, not the inland towns, would seem to have been the most likely venues; but although both cities traded with the north by land and by sea, they were preoccupied with the lucrative but furiously contested Mediterranean commerce and with their role as entrepôts. Moreover, their business organizations remained venture-oriented, even when individual enterprises coalesced temporarily or permanently into larger units, such as convoys or overseas colonies. Such cooperative arrangements were usually state-managed collaborations motivated by the need for security and overseen by state officials. In this environment, commerce was conducted mainly by individual entrepreneurs in transitory joint ventures, except in rare cases where the state maintained a substantial permanent organization, such as the arsenal of Venice.

To be sure, some businesses in these cities became very large indeed. The most striking example is that of Benedetto Zaccaria, the best known of a large and boisterous Genoese family of the late thirteenth and early fourteenth centuries. Admiral, diplomat, buccaneer, mercenary, as well as merchant on a grand scale, he built an empire of shipping, mining, and trading interests. His military and negotiating prowess brought him two enormously lucrative monopolies from the Byzantine emperor: over the cultivation of mastic on the Aegean island of Chios, and over the development of the alum mines of Phocaea in Asia Minor. Mastic, an aromatic gum much appreciated by women in the Near East for whitening teeth and freshening breath, was extracted from a shrub cultivated almost exclusively on the Aegean island of Chios. Zaccaria controlled the production and distribution of this scarce asset with a level of skill and ruthlessness that would arouse the envy of the Oppenheimers today. Alum, a fixative for dyes, was essential to the burgeoning textile industries of western Europe. Here again Zaccaria optimized profit by manipulating production, controlling distribution in his own ships, and using his political wiles and influence with the emperor to neutralize competition. But despite its size, reach, and diversity, his business had no lasting foundation. After Benedetto's death in 1307, his wealth and property passed to his heirs, but his business empire dissolved.

Merchants in the inland towns did not shun Mediterranean trade, but saw their greatest opportunity in linking it to the markets of northwestern Europe. We have already noted that, after participating in the Champagne fairs, they began to establish permanent representation in the commercial centers of northern Europe – Bruges, Paris, and London. Unlike Venice and Genoa, the inland towns lacked the military resources to enforce the establishment of colonies; instead, their merchants had to demonstrate their value to the local authorities by bringing desired goods and the means to acquire them. As a result, the more successful merchants of necessity became larger and better capitalized, with a head office in the home town and a network of representatives abroad. The largest developed enough business to warrant setting up branches with several employees in cities where opportunities were especially attractive.

THE BUSINESS NEED FOR LARGER COMPANIES

What was this business? Early in the thirteenth century, it was the usual exchange of merchandise from southern Europe and the Orient – spices, precious stones, and fine fabrics – for fine Flemish woolens and other articles, but mainly silver. Later, after 1275, when the Italians began to interpose themselves between the English wool producers and the Flemish textile manufacturers, they took over a large share of that trade.

Moreover, the Italian towns, especially Florence, began moving into the production of fine woolens themselves, first by importing Flemish semi-processed cloth for finishing, and later by importing top quality English wools for full manufacturing. These developments helped reduce the trade imbalance between north and south, but specie remained the prime "export" from northern Europe.

The northern Italian entrepreneurs were simultaneously moving in the opposite direction – to southern Italy and Sicily. There, the attraction was twofold. First, as we have seen in the previous chapter, the assistance given by Florence and other towns to the papacy and Angevins to conquer that territory opened up a splendid new market. Second, Angevin Italy possessed abundant raw materials, the most important of which was wheat of a superior grade and outstanding keeping quality. The need for this resource was increasing yearly as the population of the northern Italian towns continued to grow, outstripping their local food supplies. As early as 1258, the commune of Florence forbade the export of grain from its *contado* (the rural area surrounding the city), and in 1274 it created a special office to control the supply and distribution of grain in the city. By the early fourteenth century, the Florentine *contado* reportedly could produce food for the city for only five of the twelve months of the year, so that Florence had to import food grains on a massive scale to maintain its industrial and commercial well-being.

Opportunities thus abounded, both in the north and south, for the well-positioned merchants of north central Italy, and there was nothing inherent in any of these businesses that precluded small-scale merchants from grasping them. Ordinary firms were perfectly capable of shipping grain and raw materials of all kinds, and had done so for centuries. What made the very large concerns necessary was the fact that the rulers of England and southern Italy had become increasingly aware of the value of the commodities under their control. As their power grew, so did their expenses and the need for steady infusions of cash. To secure this cash, they were prepared to grant trading privileges to those firms that could advance large sums, the loans to be repaid from the duties or taxes levied on the exports. We have seen in the previous chapter how the Ricciardi of Lucca succeeded in appropriating a large share of the English wool trade by providing steady financing for Edward I, and how the great Florentine companies acquired a virtual monopoly of southern Italy's grain exports in exchange for a stream of large loans. By the late thirteenth century, it had become clear that only very large, handsomely capitalized companies could participate in these lucrative commodity businesses. And these same firms developed the extensive branch

networks, marketing skills, and resources necessary to distribute these
goods profitably.

A word should be said here about the larger non-Italian companies
– and there were some of significant size. Merchants from Brabant,
such as Godfrey de Mouns, and from Germany, such as Godekinus von
Revele, were important lenders to Edward III during his campaigns in
the Low Countries in the late 1330s. And the famous English wool and
textile merchant William de la Pole of Hull conducted operations on a
scale that matched that of the English branches of the Bardi and Peruzzi.
But Pole essentially led a powerful consortium of English merchants
rather than manage a complex organization under his own control.[1]
Thus, although these and other well-capitalized merchants in northern
Europe did substantial international business, none could boast the organization, branch networks, or endurance of the great Italian partnerships.

The inland Italian cities produced a stream of such companies, each
with distinctive specialties. The Bonsignori of Siena were early backers
of the Angevins in southern Italy; the Ricciardi, Frescobaldi, and Cerchi
were active in English wool; and the Scali were prestigious papal bankers
who also had a strong presence in southern Italy. Most had lengthy histories of fifty years or more, but the fourth largest of the fourteenth-
century companies, the Buonaccorsi of Florence, went through a
spectacular rise and fall in only twenty years. Although usually dominated by certain members of the family that gave the company its name,
most included outside shareholders. Each eventually overreached, stum-
bled, and fell, their business assumed by ever-larger entities.

EMERGENCE OF THE SUPER-COMPANIES

Three companies – the Bardi, Peruzzi, and Acciaiuoli of Florence – were
so large and complex as to deserve a special name to distinguish them
from merely large concerns. The term "super-company" best expresses
the nature of these organizations. They were unusually large and qualitatively different, engaged in an exceptional range of activity – general
trading, commodity trading, banking, and manufacturing – over a wide
geographical area for an extended period. These were the kind of entities noted in the discussion of the textile industry in Chapter 2 – Italian
merchant-banking concerns that had grown large enough to manage
and finance the woolen textile trade from beginning to end. The opportunity for such comprehensive oversight began in the 1320s, when
Florence's woolen cloth manufacturers began to move upscale into the
production of luxury fabrics, for which they needed a steady supply of
fine English wools. The great merchant-bankers found little to attract

them to the low-margin business of manufacturing; the Peruzzi Company, for example, had only a small production facility in Florence. Their objective was to engage in the high-profit segments of wool supply and cloth marketing, while directing the entire commercial flow from the acquisition of raw materials to the sale of finished product in the markets throughout Europe and the Mediterranean.

The process started with the steps taken to ensure continuous access to raw materials of certain qualities direct from the growers. The companies' knowledgeable agents did not merely inspect and buy from the current crop, but contracted for future clips, often years in advance, paying the growers in cash. In return, the companies earned sizeable cash discounts in addition to a guarantee of supply at preset prices. Much of the cash for these transactions arrived through circuitous channels, but with little physical movement of funds. English kings normally forbade the export of specie, including papal collections from the faithful of England. The papacy needed these funds in various parts of continental Europe, including the Holy See itself, and looked to the Italian merchant-bankers to arrange the transfers. The Italians were able to provide cash where the papacy needed it and drew on the papal collections in England for their wool purchases. Many of the wool growers in England were Cistercian monasteries, the source of some of the papal collections – so that part of the money paid to the Curia treasury was effectively recycled back to them without leaving the country!

Moving the wool out of England to Florence involved the long tortuous journey described in the transportation industry section of Chapter 2. When the wool arrived in Florence, the companies sold some, kept some for their own manufacture, and entrusted some to fabricators for their own account, holding title to the goods throughout the process. They also oversaw the dyeing and finishing to ensure that the colors and textures were appropriate for the intended markets. Then the company would distribute the finished product, selling some from the company's warehouse annex in Florence, some to merchants throughout Italy, western Europe, and the Mediterranean, and some to its branches in Italy and abroad. The entire process from beginning to end entailed many miles of transportation and many months of immobilized cash. Markups had to be substantial to compensate for these costs, in addition to normal risks of marketing and of damage or loss in transit.

Of even more importance to the super-companies was the two-way trade of grain and cloth between Florence and southern Italy. Unlike in England, where the relationship of great companies to kings was intermittent, in Italy it was continuous from about the year 1300 until the mid 1340s. And the volume of trade was huge; normal annual exports of grain from southern Italy controlled by these firms averaged around 12,000 metric tons, reaching the astonishing total of 45,000 tons in 1311. These quantities, being much greater than Florence's needs, found their way on bulk cargo ships leased from Venice, Genoa, and other maritime ports to destinations around Italy and the Mediterranean, including Muslim as well as Christian cities. The super-companies also enjoyed preferential trade in other goods of the region, especially the edible oil and wine highly desired in northern Italy. In return, they dominated the Angevin market for the better grades of cloth (local manufacture being limited to the lower end of the trade) and engaged in all kinds of commerce. They increasingly penetrated the economic life of the kingdom and in 1316 formed a syndicate that collected taxes, transported cash, paid bureaucrats' salaries and troops' wages, and managed military stores, all in addition to to their trade in grain and wine. They dealt with government officials, many of whom were fellow Florentines and even company colleagues, and enjoyed profound and steady influence with the court, especially during the long reign of King Robert.

This fruitful relationship was not sustained because of past military help or continuing good will. The predominance of the super-companies was fueled by a steady flow of massive loans to the crown, some of which were merely advances on taxes due on the export of grain. Other loans were for specific terms and were recovered from the general revenues of the realm and promptly re-loaned to keep the cycle going. Profits to the companies came mainly from the generous trading privileges granted in return for loans, rather than from interest or its equivalent on the loans themselves.

How did the three super-companies put themselves in such a happy position? They had each been in business in Naples for some years, developing slowly like others of their kind, but at the end of the thirteenth century their owners perceived great opportunities for companies with an exceptionally large pool of capital. They accordingly assembled a group of manager-investors with capital and talent from within and outside the controlling families so that they were instantly ready to do business on the scale required by the Angevins. Thus the super-companies suddenly burst on the scene and came to typify "big business" in medieval Europe over the next forty years. Of the three super-companies, the Bardi was by far the grandest. Unfortunately, specific data are lacking regarding the number of branches, employees, and capital, but fragmentary indicators of profit and assets suggest that the Bardi was at least 50 percent larger than its next-largest rival, the Peruzzi Company. It was at least the Peruzzi's equal in all markets except in France, and enjoyed a decidedly superior position in England, where it had done business from the 1270s or earlier. The Acciaiuoli, the third-ranking super-company, was active in most of the same areas as the other two and was significantly less aggressive only in England, where it avoided involvement with the king.

THE SUPER-COMPANIES

Legal structure

Although much of what will be described in this section will apply also to the not-quite-super-companies noted earlier, there are certain characteristics that are exclusively applicable to the "big three." As already noted, one is the fact that they were *created* as large enterprises to meet their objectives, rather than gradually expanding in response to business growth. Thus, the Peruzzi Company was reorganized in 1300 with capital of 124,000 *lire a fiorino*, equivalent to 85,000 golden florins, subscribed 60 percent by seven members of the Peruzzi family and 40 percent by ten outsiders from the cream of the Florentine business community. This was a staggering amount for the time and immediately established the company as one of the highest-capitalized in Europe. But although the business expanded and new branches were opened, its capital never exceeded that level, except for the years 1308–12, during the rest of the company's forty-three-year history.

The super-companies, like most Italian firms of significant size, were organized legally as quasi-permanent multiple partnerships. They were quasi-permanent in that they did not dissolve with the death or retirement of a partner, and even upon "dissolution" the partnership was immediately renewed. Each partnership lasted as long as it suited the partners, some for two years, others for as long as twelve years. The reason for closing was usually the desire for a realignment of the shareholdings, which might or might not be accompanied by a distribution of profits. In any case, the business would continue without interruption, carrying on through numerous reorganizations over decades.

We have already seen that the partnerships were multiple in the Peruzzi example of seventeen partners in the 1300 company. But a word needs to be said here to explain why we have been referring to these large firms as "companies" and their owners as "shareholders." This is because the share of ownership of each partner, and thus his share of the profits, depended upon the amount of money he contributed as a percentage of the total amount of capital. Thus the words "partner" and "shareholder" can be used interchangeably. But the companies were also partnerships in the modern sense, because each shareholder was subject

to unlimited liability against all of his personal possessions in the event
of bankruptcy of the company. As a result, any distribution of profits
was tentative, subject to subsequent adjustments, positive or negative,
years or even decades after the original allocations.

Most shareholders, both family and outsiders, contributed their talent
as well as their money and occupied key positions, including management of the more important and politically sensitive foreign branches.
The presence of these men in foreign posts gave assurance to their
clients that the company was an enduring organization, notwithstanding the frequent dissolutions. This sense of permanence was further
enhanced by the use of a company logo of distinctive or heraldic design
that was especially appreciated by the papacy as an indicator of the firm's
stability.[2] But whatever authority the managing partners may have had,
they were clearly subservient to the *capo* or chairman, who was almost
always a leading member of the family and whose name formed part
of the company title.

Organization and personnel

Although there is no direct evidence that any of the great companies
had drawn up formal divisions of responsibility or lines of authority, the
many references in the Peruzzi books to the various parts of the
company's operations in Florence and abroad offer a reasonable idea of
how they worked in practice. They suggest that the Peruzzi had a form
of organization that permitted a degree of decentralization at the operating level, but reserved important areas of decision making to the powerful chairman's central office in Florence. The facing page shows how
the organization would have looked had the Peruzzi charted it.

Operations in Florence were fairly centralized, with several "subsidiary" companies reporting directly to the chairman. Vastly oversimplified, the *tavola* dealt primarily with banking-related operations
managed in Florence, and the *mercanzia* with trading and logistics out
of Florence. The *drapperia* controlled a small textile contract manufacturing operation. "Special accounts" oversaw a number of important
foreign customers directly from Florence, such as the Order of the
Hospitalers and certain church dignitaries. The *limosina* was simply an
account through which the company's charities were channeled. About
two percent of the company's capital was set aside for God's work, from
which the *limosina* received allocations of profit. The Bardi actually des-
ignated its charity shareholding as belonging to *Messer Domeneddio*, that
is, to God. But because of the irregularity and uncertainty of dividends,

Organizational structure of the Peruzzi Company, July 1, 1335

Chairman		
Florence operations	Foreign branches	
	Headed by partners	Headed by factors
Co. della Tavola	Naples Donato Peruzzi	Barletta
Co. della Mercanzia	Sicily F. Forzetti	Cyprus
Co. della Drapperia	Avignon F. Villani	Rhodes
Co. della Limosina	England G. Baroncelli	Sardinia
Special Accounts	Bruges Pacino di Guido Peruzzi	Tunis
	Paris Filippo Peruzzi	Majorca
		Venice
		Pisa

companies also made, in January of each year, a substantial allocation of funds which were to be donated to charitable institutions and to the poor throughout the year.

Whether or not these head office "subsidiaries" were led by managers reporting to the chairman is unclear. The only firm evidence we have is that Giotto Peruzzi at one time headed the *tavola* as treasurer. Foreign branches did, however, have clearly identified managers and were organized on two levels – those headed by partners and those led by employees. Politics, more than economics, seems to have been the determining criterion. Thus, partners managed the politically sensitive branches of Naples, Sicily, England, Paris, Avignon, and Flanders, where status, social graces, intelligence, and authority in the company were necessary to deal with difficult noblemen and bureaucrats. Branches with mainly trading and logistics activities, even large ones such as Barletta, southern Italy's principal grain port, were adequately managed by well-trained employees. The level of leadership often changed with circumstances. For example, during the early difficult years of getting established, the Peruzzi's Rhodes branch was headed by a partner; later, when business became more routine, it was run by an employee.

How were all these people remunerated? For the employees, the answer is relatively simple. They earned salaries according to their age, experience, and level of responsibility. Some also earned a bonus for outstanding work. Most, especially those on foreign assignment, had access to company goods and services. Overall their pay was higher than the norm in Florence, and their salary progression was steady. In 1335, half of the Peruzzi's salaried employees earned at least seventy gold florins per year, a very handsome income. The remuneration of managing shareholders is much more problematic. Of course they received dividends. But there is no evidence of any other kind of remuneration – definitely no salaries or bonuses. They did enjoy considerable use of company resources, and it is likely that the shareholders did indeed receive substantial perquisites in the form of cloth, food, luxury goods, and services from the company. Robert Reynold's eloquent discussion of the intermingling of the expenses of a company and its managing partners may help put this anomaly into perspective. He notes that expenses that we would regard as personal were often paid by the firm, and others clearly benefiting the company were paid by the partner. "It was all one. . . . It really did not matter then; it only bothers us now when we try to appraise such matters with cost accountants' techniques."[3] But it did matter when a company entered bankruptcy proceedings. The Peruzzi's surviving accounts show a number of personal expenses from several years earlier being charged back to the partners, suggesting that what had been normal privileges were now being recovered for the company's creditors on orders from the bankruptcy court.

The employees of medieval Italian companies, both at home and in the foreign branches, had one common attribute: all were Italian, mainly from the home city. Non-Italians were no doubt hired for specific services such as transporting merchandise, but none were taken on as permanent staff. Aside from the convenience of a common language and the cardinal importance of trust, Italian employees were essential because they were trained in business systems largely unknown to foreigners. All would have studied under private tutors, or more likely, after 1300, in one of the "abacus schools."[4] There they would have learned the various computational skills, including the use of Arabic numerals, needed to deal with practical business problems. The emphasis of their training was on problem solving and developing a retentive memory, rather than the use of logic to arrive at solutions. A graduate could look forward to a rewarding career, perhaps even with one of the great companies, after a suitable period of apprenticeship.

The 133 men employed by the Peruzzi between 1331 and 1343 and the 346 who worked for the Bardi between 1310 and 1345 were drawn from the best and the brightest of Florence's mercantile families. Interestingly, though, none came from the families of the companies' main competitors, and surprisingly few were from the shareholders' own families. In the case of the Peruzzi, only 23 of the 133 factors noted above were related to the company's owners, and most worked for modest wages. The lack of competitors' offspring is not surprising, given the fact that a man's loyalty to his family was expected to transcend that to his company. But the paucity of family scions in the family firm suggests a refreshing absence of nepotism; commerce was too important to be placed in the hands of the incompetent, however near and dear. For all employees, job security was of a high order; in a going business, the usual cause for termination was fraud, which was dealt with harshly. Even during the Peruzzi's long slide into bankruptcy, enrolment declined only gradually, and no salaries were cut.

Data are lacking for most companies on numbers of employees at any given time. We do know that in 1335 the Peruzzi had, in addition to working shareholders, 90 salaried employees, 48 of whom were deployed in the branches. And we know that the somewhat smaller Acciaiuoli employed 43 factors in its foreign branches. The total for the Bardi is unknown but is likely to have ranged between 120 and 150. In addition to salaried employees, numerous people were regularly employed by the company off the payroll, such as sons of shareholders, notaries, shippers, innkeepers, and textile workers. The total numbers are not impressive by modern standards, but were considerable for the fourteenth century, and much larger than the 57 employees of the Medici Bank a century later. For perspective, the mightiest bureaucracy of the age – the Avignon papacy – had 250 administrators, and most government administrations were considerably smaller.

Accounting systems

Most of the discussion of super-companies' activity has concentrated on grain and wool, but they were much more than commodity traders. Like many other companies of significant size, they were also very active throughout western Europe and the Mediterranean in buying and selling merchandise of all kinds, manufacturing textiles on a small scale, and banking on a grand international scale for businesses, princes, governments, and the papacy. All this required a system of management and control that would enable such companies to operate successfully in an environment of slow and uncertain communications, political tumult, and pervasive violence both at home and abroad.

Unfortunately there are tantalizing gaps in the data, and no completed financial statements or analyses of operations. Nevertheless, the surviving records of companies such as the Bardi, Peruzzi, Alberti, and del Bene tell us a great deal about the organization, accounting, and control systems of the great companies of the early fourteenth century. The most complete set of accounts is that of the Peruzzi Company of 1335–43, and although it depicts a company that was sliding inexorably into bankruptcy, it provides such a wealth of detail that we can easily determine how the systems worked.

The principal ledgers of the large companies were the assets and secret books, which combined to produce something that looks broadly like the consolidation accounts of a modern multinational corporation. They open with balances carried forward from the old company, and they control certain items of income and expense, especially interest, that are not carried elsewhere. They also house the individual accounts of borrowers and depositors controlled by the head office. The difference between the assets and secret books is that the latter deals with items of special sensitivity, such as the accounts of shareholders and the payroll of employees. It is also the source of the final profit and loss statements. Because of its confidential nature, this book was normally kept by the chairman. The entries in these books reveal the existence of a number of subsidiary books, indicating an enormous accounting undertaking. One book was the merchandise trade register, which also recorded the accounts payable and receivable balances in the foreign branches. Another was a holding account for certain expenses, including advances in cash and kind to partners and employees at home and abroad, leaving no open balances of the closing of each partnership. Still others dealt with legal claims, rental charges, shareholders' capital contributions, and odds and ends of expenditures and receipts that did not fit anywhere else.

These documents tell much about the systems used by such businesses and their level of sophistication. First, they translated all local transactions and branch balances into a fictive unit of account – in the case of Florence the *lira a fiorino*. In reality, the companies did business in a bewildering variety of coinages of constantly changing relationships, and all branches reported results in the local currency. The headquarters accountants therefore had to reduce this hodgepodge into a statistical measure of value common to all the company's operations. This technique or its equivalent was used by most Italian merchants, but it required extraordinary diligence and organization in a company with the vast international reach of the Peruzzi. The effort was worthwhile then – just as it is now to the modern multinational corporation – because the managing shareholders could only understand the company's global results and ultimately receive their dividends in terms of these *lire a fiorino*.

Second, the companies used double-entry bookkeeping, with debit accounts recorded in the first half of each book and credits in the second. All entries were constructed logically, with signposts clearly informing the reader the whereabouts of the offsetting postings, making it possible to trace the evolution of each account through the life of the partnership. At the start of a new partnership, the accountants transferred the open balances from the old company by first setting up and totaling equal and opposite entries on the opening pages of the debit and credit sections of the assets book and secret book of the new company. These balances were then offset by postings to newly created individual accounts in those books or to the various existing subsidiary books, so that the new company could continue business seamlessly from the data of the old company. Those first balances, picturesquely described by Armando Sapori as the "living remains" of the old company, were actually the mirror image of them; that is, the debits are really liabilities and the credits are assets. They were the necessary offsets to the entries that had to be made to set up the accounts of the new company.

The books also show that companies meticulously assigned interest, described euphemistically as a gift of time or profit, to all balances of debtors and creditors. In the Peruzzi Company, the rate applied was a flat 8 percent until 1326, when it was lowered to 7 percent, a figure, wrote the company's treasurer, Giotto Peruzzi, that was "good and pleasing to God." In addition, the entries disclose that the accountants were familiar with the concept of accruals. For example, all employee salaries were credited to their personal accounts in the secret book in Florence. To maintain confidentiality, those employees working in foreign branches were not paid their salaries, but instead were granted living expense advances. These were charged to the employees' personal accounts in Florence, which held the accrued salaries. Any balances, positive or negative, also accrued interest at the standard rate of 7 percent per annum.

Two items are interesting because of their virtual absence from the books. The first is fixed assets. This lack of bricks and mortar was not, however, an accounting anomaly, but the result of deliberate policy. The large companies sensibly avoided tying up cash in capital goods, preferring to rent, rather than own, their shops and warehouses. And they hired all their transport, both land and sea. The second is that no inventories appear among the Peruzzi Company's assets. This indeed was a matter of accounting practice, as the company owned large stocks of raw materials and finished goods in Florence, the branches, and in transit. The reason that they do not show up in the Florence accounts is that the Peruzzi practiced venture accounting, a common procedure among medieval merchants.[5] Under this system, each lot of merchandise was controlled in a separate account. All relevant costs, such as warehousing, shipping, and damages, were debited, and all sales were credited to that account. When the goods were all disposed of, the bookkeeper closed the account, transferring the balance to profit or loss. In effect, this was an early substitute for cost accounting, enabling the managers to gain an idea of the profitability of each kind of business. Thus, a significant part of the totals reported at the end of the company's accounting period as accounts receivable are made up of inventories in the balances of open venture accounts.

The accounting at branch level is much more problematic, because none of the super-companies' branch accounts has survived, and we have had to rely on scraps of information to tell us roughly what they contained and how they were kept. The branches seem to have enjoyed a degree of independence in their reporting. Some gave only one net balance figure; others gave a figure for both receivables and payables; still others added helpful information, such as the number and type of accounts. But even at best, the information was inadequate for the central office accountants, who must have had additional data available in their subsidiary books.

The Peruzzi Company's elaborate systems of accounting and control have deservedly aroused the admiration and even astonishment of historians of all kinds. Indeed, the organization of the company's operations and their information flows reveal a level of sophistication that would not be out of place in a modern business school case study. But too much emphasis has been placed on the apparent "modernity" of the abstract conceptualizations expressed in the accounts. These were all very nice, but they were assembled much too slowly to be of practical value to the real-world running of the business; the accomplishments of the super-companies rested on the disciplined application of the knowledge, experience, and acumen of their managers to the opportunities they perceived.

Relationships with families, Florence, church, and each other

Although the three super-companies were controlled by members of their eponymous families, they do not appear to have been subordinated to the latter's interests. Put another way, the super-companies were not undertakings of lineages, but of specific individuals who devoted their time, talents, and money to the enterprise. To the family as a whole, however, the company was a source of pride and prestige, as well as profit. From a purely financial point of view, the shareholders of the super-companies would have been justified in dissolving their organizations long before such action was forced on them. But the super-companies seem to have taken on a life of their own, transcending purely family interests. In the case of the Peruzzi, the businesses had clearly become unprofitable by the close of the books in 1335, prompting the departure of three outside shareholders. But the family members of all the super-companies hung on through calamity after calamity until 1343, when the businesses simply collapsed. The Acciaiuoli succumbed around the same time as the Peruzzi, but the Bardi kept going for another three years, finally giving up in 1346.

There was considerable symbiosis between company and the lineage. Family members, both inside and outside the company, enhanced the company's power by holding influential offices in the major guilds and the commune. For example, Peruzzis were active in no fewer than four of the great guilds of Florence – the Calimala, bankers, wool, and doctors/apothecaries – and served in the priorate of the commune sixteen times between 1310 and 1342. But the super-companies were powers in their own right, as the city's ambitious foreign adventures depended heavily on them for their international connections and their unmatched capability to mobilize cash. Thus, the Bardi Company was enormously influential in municipal politics, despite the handicap that all Bardi family members had been barred from holding public office since 1293. Because of this restriction, the Bardi Company in its later years was represented not by a prominent Bardi, but by a highly capable outside shareholder, Taldo Valori, one of the most powerful figures in Florentine politics. The Bardi family members thus had good reason to cling to the company's skirts for as long as possible.

The super-companies' relationship with the commune, as suggested earlier, went beyond the interests and influence of high-ranking family members. The companies brought much business and employment to the city and were important and reliable sources of revenue for the commune, albeit mostly in the form of voluntary or forced loans. Their commercial and financial reach enhanced Florence's standing among the great rulers, papal princes, and city-states throughout Europe, an attribute that was particularly important to a city that was militarily weak. The commune was also good to the business elite, including the super-companies. It discontinued wealth and property taxes except in extraordinary crises and relied heavily on consumption taxes (gabelles) levied on a range of goods purchased mainly by the lower classes. More-over, the companies often farmed the gabelles, usually, but not always, at a profit.[6]

The commune, however, was by no means the lapdog of the merchant class. We have already seen that it controlled the grain market and kept a wary eye on prices, even employing spies for the purpose. And it could and did put enormous pressure on the super-companies to "do the right thing" in times of famine. It also had an array of laws regarding commercial activity, which, if properly administered, could yield considerable tax revenue at the expense of all companies. But this rarely happened; in fact, it was a policy of rigorous application of these laws in 1343 by the dictator of Florence, Walter of Brienne, that enraged the elite and provoked Brienne's downfall. Nevertheless, the commune had rules governing the conduct of business that were clearly defined and respected. Bankruptcy procedures, although chaotic at times, were well understood, open to public scrutiny, and produced reasonably equitable justice, at least for Florentines. Out-of-town creditors, however, were likely to fare poorly unless they were well connected.

The cosy relationship between Florentine merchants and the papacy that we saw in Chapter 4 was even more pronounced in the case of the super-companies. The church was a valued customer; its monasteries were important suppliers; the super-companies acted as papal collectors and international transfer agents; and they drew upon the immense political power and prestige of the church organization to assist them in their dealings with aristocrats and government officials. At the same time, as virtual ambassadors of the Florence commune, the super-companies were often direct political allies of the church.

The customer-supplier connection existed at many levels. The super-companies provided many of the elaborate vestments and vessels required by prelates and bishops throughout Europe. Business was especially brisk in Avignon, seat of the papacy at this time, where all super-companies maintained important branches. The church's monasteries in England were significant sources of fine wools, which the super-companies bought in large quantities, often paying years in advance, as noted earlier. Monasteries used such credits to expand production or finance their charities, but sometimes to indulge in less worthy pursuits. Warden Abbey of Bedforshire, for example, not only drew on the usual wool contract credit, but also arranged a huge loan with the Peruzzi Company to rebuild its church on a wildly extravagant scale.

The papacy's financial dealings with the super-companies, up to the mid fourteenth century, were cautious and correct. It was prepared to deposit or borrow modest sums from the Italian merchant-bankers during the latter half of the thirteenth century, but discontinued this practice until about 1350. In fact, formal ties were suspended altogether under Clement V, the first of the Avignon popes. His successor, John XXII, with his ambitious political agenda, had need of the super-companies' unmatched organizations and expertise, and resumed the relationship in 1316. Nevertheless, he restricted it to collection and transfer operations, such as those in England described earlier in this chapter. The papal treasurers felt justified in their caution by the bankruptcies of major concerns such as the Ricciardi and Frescobaldi, and after the great Scali Company collapsed in 1326, they made sure that they were not overexposed to the risk of any one firm. The collection business, encompassing all of Latin Christendom except France, involved relatively little risk to the church, but even here, the Curia opted to switch to an obscure and incompetent Sienese firm in 1341, when it appeared that the super-companies were in trouble.

The importance of the ecclesiastical business was much more than the profitability of the many transactions. In all parts of Europe, the super-companies' formal relationship with the papal treasury and their personal contact with the princes of the church gained them an entry into aristocratic society not available to ordinary merchants. At the same time, the financial sinew for many of the papacy's political adventures was provided by the super-companies.[7] This is not to suggest that the connection was always maintained consistently. In the bubbling cauldron of constantly changing political alignments, the popes and Florence found themselves on opposite sides from time to time, but for the most part, their association was sound and often even warm.

The relationship of the super-companies to each other is far from clear, given the mixed signals from the available data. There is likely to have been competition of a sort within Florence and the *contado*. They sold similar ranges of merchandise to the same types of clientele, and left no evidence of overt or tacit market sharing. And prior to the English joint venture of the Bardi and Perruzi in 1337, there is likely to have been genuine commercial contention in the search for sources of imported wool. Moreover, we know that three members of the Bardi family kept deposits with the Peruzzi, suggesting some degree of rivalry for deposit accounts. Finally, the fact that they did not employ members of each others' families indicates that they had business secrets that they wished to hide from the others. But it is difficult to argue that competition within Florence was fierce, given the fact that many prices were regulated by the guilds or the commune (especially for grains).

Outside Florence, there was vicious rivalry between the merchants of different cities; but those from the same city, with the notable exception of Genoa, were likely to be cooperative. In the case of the super-companies, we have already seen market sharing on a grand scale in southern Italy and in the joint venture of the Bardi with the Peruzzi in England. Nevertheless, the great companies did compete abroad for the best wool and for merchandise at the best price. And each strove to find marine shipping space at the best rates while maintaining its own network of innkeepers for overland transport. But their natural competitive urge was attenuated by the fact they were political allies in Florence and abroad, with frequently coinciding interests.

EXPLANATIONS FOR THE COLLAPSE OF THE SUPER-COMPANIES

One of the best-chronicled business news events of the Middle Ages was the sudden crash of the super-companies in the 1340s. The conventional reason for the collapse is that the super-companies were victims of their own greed, suffering huge losses on their excessive loans to finance Edward III of England during the opening years of the Hundred Years' War. More thoughtful scholars of economic history have attributed the demise of the super-companies to an adverse change in the gold–silver ratio. We will discuss both of these rationales and then offer what we believe to be a more compelling reason for the bankruptcies — adverse developments in the international grain trade.

Losses on loans to Edward III

The primary basis for this explanation is the assertion that the English king reneged on debts totaling 600,000 florins to the Peruzzi and 900,000 florins to the Bardi. Even today, historians continue to trot out this one-sentence rationale for the companies' fate, despite the existence of much contradictory information. At the very least, it has long been known that the English crown never actually defaulted, but rather forced the companies to recognize a much smaller amount of debt after subjecting them to a series of audits.

The person most responsible for establishing this traditional version of events is the fourteenth-century chronicler Giovanni Villani, who described the collapse of the super-companies in his history of Florence and identified Edward III as the principal culprit. Villani has been regarded by many historians as a trustworthy authority because he was a contemporary businessman well versed in the commerce and politics of early fourteenth-century Florence, which indeed he was. He joined the Peruzzi Company of 1300 as a shareholder-manager at a very early age, establishing himself as a man of means and social position. He left the company in 1308 and later became a managing shareholder of the Buonaccorsi Company, which rapidly grew to be Florence's fourth-largest firm. Villani was also active politically, holding several prestigious offices, including that of chamberlain of the construction of the new set of walls around Florence. His reputation began to suffer, however, when he indulged in legal delaying tactics in response to allegations of bribe-taking and although never convicted of wrongdoing, he was relegated to minor posts thereafter. Moreover, the Buonaccorsi Company, in which Villani was still a partner, went spectacularly bust in 1342, as its representatives in Naples and Avignon disappeared, leaving a swarm of angry creditors. The company managed to stall proceedings in Florence for some years, but in February 1346, Villani was imprisoned in the notorious *Stinche*, where he died of the plague in 1348.

What these facts suggest is that Giovanni Villani, rather than being a well-informed man-about-town during the last years of the super-companies, had long been on the sidelines and was preoccupied with his own predicament. His estimates of the Bardi and Peruzzi losses were thus most likely based on street gossip around the communal courts. Indeed, the public record is vague and confusing. The initial report after the bankruptcy filing of the Peruzzi Company gave no figures, merely mentioning that most of the liabilities were huge sums due from debtors in England, France, Sicily, and other foreign locations, "unrecoverable because of the war."

The eventual settlements suggest a much more modest scale of losses. The Peruzzi accord of 1347 provided for recoveries to the creditors of around 35 percent of their claims. The Bardi concordat, arranged with amazing swiftness following the company's insolvency filing in early 1346, awarded creditors over 46 percent of their claims. These returns belie the gargantuan English losses, which Villani also asserted were suffered mainly by Florentines. The Acciaiuoli Company, which had avoided lending money to Edward III, expired at the same time as the Peruzzi, and paid off its creditors at a rate of 50 percent, only slightly above that for the other two super-companies. Finally, a close examination of the records in England shows that the two companies, especially the Peruzzi, were able to claw back a good portion of the money loaned to the crown. Although they did suffer losses on their loans, they were nowhere near the level suggested by Villani, and were further attenuated by profits earned on the privileged export of wool.

Change in the gold-silver ratio

The business of western Europe operated under a bimetallic system, in the sense that gold and silver money existed side by side throughout most of the High and late Middle Ages. Before the mid thirteenth century, silver overwhelmingly dominated the coinage in circulation, but in 1252 both Genoa and Florence began to mint gold coins on a significant scale. The Florentine gold florin became instantly popular, especially with the papacy, and soon acquired the status of an international currency. The Venetians moved more slowly because of the importance of their silver grosso, but in 1284 began minting their famous ducat. Although Europe had a bimetallic system, it did not amount to a standard, despite attempts from time to time to fix the ratio between the two metals. In practice, the ratio fluctuated according to changes in supply and demand for each metal in each region. As a result, there developed considerable commerce in gold and silver coinage and bullion that was at least partly driven by a kind of slow-motion arbitrage.

For businessmen there were additional effects of changing ratios beyond the arbitrage opportunities. A significant part of their expense, especially wages, was incurred in silver, while much of their sales in the international markets were in gold, especially gold florins. Grossly oversimplified, therefore, an increase in the price of gold relative to that of silver was expansionary and favorable to businessmen, whereas an increase in the price of silver relative to gold was depressing and unfavorable to them. When the gold florin was first minted in 1252, the ratio was briefly fixed at 8.96 ounces of silver to one ounce of gold, or roughly 9:1. The ratio increased to 10:1 by 1280 and continued to rise until it crested at 14:1 between 1310 and the late 1320s, when it began to decline. The reversal proceeded at varying rates around Europe, affecting Venice sharply by 1331, Florence by 1334, France by 1337, and England by 1344.

The trend of the ratio from the latter half of the thirteenth century through the first quarter of the fourteenth was of course highly advantageous to international businessmen. And its reversal from the mid 1330s has been cited by many economic historians as a significant contributor to the demise of the super-companies. This is a plausible argument, but on close examination it has weaknesses of timing and specifics. The fact is that the relationship of the Florentine gold florin to the silver currencies of the super-companies' most important trading areas – southern Italy, the Mediterranean, and England – changed relatively little between 1325 and 1345, the period of the companies' decline and fall. To be sure, the convulsion in the bullion markets was an unwelcome addition to the super-companies' difficulties, but this was a challenge that such firms, with their network of international traders, were particularly well equipped to manage. And the most serious changes and their deleterious effects on business did not occur until the super-companies were already in terminal decline from other causes.

Deterioration of the international grain trade

The Peruzzi Company records for the partnership of 1331–35 reveal a company clearly drifting toward insolvency before it entered the English venture and before the changes in the gold-silver ratio could have had any measurable effect on its fortunes. It had suffered a stunning loss, and even the mighty Bardi, although shielded by its profitable business in English wool, is believed to have recorded a sharp decline in profit. The problem for both, as well as for the Acciaiuoli and Buonaccorsi, was a fundamental deterioration of the international grain trade on which their prosperity had always been founded.

The companies had been weakened by a series of costly and futile wars in the 1320s and 1330s that curtailed commercial activity and raised taxes; by intermittent bad harvests; and by a devastating flood in 1333, the like of which was not seen again until 1966. Of these, the famines were the most troublesome, producing a profound change in the attitude of governments toward the provisioning of their citizens. The terrible famine of 1329, far from being a boon to grain distributors, was so severe and widespread that the great grain companies were forced into a classic price squeeze. They were required to supply grain at "politically correct" prices while having to scramble for sources in a seller's market. Then, as the 1330s wore on, city governments increasingly dealt with the grain authorities in southern Italy and Sicily, bypassing the super-companies. As a result, this declining commodity business no longer provided the volume and profit necessary to carry the complex organizations built to manage it. The super-companies were gradually crushed under the weight of their own overhead.

THE DISAPPEARANCE OF THE SUPER-COMPANIES

One of the most curious aspects of the super-companies is that they all crashed within a period of thirty months, never to reappear. Some quite large firms, such as the Alberti, did manage to survive, but they were essentially general merchant-bankers, not in the same class as the super-companies. Also, some very large concerns, most notably the Medici, grew up in the following century, but these were of a different character, focused on manufacturing and banking and not nearly as dominant or widespread as their fourteenth-century forebears.[8] The trend toward gigantism that had begun in the thirteenth century, wherein large companies that failed were consistently replaced by larger firms, abruptly reversed. Why? The answers are most likely to be found in the economic phenomena that gave rise to the super-companies in the first place – the commodity markets and the needs of the monarchs who controlled them.

The demise of the super-companies cannot be attributed to the Black Death, as all of them perished shortly before this cataclysm of 1347–50. But their re-emergence was decidedly thwarted by the plunge in population caused by the Black Death and associated calamities, especially in the thriving, overcrowded cities of Italy. Moreover, repeated outbreaks of various forms of the plague over the years ensured that population levels would remain depressed. One result of this new environment was a greatly reduced grain trade. Food production in the areas surrounding the cities also suffered from population loss, but the amount needed to make up for any shortfall was much less than before. And in those years when large-scale imports were necessitated by famine, they continued to be organized by the municipalities. As a result, the grain trade never revived as the volume business it used to be, and it no longer required exceptionally large private organizations to manage it.

The English wool business was another matter altogether. The demand for this commodity actually appears to have increased in the years following the Black Death. Exports in the 1350s and 1360s reached levels not attained since the beginning of the fourteenth century and continued robustly into the 1370s. But Italian companies never recovered their grip on this business because the administrators of the English crown had become more adroit in their handling of the king's affairs, obviating the need for continuous financing by private companies, domestic or foreign. William Edington, bishop of Winchester, reformed the government's bookkeeping, financial information systems, and customs procedures, greatly improving the control of expenditures and enhancing revenues. This is not to suggest that Edward III and his successors no longer needed frequent recourse to borrowing, but never again did they do so on the former scale or with such concentration on a few lenders. Nor had the Florentine merchants abandoned the English wool trade, but although they remained very active for a time, they had lost position. By 1376 they had yielded primacy to the now-dominant English merchants.

The disappearance of the large-scale commodity business affected the organization of business in two ways. The first is that, as we have noted, there was no longer the volume to support the elaborate and costly structure of a great international network. And the sheer amount of effort and energy required to maintain an organization of super-company dimensions in an environment of mounting risk required commensurate rewards that were no longer attainable. The second is that there was no longer a *need* for such a big organization. The business of general merchandising, manufacturing, and banking could be conducted satisfactorily on any scale, large or small, that suited the ambitions of the entrepreneurs. Given the chaotic state of commerce in war-torn Europe, most businessmen opted for a constrained level of activity, and although some developed quite large organizations, none approached super-company size until the middle of the fifteenth century.

THE END OF THE GREAT EXPANSION

The onset of the Black Death can arguably be said to mark the end of one of the longest and most dynamic economic expansions in European history. Although the forward thrust had already diminished by the beginning of the fourteenth century and had even been reversed in some areas, economic activity had generally remained vigorous until the 1340s. Perhaps the expansion would have ended at that point in any case, but the massive depopulation occasioned by the Black Death ensured that business would not continue on its previous course.

Historians have tended to view this pre-plague reversal in terms of "overextension" of the medieval European economies beyond the limits of their technological capacity. As this is not an economic but a business history, it is not our intention to join the great Malthusian debate concerning this period. But there are also historians who have applied the "overextension" cachet to the collapse of the large international companies of the fourteenth century. Here the argument runs that such companies, especially the super-companies, had in effect become dinosaurs of business, too large and too complex for fourteenth-century businessmen to manage successfully. The great Italian companies had indeed become large and complex, but primarily because they had succeeded in simplifying international business through the establishment of smoothly functioning branch networks and the use of sophisticated techniques of control and money transfer. By these means, the large international companies achieved significant cost advantages over their smaller competitors; the proposition that these advantages were inherent in the structure of such companies is supported by the fact that large companies with branch networks, such as Alberti of Florence, Guinigi of Lucca, and Datini of Prato, continued to emerge and prosper long after the collapse of the super-companies. As for the super-companies, they had been created extraordinarily large to capitalize on specific opportunities of large-scale commodity trading – in other words, they were a short-run reaction to a short-run phenomenon. Their downfall occurred only when those opportunities disappeared.

In the year 1200, at the beginning of our period, economic expansion had been in progress for about two centuries. But at this point businessmen were only starting to recognize the scope of their opportunities and to develop the tools to exploit them. Over the next 150 years, they invented devices to transfer funds and systems to manage and account for the increasingly complex operations that expanded the scope and reduced the cost of business. And when the boom had run its course, businessmen did not forget what they had learned; they were able to use their knowledge to help them adapt to changed conditions. The second part of this book deals with those conditions, the new technologies, and the adaptations achieved to cope with them.

PART II

BUSINESS IN THE LATE MIDDLE AGES: A HARVEST OF ADVERSITY

---•---

INTRODUCTION

---•---

In nearly every respect, the conditions that had contributed most to medieval Europe's escape from economic backwardness between 1000 and 1300 – benign weather, relatively peaceful internal politics, steady demographic growth, agrarian and settlement expansion – were changed and in many areas even reversed in the course of the next century and a half. Historians have attached a whole series of disparaging descriptions to this unfortunate epoch: calamitous, depressed, demographically disastrous, war bound, famine and plague ridden, to name a few. In short, the traditional image of the European economy in the interval between Dante and Columbus is that of a slump coming between the remarkable growth of the earlier age and the no less remarkable expansion into the Atlantic and beyond after 1450.

This conventional picture has been radically altered in recent years. A generation of research has dispelled much of the doom and gloom surrounding the period to show, on the contrary, that it was one of the most formative and important eras in the business history of Europe. Having said this, however, it is important to avoid understating the magnitude of the challenges facing business in an era when the Four Horsemen of the Apocalypse were anything but an abstraction. This introduction will provide a brief overview of the problems presented by the scourges of famine, pestilence, and war during the fourteenth and fifteenth centuries.

First, the success of the grain-based rural economy described in Part I concealed a great danger, for much of northern Europe was barely suited for grain cultivation, particularly for the ever-fickle wheat grain. Thus even a slight shift in weather, rainfall patterns, or soil conditions would have a significant effect on crop yields. In fact, European weather appears to have altered during the period, leading to increased rainfall and colder temperatures in the north, increased drought in areas of the south, and general instability in both. This change and European vulnerability to it manifested themselves most strikingly in the second and third decades of the fourteenth century. In northern Europe, the period 1315–22 embodied the greatest sustained famine of the second millennium of European history. The initial trigger was unusually wet weather across all of northern Europe, which destroyed the grain crop in 1315 and produced mediocre harvests over the succeeding three years, with ravages further extended by an outbreak of animal disease in 1321–2. And although grain harvests in Italy in those same years were so good as to evoke lyrical praise to God from the Florentine chronicler Domenico Lenzi, Mediterranean Europe's turn to suffer came with a vengeance in the late 1320s and the 1340s. To a certain extent, such failures and their attendant famines should have created opportunities for international grain dealers. But, as we have seen, the severity of the shortages provoked increasing government intervention in the markets, which, although often helpful, tended to freeze the imbalances of glut and scarcity. Thus starvation and suffering were great throughout most of Europe in the immediate aftermath. But most significant was the role of famine as the herald of a new economic age in which previous economic strengths became deadly weaknesses.

The persistence of inclement weather spelled hardship for the great grain belt of northern Europe, leading to declining production and abandonment of inferior land in many areas. In the south, the productivity of the traditionally fertile plains of Sicily and southern Italy declined. Clearance and reclamation projects slowed or ceased, and European external colonization came to a halt in the eastern Mediterranean, central Europe, and even the British Isles. Allowing for wide variations of extent and tempo, it can be said that the age of agrarian growth and stability had ended across Europe by 1350. Yet population pressure continued even after the famines. England's growth remained unchecked, and despite signs of decline elsewhere – as in the town of Pistoia and the Florentine *contado* – population losses due to famine were insufficient to redress the imbalance between population and declining crop yields.

The advent of the Great Pestilence, as contemporaries called it, or the Black Death, as it became known in the sixteenth century, signaled a further change in the human ecology of the fourteenth century. The plague entered Europe via the trade routes from China, rolled along the Mediterranean and northwards like a great tidal wave, and reached even the remote outposts of European colonization in Greenland and Iceland. The very success of the European trading system in distributing goods thus served to distribute plague as well.

All centers of international commerce, Christian and Islamic alike, were affected, some more than others. Many Italian cities suffered 50–80 percent mortality, and although the cities of Flanders were less severely affected by the plague of 1347–52, they were not as fortunate as once believed and suffered heavily during the outbreaks of the 1360s. This tendency to recur was an especially devastating characteristic of the disease, as it appeared again and again over the following centuries, often in its particularly deadly pneumonic and septicemic forms. Although local and regional variations abounded, the range, intensity, and repetitiveness of the bubonic plague worked to still the engine of demographic growth so characteristic of the previous era of expansion.

While the black horse of famine and the pale horse of plague were frequent visitors, the red horse of war had become almost a permanent menace. Aside from the storied Anglo-French wars, there were intermittent but vicious local conflicts and civil wars in Flanders, Germany, Scandinavia, and the Iberian and Italian peninsulas. Of special significance to Mediterranean commerce were the loss of the last Christian outposts in the Holy Land, the great naval struggles between Genoa and Venice, and the push of the Ottoman Turks into Europe.

War's attendant problems meant more to business than simply greater danger of loss of cargo or increases in rates of brigandage and piracy. Interference with business was caused by crushing trade embargoes, reflecting the tendency of expanding nation-states to strike the economies of their rivals. Thus the English periodically forbade shipments of wool to Flanders, and the French hired Genoese fleets to plunder English seaports and harass English shipping. The English in their turn perfected the *chevauchée*, the wholesale destruction of the French countryside, as a weapon of war. But beyond destruction and disruption, businessmen had to cope with the growing assertiveness of government bureaucracies. Taxes were needed to finance wars and they were pursued with unprecedented sophistication by many European states and communes. Governments also moved to control commodities such as wool and precious metals and to influence the cost of services by fixing wages. And they sought to raise funds by debasing the coinage, the medieval equivalent of printing money. These actions were often carried out with little concern about their effect on commerce and even less understanding as to their economic impact on the populace. But occasionally the authorities acted with constructive business insight, even though their objectives were to secure increased revenues and power for themselves. They increasingly regulated all important commercial activity, often in minute detail, sometimes providing capital and even directly entering into the conduct of business. Government became, by the standards of the day, more businesslike, and in so doing became a force to be recognized in every business enterprise.

Periodic famine, disease, and endemic warfare – what did all this mean for European business after 1300? First, it meant severe depopulation, from one-third to one-half by 1400. Second, it meant disruption and disorder. All business history of the fourteenth and fifteenth centuries must be understood against this background of adversity. For what had changed was nothing less than the ecological and political conditions so instrumental in Europe's great expansion and escape from economic backwardness of the early Middle Ages. Remarkably, however, European business was able to adapt to the groundswells of change in ways that are both consistent and continuous with business enterprise of the previous era. And business enterprise did more than simply survive; it took advantage of new opportunities, even among the disasters of this period. Paradoxically, then, the story of the second part of this history is of the rich harvest of an age of adversity.

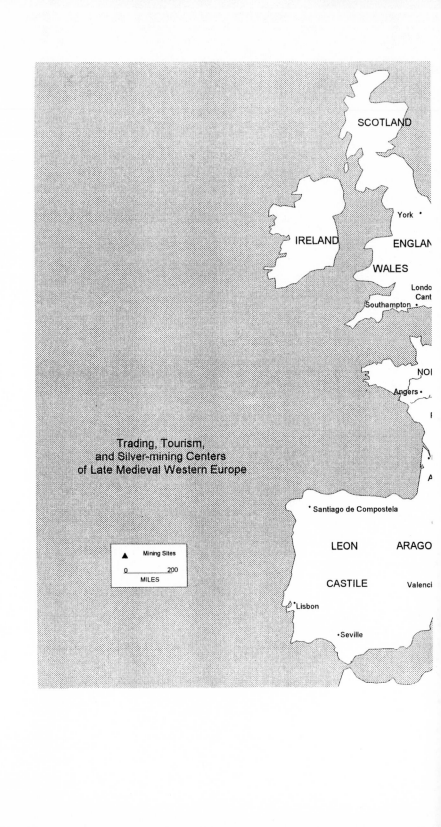

SCOTLAND

York •

IRELAND

ENGLAN

WALES

Londo
Cant
Southampton •

NOI

Angers •

Trading, Tourism,
and Silver-mining Centers
of Late Medieval Western Europe

• Santiago de Compostela

LEON

ARAGO

CASTILE

Valenci

▲ Mining Sites

0 _____ 200
MILES

Lisbon

• Seville

6

THE NEW BUSINESS ENVIRONMENT OF THE LATE MIDDLE AGES

•

In contemporary understanding, business is often linked to entrepreneurship – the quality of acting as a go-between or agent matching supply and demand. The word "entrepreneur" was borrowed from the French in the fifteenth century to describe a military commander leading troops into battle; only gradually was its meaning extended to the battlefield of business. But the military image is an apt one, for businessmen of any age seek to command forces that are not of their own making, under conditions they cannot choose, with outcomes they cannot foresee. Of course, good businessmen, like good generals, seek to reduce the level of uncertainty, and we have seen that in the fourteenth century they were fully challenged in this regard. Many business enterprises, including the mighty super-companies, were unable to cope with the unprecedented changes in the natural and human world and disappeared. Others, using many of the same business techniques, adjusted to change, turned it to their advantage and prospered. Given such diverse challenges and enigmatic outcomes, we have divided our discussion, treating the many changes to the business environment in this chapter and leaving the effects of these changes and business's adaptations to them for the following chapter.

EVOLUTION OF AGRICULTURE IN THE FOURTEENTH CENTURY

We have seen in Chapter 1 that agriculture was fundamental in medieval society and economy to a much greater degree than in the modern world. The very fact that in today's developed economies only 2 to 6 percent of people are farmers, while in the Middle Ages roughly the same percentages were not farmers, gives some idea of the magnitude of the difference. Thus business could not escape an intimate attachment to agriculture. Indeed, in the centuries after 1000, business often arose as a result of developments in the countryside, where businessmen furthered and profited from the cooperation of Europe's lords and peasants. However, in the north, a subtle shift occurred in the relationship between business and agrarian enterprise in the fourteenth and fifteenth centuries. Whereas the former had been almost entirely dependent on the latter, after 1300 the relationship began to take on the characteristics of the south, where agricultural advance was fueled by urban investment responding to often distant market demand. In other words, businessmen were moving increasingly from a reactive role of marketing agricultural surpluses to a more active one, directing new demand to encourage new uses of productive land.

Complicating the relationship between business and agriculture was the extreme sensitivity of municipal authorities to the provision of foodstuffs for a populace whose reaction to failure was likely to be violent. Following the widespread and severe famines of the early fourteenth century, this concern became obsessive, resulting in very conservative and localized stockpiling policies for all comestibles deemed essential. Almost everywhere, from Flanders to Tuscany, exports of grain and other "necessary" goods were strictly controlled by local governments, even for destinations within the same polity. This drive for self-sufficiency began to reduce international and regional trade in these vital commodities and often exacerbated the local effects of a single bad harvest. But although governments increasingly managed the procurement and distribution of foodstuffs, they were alert to the need to break the vicious circle of poor crop yields and over-reliance on a monoculture of grain. Their priorities therefore did not appear to hinder those entrepreneurs who were eager to promote crop diversification, expanded animal husbandry, and specialty products for long-distance trade. Thus, both in the late medieval countryside and in the city, production and exchange of agricultural commodities became the object of investment and regulation.

Population loss was certainly a driving force for change after 1350. The European diet, for example, underwent a profound modification as a result of depopulation. Historians have calculated that in the century before the Black Death population pressures and high food prices caused roughly two-thirds of household food expenditure to be devoted to grain in the form of bread, meal, or ale, and only 20 percent to fish or meat. This of course is a very rough average; the poor expended proportionately more for bread, the rich considerably less.[1] Severe mortality relieved the pressure on European farming to produce ever more grain; and it enriched the survivors with the goods of the dead, allowing the living to shape their diets more to their liking. The results could be dramatic, as shown by a comparison of harvest workers' diets between the years 1256 and 1424 compiled by Christopher Dyer. When analyzed in terms of calories, the harvest worker of 1256 received meals with bread supplying 75 percent of the nutrition and meat a scant 2.5 percent. In 1424, in contrast, meat constituted nearly 20 percent of the food value and bread 37.5 percent. Although these workers were something of an exception, in general household expenditure on grain fell to about 40–50 percent of the total, leaving 35–40 percent free for the purchase of meat and fish by the early fifteenth century. Some peasants and many townspeople ate more like lords after 1350, and lords devoted their greater buying power to spending even more lavishly on wine, spices, and other delicacies.

Three regions of Europe excelled all others in their adaptation to these dietary preferences: southeast England, the Low Countries (particularly Brabant and Flanders), and northern Italy. Not coincidentally, they were also three of the most urbanized areas of Europe, for cities are nothing more than concentrations of consumers, who in the later Middle Ages were able to buy and invest in the objects of their dietary preference. The results were impressive: new crops for widespread consumption included peas and legumes, hops for beer, spinach, celery, melons, asparagus, artichokes, and rice. All are found as significant specialty crops in one or another area in this period. Fruits became another item of consumer demand and local specialization. The region around Erfurt supplied much of the German Empire with fruit, while Italy and Spain provided citrus fruits to the north. Figs, dates, and raisins from North Africa and Spain became common trade goods as well.

The most striking change brought by the enhanced urban influence on late medieval agriculture was an increased consumption of meat and fish. Beef, pork, and mutton were consumed in large quantities. Butchers were at least twice as numerous in most medieval cities as they are today and were among the richest and most powerful of all guildsmen. In Toulouse in 1322, for example, there were 177 butchers, roughly one per 226 inhabitants. And in fourteenth and fifteenth century Ghent, the wealth and power of the butchers' guild was symbolized by their large and lavish guild hall, which still stands today along one of the market squares of the city.

Fish had long been of great dietary importance to the average European for religious reasons, especially after the Lateran Council of 1215 demanded stricter observance of fast days by the general population. Demand had outrun local supplies, propelling fishing fleets further from shore in pursuit of herring and cod that could be preserved by salting or smoking. The story of the investments and innovations that transformed the Dutch herring industry will be told later in this book.

To meet the new demands, business and urban investment transformed the face of the medieval countryside. In England, land once used for grain was converted to pasture, sometimes by enclosure, to feed large numbers of sheep and cattle. Urban butchers in France, Germany, and Flanders organized the raising of pigs and sheep in the countryside around their cities, integrating urban capital and rural production. New animals that could flourish in areas with poor soil, such as the rabbit, were also raised for food and pelts. Historians have also noted a tighter integration of animal raising and crop raising – farmers used the same land alternately for crops and pasturage, while reconciling the demand for animal fodder by sowing legumes and clover that coincidentally provided nitrogen fixing for fertilizing the soil.

Despite these changes, Europeans still depended on grain for the majority of their calories. Yet even the grain market did not escape from the forces sketched above. In the north, certain areas in northern France, southeastern England, and Prussia and Poland came increasingly to specialize in grain farming, shipping their surplus to urban consumers in London, Flanders, and northern Germany. In the south, the swift and severe depopulation of the towns completed a change in the dynamics of the grain trade already under way in the 1330s. As we have seen, the role of the large Florentine companies as the prime international grain traders ended abruptly with their collapse just prior to the first onslaught of the Black Death. Their place as large-scale providers was taken, for the most part, by urban governments. To be sure, merchants continued to be involved in the grain trade, but mostly on a small scale. In the voluminous records of the Datini and Medici companies, for example, we find references to only a few insignificant grain transactions.

Grain trade on a substantial scale nonetheless continued in the Mediterranean basin throughout the late Middle Ages. Despite the smaller urban population and increased attention to self-sufficiency, there were persistent deficiencies in food supplies in one area or another that had to be made up by imports. One reason for the shortfalls is that the population of the countryside surrounding the towns were also depleted, often more severely than that of the towns themselves, resulting in reduced local production. Another is that the survivors were, on average, more affluent and better able to afford greater quantities and varieties of food. The traditional granaries – southern Italy, Sicily, North Africa,

Egypt, and the Crimea – continued to have surpluses available, albeit smaller and less reliable ones, due to the vagaries of their own weather, deteriorating infrastructure, export policies, and shipping disruptions. Thus we find that a perennial grain basket, Egypt – suffering from depopulation, land flight, neglect of irrigation canals, and low prices – from time to time had to import quantities of wheat from Sicily to avert shortages.[2]

The main operators in the Mediterranean grain trade were the big shippers: the Venetians, Genoese, and Catalans. They were also major consumers, and having limited hinterlands of their own, they were particularly careful to ensure that they had adequate supplies of low-cost sea-borne grain. Venice offers a useful example of the level of sophistication applied to the management of supplies, even after achieving control over an increasing spread of agricultural hinterland. As a great international entrepôt, Venice was in an especially strong position, able to divert any part of grain cargoes it needed for its own use. The commune maintained two authorities to manage grain supplies, one for buying and selling and the other for financing. The former reported daily to the doge's office the size of the reserves in the city's two large grain warehouses. In times of low supplies or forecast scarcity, this office was empowered to guarantee attractive prices to merchants who were prepared to bring grain from specified places within a specified time. The importers could choose to sell this grain on the open market, but had to reckon with the fact that prices on this market were manipulated by the government. In the first place, prices were partially controlled by the same device used in today's commodity markets – imposing limits on the amount prices could rise in one day. Secondly, the grain office used its reserves as a price moderator, drawing from or adding to its warehouse stockpiles as appropriate. It had the means to exercise this control, as it carefully registered all incoming grain and allocated supplies to bakers, fixing the prices and sizes of loaves.

Apart from grain, the foodstuffs of the Mediterranean towns generally came from the same sources as they had before the Black Death. Most livestock was acquired from nearby localities, although northern Italian cities obtained cattle from the south, and the Venetians imported some of theirs from Hungary. And as before, fish, fruit, and vegetables from local providers added variety to urban diets. The main change was the increasing availability of exotic fruits and condiments, now that Spain had moved firmly into the trading orbit of Christian Europe. Italian, especially Genoese, merchants did a lively business in dates and almonds from Valencia and raisins and figs from Malaga, products which, as noted earlier, also found their way to the tables of the well-to-do in England and Flanders. And throughout the Mediterranean, trade in such diverse comestibles as citrus fruits, sweet wines, sugar, edible spices, rice, olive oil, apples, cheese, butter, tuna, and sardines continued to crisscross north and south, east and west. Most of this business was handled by numerous merchants of relatively modest means in large numbers of small transactions. Indeed, it was the nimbleness of small-scale merchants that enabled such commerce to carry on relatively steadily despite endemic piracy and the periodic conflicts between the major shippers.

A considerable acreage of agricultural land had long been devoted to the production of nonedible materials for regional and long-distance trade. Pasturage for sheep dotted central and northern Italy, Spain and southern France. Extensive cotton fields appeared in southern Italy, Sicily, and southeastern Spain as early as the twelfth century. Mulberry trees were cultivated for silk in Tuscany and Spain, woad for dyes in Lombardy, and crocuses for saffron around San Gimignano. These applications continued into the later Middle Ages and expanded substantially in some regions, the most notable being the vast transhumance pastures for wool production in Spain.

To generalize about the role of agriculture in late medieval business is difficult, but a distinct shift is perceptible after 1350. Almost everywhere, urban markets and urban capital began to play a greater part in the countryside; and rural populations, despite their own losses, were tapped to fill the decimated ranks of urban dwellers after the plagues. This increasing urban orientation continued the trend toward the increasing specialization in crops for sale for cash, a movement that was most pronounced in the north. Farmers in the south, with its extensive urban population and relatively easy maritime transportation links, had already since the eleventh century been more highly motivated to produce cash crops than had those in the north. Despite the disruptions of the fourteenth century, rural populations in both north and south resisted the pressures to revert to subsistence farming. And where they could not produce for the market, they often found profitable outlets for their energies in textile manufacturing, becoming laborers once removed in urban industries.

MONEY SUPPLY DURING THE LATE MIDDLE AGES

In one sense, the changes described here represent a continuation of the trend toward commercialization of agriculture noted in the first part of this book. In this increasingly cash-oriented society, money supply became a subject of considerable importance, and the economic forces affecting it deserve careful attention. A great deal has been written by thoughtful economic historians on the nature of the post-plague economy of western Europe and the reasons behind the observed gyrations. Scholars such as Day, Lane and Mueller, Munro, and Spufford have puzzled over voluminous economic data of the late Middle Ages and have sought explanations that would encompass the seeming inconsistencies therein.[3] Again, it is not the purpose of this book to enter into this fascinating discussion; but it is appropriate here to attempt an analysis of the information developed by these and other authors as a guide to the economic environment in which businessmen operated throughout this period. Moreover, because the subject has received so much attention, it is useful to present it here as a single issue covering the entire late Middle Ages, providing a point of reference for discussions of monetary topics as they come up in the later chapters.

Such an analysis will of course risk oversimplification; even to talk about a collection of disarticulated local and regional economies as "the economy of western Europe" requires a leap of the imagination. But despite the very great divergences among the localities, there were indeed large economic forces that, like the tides, lifted or lowered all boats, albeit with differences in timing and degree. Our approach will therefore be to attempt a very broad-brush examination of these forces in terms of their effects on the money supply, an element of crucial importance to businessmen anywhere at any time.

The most obvious component of money supply, currency in circulation. remained through the late Middle Ages much as described on page 63 for the thirteenth century – overwhelmingly in the form of minted coins of precious metals and alloys. Money supply for commerce was therefore affected largely by the physical availability of precious metals and by the minting policies of princes and communes. However, there were also important "extenders" of money supply, including barter, as well as financial devices, such as bills of exchange and bank transfers, that did not add directly to money supply but enhanced the efficiency and transferability of existing cash. A few banks created credit in some major centers by operating with fractional reserves, but the amount provided was limited and sporadic, tending to be least available when most needed (see Chapter 9).

The table presented on page 141 attempts to plot the direction of forces affecting money supply in six periods of discernibly different levels of economic activity during the two centuries following the Black Death. The first two columns relate to physical changes in money supply.

The first, *specie supply* reflects mining output minus losses of specie through shipwreck and other disappearances, coinage wear and tear, and the outflow of precious metals in trade with the East.[4] The net change in this latter category was firmly negative through most of the fifteenth century, as increasing demand for Eastern goods more than offset the growing array of Western goods, especially cheap textiles and copper, that made their way to the Levant. Late in that century, the outflow of specie to the East declined owing to the continued growth of exports and the displacement of imports as a result of the discovery of rich deposits of alum north of Rome, and the cultivation of sugar in Sicily and Spain. At the same time, that still-negative balance was offset by increased production of silver in the West. In the first half of the sixteenth century, continued growth in mining production was supplemented by inflows of specie from Africa and America. The next column, *hidden reserves*, deals with the precious metals squirreled away in hoards or converted into plate and objects of art. Accumulation of these reserves, which reduces money supply, could occur in good times or bad, but significant dishoarding was usually involuntary, resulting from looting or confiscatory taxation. One important example of voluntary dishoarding occurred in the years immediately following the Black Death, when hedonistic spending was a significant drain on the reserves.[5]

The next two columns suggest the effect of the responses of rulers (*currency maneuvers*) and businessmen (*money extenders*) to money supply problems. Data in the first of these columns are especially difficult to rationalize due to differing policies at different times by different princes and communes, often in opposite directions. The most startling example is France, where massive debasements during the first half of the fourteenth century were followed by equally extreme revaluations. Philosophically, most princes leaned toward strong currencies, which favored the aristocratic rentier class and which enjoyed the theoretical support of Nicholas Oresme's famous treatise *De Moneta* published in 1358.[6] But rulers also found that, over time, debasement to a limited degree was a practical necessity to offset coinage wear and tear; and in times of war they often found the income generated by large-scale debasement to be downright irresistible. On a net basis, the currencies of most locations in western Europe – even including France, Burgundy, and Flanders – despite their occasional huge fluctuations, were relatively stable. English sterling kept remarkably steady until the devaluations of Henry VIII in the sixteenth century. Only the coinage of Castile and of some German polities suffered consistent and severe long-term erosion. By and large, therefore, currency manipulation tended to increase money supply only to a limited extent over the period under review here.[7] In the *money extenders* column, changes had little perceivable net effect on money supply until the late fifteenth century, when the use of financial instruments became more widespread in southern Germany and northern Europe. Until then, any improved efficiencies in exchange were more than offset by the severe restrictions on international exchange of specie imposed by most rulers. A more reliable extender was barter, always present in medieval commerce, which was often usefully employed to mitigate the severest effects of monetary shortage.

The last two columns reflect an attempt at a rough consensus of scholarly opinion on the observed status of the money supply and price levels in highly generalized terms. As regards *money supply*, notwithstanding the inexactness of the cited periods, there seems to be rough agreement that during the periods 1350–80 and 1500–50 money supply was not a great problem in most areas, and that during 1381–1415 and 1431–65 money was so scarce as to warrant the term "famine." The other periods, characterized by differing supply situations in different locations as well as differing opinions of scholars, can best be described as "variable." The *prices* column is an attempt to show in very simplistic terms the direction of prices and their relationship to money supply. Here, the data are especially diverse, with variations in price levels occurring not only across time and place but also by commodity. The characterization of "inflation" or "deflation" is therefore extremely broad, encompassing a collection of plus and minus factors.

The sources for this table are too numerous and varied to list in the usual place below the table, but an interested reader can find most of the data in the works of the authors cited in note 3, page 254.

We cannot leave this highly compressed review without acknowledging the oversimplification of lumping gold and silver together as a single factor, "specie supply," and thus ignoring the important and vexing question of gold and silver price relationships. Our argument late in the previous chapter, that the dramatic drop in the price of gold relative to silver came too late to have contributed materially to the collapse of the super-companies, was not intended to discount the significance of this development. The surge of gold from the new discoveries in Hungary along with a shortage of silver prompted the spread of large-scale minting of gold coins from Italy to northern Europe from the 1330s onward. Gold thus became the exchange medium of choice for large political and commercial payments because of its convenience and availability. At the same time, price differentials between the metals in different parts of Europe and the Mediterranean meant that one metal

Principal factors affecting money supply in medieval Europe, 1350–1550

	Changes in money supply due to:				Observed status of:	
Period	Specie supply	Hidden reserves[a]	Currency maneuvers[b]	Money extenders	Money supply	Prices
1350–80	negative	positive	positive	positive	adequate	inflation
1381–1410	negative	negative	neutral	neutral	"famine"	deflation
1411–30	negative	positive	positive	negative	variable	inflation
1431–65	negative	neutral	neutral	positive	"famine"	deflation
1466–1500	neutral	negative	positive	neutral	variable	deflation
1501–50	positive	negative	positive	positive	adequate	inflation

[a] Hoarding has negative effect, dishoarding positive.
[b] Devaluation has positive effect, revaluation negative.

might be preferred over the other in making payments. And often the differentials were so wide as to make arbitrage profitable enough to overcome the cost of shipping specie from place to place. All this added complexity, risk, and opportunity for businessmen, but essentially within the specie-supply dynamics cited in the table.

This analysis, despite its shortcomings, does enable us to make two observations. The first is that behind the smoke screen of confusing distortions caused by governmental bullion export prohibitions, exchange-rate manipulations, and minting policies, the main determinant of bullion movements and bimetallic ratios was the continuing demand in the West for oriental merchandise that had to be met mainly by the only commodities assured of ready acceptance in the East – precious metals. The second is that the 150 years following the Black Death did not constitute one long period of depression but a series of ups and downs, each of about thirty years' duration, albeit with variations of incidence and timing around Europe. But irrespective of the individual situations, the data strongly suggest that most businessmen faced significantly changing circumstances during their careers. Business life in the late Middle Ages was characterized not by stultifying tradition but by challenging volatility requiring frequent adaptation. Much of the discussion in the following chapters is about the varying success of businessmen in meeting this challenge in different industries in different parts of Europe.

WAGES, PRICES, AND GUILD ORGANIZATION IN THE FOURTEENTH CENTURY

The complications caused by the political, social, and monetary disruptions of the second half of the fourteenth century make it difficult to isolate the early effects of the Black Death on business activity. And taken by itself, the Black Death cannot be said to have had a lasting economic effect. But this catastrophe did suddenly create new economic conditions for businessmen – a scarcity of labor and a sharp decline in demand for food grains – that were extended well into the following century by the reinforcement of the subsequent pandemics. Thus the macroeconomic environment to which businessmen had to adapt was one of rising costs of labor and fluctuating prices of key commodities.

The rise in the cost of labor was virtually immediate and relatively easy to identify, despite the blurring effect of coinage debasements. Abundant evidence comes from a variety of sources – complaints of wage increases and worker arrogance by contemporary chroniclers, statistical data from various parts of Europe, and ordinances in England, France, and Christian Spain attempting to roll back "excessive" wages. The latter are of special interest, reflecting as they do the direct intervention of royal governments in the economic lives of their subjects. The French king in 1351 tried to establish pay scales at only one-third higher than pre-plague levels, when actual wages had doubled or tripled. In England the king reacted even more swiftly, ordering in 1349 that wages be fixed at their 1346–7 level. This ordinance failed, judging by parliamentary discussions leading to the Statute of Labourers in 1351, which again rolled back wages to 1346–7 rates and enforced them throughout the kingdom with severe penalties. Aragon and Castile also issued decrees to control pay scales, but were more flexible in their application. All of these laws touched on the shortage as well as the cost of labor and bore down particularly heavily on able-bodied beggars. Overall, however, the regulations were only partially and temporarily effective, save in England, where the full force of the king's bureaucracy made them fairly efficacious; and even there wage increases were significant, especially in the countryside. John Hatcher has recently made a convincing case that rural wage earners obtained considerable noncash and other unreported income, giving them much more purchasing power than suggested by the statistical evidence.[8]

Price changes are much more problematical. All things being equal, one would expect commodity prices, especially foodstuffs, to decline in the face of huge drop in the number of consumers. But all things were not equal. Europe's climate appears to have been especially capricious throughout the fourteenth century, causing wildly fluctuating crop yields from year to year and region to region, with concomitant effects on prices. Then the disruptions of war and pestilence affected both agricultural and industrial production. And the quantity of money did not decline, while its velocity actually increased, as the plagues and wars redistributed wealth on a grand scale through accelerated inheritance, taxation, and looting. We have seen in discussing agriculture that the resulting per capita increase in wealth provided individuals with more purchasing power to deploy against a wider variety of goods and services. However, the increase in spending power did not reach all individuals, and in many cases the apparent gain was offset by price inflation, leaving them no better off than before. Moreover, bottlenecks caused by the dislocations of mortality and warfare meant that some areas suffered from scarcity, others from glut, while still others enjoyed the happy medium.

Finally, most communes, along with the kingdoms that rolled back wages, did their best to impose price controls, especially on critical foodstuffs. We have already seen Venice's elegant indirect management of grain prices; the methods of other polities were cruder and more direct. Again, as in the case of wage controls, results were mixed. Prices of most comestibles in England in the second half of the fourteenth century were stable or lower, while those of industrial goods showed a significant increase.[9] In most continental areas, however, prices were much more volatile. All these forces, along with intermittent coinage devaluations and revaluations and gaping holes in the data, have given economic historians endless difficulty in deciphering the underlying effect of the changed demographics. The businessmen of that period, however, were concerned not with explaining the macroeconomics of their situation, but with the new day-to-day realities that they faced. Those realities were higher costs, higher risks, and changing markets.

During the years leading up to the Black Death, in what Steven A. Epstein characterizes as a "crisis" of the fourteenth century, subtle changes had been taking place in the guild system with regard to wage labor.[10] As usual, specifics and timing varied by community, but it can be said that broadly across Europe apprentices and journeymen were finding it increasingly difficult to achieve the status of independent masters. More and more, that prize was going to a master's direct descendant. And masters were often expanding the scale of their businesses by starting up an additional "family workshop" headed by an employee, paying the extra fee to the guild, but not enrolling the employee as a member. In this way, many masters were becoming entrepreneurs. At the same time, apprenticeships were being lengthened without reference to the requirements of experience or skill. And at the end of their terms, most apprentices could now expect journeyman status to be a permanent condition, rather than a stage on the way to becoming a master. On the positive side, there was increasing division of labor in the textile, shipbuilding, and metalworking industries and new specialties in the manufacture of clocks, cannons, crossbows, special tools, paper, and mining equipment, giving rise to new skill groupings. These trades were mostly too small and scattered to become institutionalized as guilds in their own right, but did enjoy some prosperity and prestige. And economically if not socially advantageous, the growing pool of wage labor fostered increasing mobility, aiding the transfer of technology from town to town.

Artisanal and industrial trades are being treated jointly here because they were affected in roughly the same ways by the economic changes of the late fourteenth century. Among artisans, the immediate shock of the plague had relatively little economic effect on single proprietors, especially those producing goods for the luxury trade. Survivors in this category were able to continue supplying flourishing markets and could exact steadily higher prices. However, those artisans and industrialists who had to rely on numbers of apprentices and journeymen to meet their production requirements suddenly found themselves faced with a shortage of adequately trained labor. And despite the legal restrictions applying to wages, employers had to find ways to attract workers or lose production. These artisan-entrepreneurs therefore faced increasing costs that were not always recoverable in price-controlled businesses, particularly those providing basic foodstuffs. Bakeries, for example, were a special target of the regulators. But the fact that many such businessmen did manage to pull through, despite having few resources in reserve, suggests that they succeeded in recovering their rising costs, despite the pricing regulations. It is probable the guilds played a part in this feat; for notwithstanding the fact that they were brushed aside by the royal and communal governments that instituted the controls, the guilds remained a powerful force in their communities and were able to mitigate the more unrealistic aspects of the regulations.

The guilds adapted to a certain extent to the new realities of labor supply and demand. For example, they quickly scaled back the excessive length of pre-plague apprenticeship terms. In one instance, the apprenticeships of Parisian leather workers dropped from nine to two years – an extreme case, obviously, but demonstrating the absurd inequity of the earlier requirements. Entry into the ranks of masters, however, remained as restricted as before, with kinship continuing as the prime requisite for matriculation into most guilds. Wage earners enjoyed a period of relative prosperity in many localities in the decades immediately following 1350, but they lacked security, and frequently vented their frustrations in violence in times of economic downturn. It is of course risky to attempt to draw close parallels among the underclass uprisings in various parts of Europe in the second half of the fourteenth century. Each was triggered by a different set of circumstances – the Paris riots and Jacquerie in 1358 stemmed from the absence of royal authority after the capture of King John at the Battle of Poitiers; the Ciompi Revolt of 1378 in Florence followed an economic depression and devaluation; and the English Peasants' Revolt of 1381 was sparked by an ill-advised poll tax.[11] But the connecting link was the participation of disaffected tradesmen, both urban and rural, in all these insurrections, despite the "peasant" labels in two cases. The main problem of the wage earners was that they were disconnected from any system of power; they were controlled by the guilds, but often were not members of them.[12] This was especially evident in the Ciompi Revolt, wherein the rebels enforced the formation of new guilds for dyers, shirtmakers, and the Ciompi, the latter guild being a contradiction in terms as it included no masters. They even insisted on having the currency revalued to the level it had held in more prosperous times. Of course, all the rebellions were suppressed – the Jacquerie savagely, the English revolt ruthlessly, the Ciompi more gently, but effectively.

THE TRANSPORTATION INDUSTRY

Transportation was swiftly and seriously affected by the troubles of the fourteenth century, as warfare, embargoes, robbery, and civil strife swept along the roads and sea lanes of Europe. The economic historian Herman van der Wee has seized upon changes in transport as the key force driving many of the structural changes in the European economy from the thirteenth to eighteenth centuries. He argues that the growth and prosperity of the high medieval economy had depended upon the vitality of overland continental trade routes, particularly those linking Italy and the Low Countries. With the fourteenth-century disruption of those routes, commerce contracted, which in turn reduced investment and incomes. The first victims were the Champagne fairs, which had declined precipitously by the 1330s, affecting hundreds of towns and villages along the arterial routes leading to the continental hinterland. Trade tended to fall back to smaller networks organized around regional fairs.

Longer-distance trade was partially redirected to new sea routes to northern Europe, as the great Italian port cities regularly dispatched fleets of ships to London and Bruges each year. This shift tended to concentrate wealth and income flows into the important maritime towns of the north, notably Bruges and the Hanse towns, with the concomitant effect of starving inland Europe of economic growth. Thus seafaring experienced the greatest expansion and innovation of all modes of transport.

Nonetheless, shipbuilders and shippers in the late fourteenth century faced three big problems: shrinking markets, escalating crew costs, and surplus capacity. The diminishing markets particularly affected goods for which marine transport was most efficacious – bulk commodities, including food grains. As the market price of grains dropped relative to the expense of moving them, transport cost began to make up an increasing share of the landed price at destination, reaching almost half that figure in the case of Baltic grain shipped to Bruges. Rising crew costs were a function not only of higher wages, but also of the scarcity of able-bodied men, especially for rowing the galleys, and of extra hands needed for defense in these troubled times. And excess capacity was caused by lower consumption of commodities usually transported by sea as well as a supply of unused shipping. This latter problem delayed the introduction of new, more efficient ship designs.

Another environmental change affecting shipbuilding and transport was the trend toward bureaucratic intervention, as governments increasingly recognized the importance of these activities to the economy and to defense. Intervention sometimes took the form of direct aid; for example, the great galleys of Venice that will be discussed later were all built with the help of subsidies from the state. The king of Portugal promoted the construction of larger ships to compete in the bulk trade and even organized a scheme of obligatory mutual insurance. And galleys built in northern Europe were funded by the French crown. But government involvement most often occurred in formulating regulations for safety, loading limits, inspections, scheduling, ship design, and for the control of technology transfers. The great ports of Venice and Genoa had long enforced regulations on all aspects of shipbuilding and sailing, but such controls were now becoming more detailed, pervasive, and widespread across Europe.

Despite the preponderance of sea transport, land routes and inland waterways were not entirely insignificant. Land routes revived quickly when road security improved, so that on the better European roads carts and even four-wheeled wagons could link important trading cities. The latter vehicles began to be built with a sway bar and front wheels smaller than rear wheels, which gave them improved stability and maneuver-ability. But for the most part, land transport in Europe continued to depend upon beasts of burden, chiefly the mule. Mule trains traversed the great mountain routes linking Italy with Switzerland and southern Germany, Spain with France, and also joined trading centers within France and Italy that were separated by difficult terrain. The mule could carry up to 350 pounds and could navigate the narrowest of mountain paths. It was entrusted with precious cargoes, such as silver and gold bullion between Italy and Germany, as well as with homelier goods, such as salt between Provence and Piedmont. By the late fifteenth century, the salt trade alone accounted for some 21,000 mules passing the toll booths between Mount Viso and Milan. In the same century, there were over 60,000 mules per year plying the roads between Genoa and Milan.

Inland waterways, widely used in the commercial areas of the Low Countries and northern Italy in the twelfth and thirteenth centuries, also suffered from the collapse of public order in the fourteenth century, but remained crucial to the economies of those areas. In Flanders, the inland waterways linking the plains of northern France and the chief Flemish cities, notably Ghent, were improved and patrolled vigilantly. So zealous were the people of Ghent in this regard that in 1379 they attacked a work crew from Bruges digging a canal to link that city to the Leie River, plunging the county into a devastating civil war. Other areas of Europe improved their canal and river systems. The course of the Loire River, for example, was rendered more navigable by the con-struction of levees and deepening of channels. In the Low Countries, the improvement of sluice-gate and watermill technologies permitted water transport across more varied territories and over greater distances. Above all, in the Po river valley the completion of a complicated network of canals and alteration of the course of the mighty Po itself made low-cost transport possible for the entire region. The city of Milan and a host of smaller cities were beneficiaries of these late medieval infrastructure projects.

INTERNATIONAL COMMERCE

International commerce in the second half of the fourteenth century faced enormous disruption. Following the Black Death, the great rival polities in north and south quickly mustered the men and resources to mount devastating military campaigns over the next three decades, even in the face of further severe plagues in 1361, 1369, and 1374–5, in addi-tion to several regional epidemics. During this same period, there was a rapid transfer of wealth from the older victims of plague and war to younger generations, who had an unsurprisingly pessimistic view of life expectancy. Many were accordingly determined to enjoy life to the fullest while they could and embarked on a spending spree of gargantuan proportions. The resulting surge in demand for luxury goods of all kinds – fine clothing, jewelry, exotic foods and spices – sharply boosted international commerce, especially long-distance trade with the East. Meeting this demand in a chaotic environment presented a not unwelcome, but nevertheless challenging problem to the businessmen involved.

In order to grasp the full effect of these stresses, it may be helpful, at the risk of belaboring the obvious to some readers, to offer further detail on the mechanics of medieval international commerce. The first point to note is that although most artisans in local trade sold their wares retail, those involved in regional or international activity usually sold to merchants, who took the risks and rewards of marketing. To be sure, there were numerous exceptions in both areas – artisans who sold to local wholesalers or who filled special orders from foreign customers for personalized tapestry, jewelry, or armor. But even in the latter case, the complexity of international transport, finance, and collection prompted the fabricators to use merchants as intermediaries. For the most part, therefore, international trade was conducted by merchant adventurers seeking goods for markets and markets for goods.

We have seen in Chapter 3 how sedentary merchants entrusted their wares to their travelling partners through *commenda* contracts, or shipped merchandise to their branch managers, factors, or correspondents in foreign locations. In all cases, ownership of the goods remained with the sedentary merchant-investor or company, while the traveling partner or company manager or correspondent acted as agent, with the rights to transfer title, pay expenses, collect money, and make purchases on behalf of the principal. The agent's reward, if partner, was a share of the profit; if employee, a salary; or if correspondent, an ad valorem commission. In effect, most international merchandise was shipped on consignment, and even a consignee who was the merchant's own partner or employee might transfer part or all of the shipment to a correspondent in his territory.[13] Trust, as well as business acumen, was a critical ingredient in these arrangements, given that communications were slow and uncertain, and fine judgments had to be made independently on how to secure the optimum result for all concerned. Such judgments included whether to move the goods to another market for a better price: merchant ventures frequently reflected changed routings in response to new intelligence gathered on market conditions. But rarely did the consignee in long-distance trade resort to his ultimate option – returning the unsold goods to the owner.[14]

Another important feature of the consignment system was a lengthy immobilization of the owning merchant's cash, especially on shipments to the Levant and beyond; even shorter overland or marine ventures required considerable time for the merchant to recover his money. The initial impact of the Black Death on this finely tuned, highly vulnerable system was undoubtedly devastating, as so many trusted intermediaries, Christian and Muslim alike, in this long chain of commercial transactions met untimely deaths. Moreover, this new catastrophe followed closely upon the failure of hundreds of Italian companies, large and small, in the 1340s. The surviving international merchants were suddenly faced with the problem of keeping old transactions from unravelling, recovering their cash, and building a new structure of effective commercial relationships to take advantage of the rush of orders from eager new customers in the West.

Surprisingly, international commerce did not collapse, a testimony to the resilience of the system and the good faith of the survivors. But the initial increase in trade generated by spendthrift heirs had played out by about 1380, and as time wore on and the effects of the greatly reduced population made themselves felt, the demand/supply dynamics began a long-term change. Merchant-adventurers could no longer be as confident that lucrative markets would be awaiting their wares. And the risks of getting goods to market were increasing, mainly from acts of war and piracy, although the victims were not always without legal recourse.[15] The initiative for trade was accordingly passing to producers, especially of raw materials, who in the past had largely been responding to demand, but now began aggressively competing for customers. We shall see how these changes developed, and how the merchants dealt with them, in the next chapter.

It is difficult to imagine an era richer in uncertainty for businessmen than the fourteenth and early fifteenth centuries. Within a typical lifetime, presuming it was not shortened by disease or violent death, a businessman would almost certainly experience currency fluctuations, trade routes made unsafe by war, embargoes and blockades, to name but a few of the impediments he might face. This "certainty of uncertainty" for business claimed many victims; but remarkably, throughout the era dozens of new businesses arose and flourished. When challenged, European business responded with a show of recombinant and adaptive force that preserved traditional business customs on the one hand, but at the same time arranged them into new organizational structures that were better suited to the changed environment. The result of all this, as we shall see, was not simply survival but success, in areas of business enterprise never before attempted by Europeans.

7

BUSINESS RESPONSES TO
THE NEW ENVIRONMENT

—————— • ——————

In the daunting new environment following the Black Death, business-men had a number of advantages working for them. The accumulation of technological advances, business knowledge, and management techniques through the High Middle Ages had not been lost: it was available to be used and built upon. This legacy had come down partly by word of mouth and also through the wide distribution of written material.[1] We have already noted the positive side of higher labor costs – more consumers with income to buy goods – and the opportunities for trade created by the disruptions of war. These advantages, along with the redistribution of wealth discussed earlier, offered possibilities to the alert and the agile.

COST CONTROL AND TECHNOLOGY

Business people, both urban and rural, responded to the new realities of the post-plague era in many ways.[2] We will offer examples in this chapter, such as the invasion of the international cloth markets by English producers and the market specialization of Flemish and Italian textile manufacturers. But the primary response of most businessmen was an intensified focus on cost control as the surest way to satisfy demand profitably. Crucial to this objective was more accurate measurement of time and of results. Determining the divisions of the workday was useful in helping mitigate the effect of higher wages, but initially not as important in controlling costs as accurate measurement of results, which entailed great emphasis on disciplined accounting, along with timely and *regular* reporting. And this, in turn, depended upon a responsive organization. As we shall see, businessmen were amazingly quick to react to these needs to measure results.

Yet another form of business response was the application of new or improved technology to meet demand or cut costs. The role of technology in this regard, however, is somewhat ambiguous. Nearly all of the technology in use up to the fourteenth century was either inherited from Rome or borrowed from Chinese, Indian, or Arabic sources. We have already referred to examples of the former in the discussion of watermills, and of the latter in describing textile technology. Even the outstanding indigenous invention of the High Middle Ages, the windmill, drew heavily upon existing watermill knowledge. Medieval Europe's great and unique contribution was its open-minded approach to solving problems, expressed as a willingness to experiment by trial and error, to consider applications for imported inventions not dreamed of by the originators, and to press continually for improvements. Progress came not through centrally directed investment and managed procedures, but through learning by doing, achieving better recipes and formulating them, acquiring new skills and passing them on, with only limited understanding of why things worked the way they did.

This is not to suggest an absence of scientific thought or exploration in medieval Europe. By the late Middle Ages, the principal Greek and Arabic writings on physics, astronomy, mathematics, geometry, and geography had long been translated into Latin and widely disseminated. The increasing acceptance of the sphericity of the earth, and the application of scientific method to cartography were to have significant importance in the explorations of the late fifteenth century. Even such preoccupations of scientists as alchemy and perpetual motion machines had useful technological fallout in fields as disparate as mining, chemistry, and physics. But while all this effort was of little direct value to medieval businessmen, the combination of a few scientific insights and the cumulative effect of the gradual spread of modest practical adaptations resulted by 1500 in technological capability vastly superior to that of 1300.

A case in point is the development of the mechanical clock. The interest in this device came from two sources, the first being astronomers and astrologers seeking precision instruments to track the movements of stars and planets. The second was the merchants, industrialists, and governors who perceived the value of having public timekeeping devices independent of the ecclesiastical daily rhythm and thus better suited to commercial life.[3] In 1370, Charles V of France had three clocks built and demanded that all citizens of Paris regulate their personal and business lives according to equinoctial hours. At the same time, he required the churches to ring their bells on the hour, departing from their liturgical divisions of the day. The earliest public clocks that began to appear in the larger cities in the middle of the fourteenth century were clumsy, inaccurate affairs, but they apparently were useful enough to attract further development. By the early fifteenth century clocks had greatly improved and spread throughout Europe, and had begun appearing in houses as well as in public places. In the late fifteenth century, the invention of the mainspring made timepieces portable, inexpensive, and suitable for use at sea, where they were eventually to become an invaluable aid to navigation.

The predominance of the trial-and-error and learning-by-doing methodology meant that improvements came slowly and unevenly, and their geographical spread occurred at varying speeds. Moreover, in different industries the impetus for innovation came from different sources, so that easy generalization is difficult. For example, in mining and metallurgy, progress was driven by insistent demand forcing repeated trial and error until breakthroughs were achieved. Conversely, the invention of the mechanical clock was not initially stimulated by any particular need, but its use spread fairly rapidly once its utility was perceived. The great improvements in weaponry of all kinds were compelled by the rivalry of princes and concentration of wealth in their hands, whereas the hugely important advances in ship design were essentially a response to commercial need.

Business entrepreneurs undoubtedly played a part in the diffusion of technological change, but their pragmatism, which tended to keep building upon existing technology and systems, did not stimulate the spread of new ideas. Rather, the pace and direction of innovations owed most to the efforts of princes and communal governments. We will encounter numerous examples in which the technological evolution of various industries was hugely influenced by the positive or negative intervention of governments. Because there were very few identifiable original inventors, and because the process of important innovations was rarely written down, the transfer of technology largely had to come from the hands and minds of experienced practitioners.[4] Thus princes desiring to found or improve industries in their territories tried to lure expert artisans to their domains with offers of money and privileges. In this manner, Louis XI attracted Italian specialists to start up the silk industry in France; the Venetian senate encouraged foreign ship designers to settle in that city; and the English aided the remarkable expansion of their cloth industry by importing Flemish weavers and dyers. And inventors or merely introducers of new and useful processes were granted monopolies from Italian cities, especially Venice, which began issuing time-specific patents as early as 1416. That same city promulgated a formal law of patents in 1474, which attracted technicians from all over Europe seeking generous reward for their innovations. But governments also impeded the spread of technology by reversing this process – forbidding valued specialists from emigrating, under threat of severe punishment, even death. Venice went as far as to prevent the teaching of glassmaking to foreigners legally residing in the city. And governments also resisted the introduction of new materials or technology that would reduce the flow of taxes from existing processes.

The diffusion of innovations in systems of business organization and control were of course matters strictly within the ambit of the businessmen themselves. Here we find that merchants in the southern trading orbits observed each other's methods and adopted many of them. Northern merchants too adopted more sophisticated methods, involving elaborate systems of book transfers. But systems did not seem to migrate between the north and south until the late fifteenth century, when southern accounting and control methods began to penetrate the north, as will be discussed in Chapter 10.

MERCHANT ADAPTATIONS — ITALIAN

The significant organizational advances, in particular the multiple partnerships described in Part I, occurred mainly among the Tuscan companies. Venetian and Genoese businesses continued largely as sole or family proprietorships, with accounting controls based on the management of individual ventures. Following the financial crises of the 1340s and the disruptions of the Black Death, the Venetians and Genoese carried on more or less as before, adding useful but minor improvements to their existing systems. The Tuscans, especially the Florentines, who had invested most heavily in complex international financial and trading organization, were the most vulnerable to these powerful events. Accordingly, they had to make the greatest adaptations.

Organization: Alberti and Datini companies

The most obvious casualty was the large multiple partnership described in Chapter 5. This form of organization, so prominent before the Black Death, largely disappeared from the business scene after 1350. One reason for this change was that the high mortality from the recurring plagues made long-term commercial associations very tenuous, especially when many heirs had become more interested in spending their inheritance than in perpetuating the business. And such businesses had become increasingly risky, requiring the close and dedicated attention of the owner-managers. To be sure, significant firms, such as the Guinigi of Lucca, and the Malabayla of Asti, did survive and prosper as international traders and financiers, but they were a shadow of the mighty super-companies of the first half of the fourteenth century. The most important of the survivors, however, was the Alberti of Florence, whose unique and remarkably successful adaptation is deserving of special comment.

The original Alberti partnership, dating back to 1302, was concerned mainly with general trading, and with finishing and dyeing imported Flemish cloth. After surviving a brush with bankruptcy between 1312 and 1315, the firm gradually shifted its emphasis, and by the 1340s was a significant participant in international trade and finance with a typical branch network. In 1347, shortly after the crash of the super-companies, the Alberti split into two competing partnerships, familiarly known as the elder and new branches, "Alberti antichi" and "Alberti nuovi." Both were substantial companies, but the "antichi" was by far the more successful, becoming the largest merchant-banking organization of western Europe and the papacy's banker of choice. As the company grew, it split again, first in 1372 and then again in 1387, 1393, and 1401, as various members of the family and finally the entire family were exiled from Florence for political reasons. The exiles settled in the major commercial centers in Italy, England, Flanders, France, Catalonia, Spain, North Africa, and the eastern Mediterranean, and joined or formed Alberti branches in those locations. These branches were essentially independent (and in some places there was more than one branch); they were connected through family relationships, trust, and linked investments rather than through corporate control.

The Alberti of the late fourteenth and early fifteenth centuries was thus a very large, wealthy family association in terms of the sum of its parts, but unlike the earlier super-companies it was entirely decentralized. Certain branches were indeed very important; the English branch, for example, renewed the super-companies' practice of advancing credit to wool producers and even organized its own shipping to take English wool and cloth to Italian ports. The decline of the Alberti association finally occurred, oddly enough, a few years after the family's welcome back to Florence in 1428, when the business suffered an unexplained reversal there and family members began to live off the revenues of their property. In a further irony, Leon Battista, the most famous of the Alberti, had drafted his treatise *Della Famiglia* in the early 1430s and circulated it among family members in the forlorn hope of encouraging family solidarity. Once again we find that a business built on family affinity, although enduring, was not proof against decline.

The venerable families deservedly attract the attention of historians, who also note the brief appearance of individuals or partnerships named Peruzzi, Bardi, Strozzi, or Frescobaldi in the post-plague period. But most international business was transacted by a host of obscure individuals and relatively small family organizations operating in narrowly defined product or geographical niches. These smaller concerns were much more cautious and control-minded than their forebears, given the greater risks and more uncertain rewards that they faced. One of the largest and certainly the best-known of the smaller units was that headed by Francesco di Marco Datini, the merchant-banker from Prato, near Florence. Datini, born about 1335, orphaned by the Black Death, moved to Avignon in 1350 and worked there until he had acquired enough capital to invest in a small partnership in 1363. This he developed into a very profitable business, trading initially in armor and armor plate, and expanding into general merchandise. He remained in Avignon well after the papacy's return to Rome in 1378, finally returning to Prato in 1382. There he built his main residence, joined a cloth-manufacturing partnership, and soon expanded his business in Prato and in nearby Florence, eventually also becoming a citizen of the latter city. By 1395, he had successfully founded companies in Pisa, Genoa, Avignon, Barcelona, Valencia, and Majorca, and dealt with correspondents throughout Europe and the Mediterranean. His operations were wide-ranging – domestic and international, wholesale and retail, staple goods and luxuries, manufacturing and financing (he was even briefly a partner in a highly successful bank).

Datini's organization differed significantly from that of the super-companies. The latter were single legal entities that wholly owned their branches and managed them with company shareholders or employees. Datini was the dominating partner of a series of businesses, domestic and foreign, each with different people and partnership arrangements. All partners were men well known and loyal to Datini, and several were employees promoted to partnership (something that never occurred in the super-companies). Datini combined this part-ownership incentive with a regime of rigorous controls to ensure that his interests were being served. The extraordinarily well documented story of this company provides an almost perfect case study of the new challenges of business in the late fourteenth century and the qualities now essential for success in this environment – control, nimbleness, flexibility, and risk management.

Accounting, costing, and reporting

How did Datini achieve effective control over his far-flung empire? In part, it was his deep understanding of business and his relentless follow-up on the activities of his managers, reflected in reams of correspondence. But such follow-up required large amounts of timely data in forms that could be readily analyzed and acted upon by Datini at the center of his web. As we have seen in Part I, significant advances in accounting and control techniques had occurred in Italy between 1300 and 1350. Sophisticated bookkeeping had helped the largest Italian companies control their international operations over a period of decades, and even municipal governments had embraced versions of the new systems. These techniques not only survived the financial and social collapses of the 1340s, but also were improved and refined. For example, Datini's Avignon company accounts of the 1360s and 1370s followed the familiar Florentine pattern, with debits in the first half of the ledger and credits in the second. But after the move to Prato, Datini learned about the new Venetian bilateral method of presentation – debits on the left side, credits on the right side of each page – and installed it throughout the entire company by 1393. More important, Datini insisted that all ledgers be balanced and statements prepared annually, giving him a regularly updated picture of all parts of the business and the means to harass his managers. This was a far cry from the dilatory approach of the super-companies, which struck balances only when there was need to close a partnership, and then often with considerable delay.

Although Datini was something of a trailblazer, by 1400 other Italian merchants were also using accounting as a tool of management and control. They may not have gone as far as Datini, whose Barcelona branch even recorded "Martha, our slave" as a depreciable asset, but they were making increasing use of notions such as reserves, accruals, deferrals, fixed assets, depreciation, and audits. And those with manufacturing operations, driven by the need to monitor higher labor costs, were steadily refining their methods of industrial cost accounting.

Medieval merchants had long been familiar with cost accounting concepts, given that so much of their business, even in the large Florentine firms, was organized and controlled on an individual venture basis. Merchants with manufacturing operations, however, often did not cost them separately; the 1318 accounts of the Del Bene Company of Florence, for example, reflected manufacturing costs in the main books along with other expenses. But as the fourteenth century wore on, companies, including the Peruzzi, increasingly kept separate books for mercantile and manufacturing activities, and by mid century the transition was

complete. Thus, by 1368 the same Del Bene Company had divided its
industrial textile accounts into three books, each with as many subac-
counts as deemed useful by the owner. One book detailed the cost of
raw wool, the second contained the cost of labor – washing, beating,
carding, weaving, etc. – to produce a certain quantity of cloth, and the
third recorded the wages of the specialist dyers by individual. Results
from the three books could be combined to produce a cost of goods
for a given quantity of cloth, identified by type and quality. Datini took
this process a very "modern" step further, allocating indirect overhead
expense to product cost by means of a system of commonsense ratios.

Risk management and insurance

Although all these improved accounting techniques were helpful, they
could make only a limited contribution to the owner's control of his
business. As always, the establishment of trust and obligation was essential, and the owner continued to select partners and employees, especially those serving abroad, who were connected to him by ties of
kinship, friendship, or obligation. Fraud or incompetence would be
promptly reported back to the offender's family. But what was different
in the late fourteenth century was the emphasis on caution and the
spreading of risk. Datini was almost fanatical on this point; he avoided
overcommitment to any one venture or line of business, insured his
cargoes or split them among several ships, never made loans to princes,
and kept out of politics to the extent possible for a man of his wealth.
At the same time, he was dogged in his pursuit of ventures to a successful conclusion. In one noteworthy case, he ordered wool to be
bought in Majorca for conversion in Florence into finished cloth, which
was to be sold in Majorca and Spain. The process from order to final
sale took three and a half years, due partly to the need to reroute shipments because of hostile action and partly to poor market reception of
the goods. Plague had reduced demand, and the color was unpopular,
so that the unsold cloth had to be moved through Majorca to Valencia
to North Africa and back to Majorca before it was finally sold. But
despite the unexpected costs associated with the delays and markdowns,
the venture made a profit reckoned at about nine percent – a derisory
return for the expenditure of time and effort, but at least a profit.

The increased emphasis on caution among Venetian and Genoese
businessmen after the Black Death has been described at some length
in a well-documented book by Benjamin Kedar.[5] The author interprets
this phenomenon as a loss of confidence and declining entrepreneur-

ship among merchants from these cities, even noting that the word "risk" had changed from a positive to negative connotation. But the reaction seems better explained as a rational response to a more difficult environment. The intense activity of the Genoese in the western Mediterranean and Atlantic and the vigorous defense by the Venetians of their eastern Mediterranean trade that we find in the fifteenth century (see Chapter 8) suggest that any retreat from entrepreneurship, if indeed it did occur, was short lived.

It is worth pausing at this point to elaborate on the development of insurance in the Mediterranean area in the late Middle Ages. We have seen in the section on managing risk in Chapter 3 that maritime traders used a number of devices, including the sea loan and other indirect methods, to spread commercial risk, but that direct insurance was slow to develop. From the Datini records, it is clear that marine insurance had become widely used by the late fourteenth century and had evolved into a recognizably modern form. Underwriting continued to be dominated by the Genoese, several of whom insured cargoes as a main line of business and developed a reasonably sophisticated system for settling claims. Venice was also an important insurance center; the Venice branch of the Medici Company normally took out insurance for its affiliates. There is evidence also of overland insurance and even of life insurance, but the predominant form of risk underwriting continued to be marine insurance. There the risks were carefully considered, with premiums calculated according to the routes, the current conditions on those routes, the types of cargo, and importantly, the type of ship. For example, armed galleys sailing in convoys were usually deemed so safe that shippers would often forego insurance altogether, even for valuable goods. Large bulk-carrying cogs with high freeboard and crews supplemented by soldiers were also considered low-risk. Medici Company records of the mid fifteenth century show premium rates of three percent of the value of the goods on Venetian state galleys for a trip from England to Venice, whereas the rate on less secure ships was six and seven percent for a shorter voyage.

This is not to suggest that risk management had become rationalized and monetized, however. Underwriting was still in its infancy and concentrated in the hands of a very few practitioners. But businessmen were increasingly seeking means to assess and control risk, including the gathering of statistical evidence. Datini, for instance, kept documents that showed the estimated loss of Genoese ships on trips to Flanders to be less than two percent. The idea, if not the universal practice, of insurance was clearly taking hold in the late Middle Ages.

MERCHANT ADAPTATIONS — FLEMISH

Prior to the fourteenth century, the most intensive trading in the vast regions of northern Europe from the Atlantic to western Russia took place between England and Flanders in the productive symbiosis of the cloth industry. Although large quantities of wool were produced in Flanders, Flemish merchants also bought thousands of sacks of English wool and supervised the transformation of the wool into finished cloth by Flemish weavers, fullers, and dyers. Credit and other trade goods flowed between Flemish merchants and English producers as well, leading to considerable integration of the domestic economies of the two regions, with the Flemings as the system's driving force.

The unique interdependence of these two economies was one of the first victims of the late medieval time of troubles. Trade relations and economic interests mattered little in the renewal of conflicts between the English and French kings, placing Flanders, essentially part of France yet economically tied to England, squarely in the middle. A series of embargoes, retaliatory confiscations, taxes, and acts of piracy associated with French-English warfare contributed to far-reaching changes in the nature of business in the region. Flemish merchants felt the effects almost immediately, losing their supremacy in the English wool trade to Italian businessmen after 1270. They also faced increasing competition from both Dutch and German merchants and shippers in the North Sea area. Step by step, the Flemish reoriented their efforts away from transporting and direct trading in commodities after 1300, favoring instead the sedentary and stable role of broker, partner, and entrepreneur. These changes, along with the increased importance of sea routes, Italian commercial interests, and the growing incorporation of northern and eastern traders of the German Hanse, combined to create a new business environment. Nowhere was this new regime more readily apparent than in the Flemish city of Bruges, which became one of the "great merchant cities of Christendom," in the words of a contemporary.

Bruges's new status owed much to a favorable geographical position and the disruption of the overland trade routes that sharply reduced the importance of the Champagne fairs after 1300. The city was situated at the intersection of several trading spheres in the European north, and from 1287 had begun to receive regular visits from the Italian trading fleets. Because of its traditional role in the English wool and Flemish cloth trades, Bruges was able to provide profitable return trade for the Italian ships. And the "Easterners," as German and other Hanse members were called, were themselves attracted by the merchandise conveyed by the Italians and by the chance to sell the products of their own regions:

furs, forest products, amber, and later grain, beer, and metal. Another reason to journey to Bruges was to take advantage of the demand generated by the populous and wealthy hinterland of the Low Countries and northern France. The flow of foreign merchants and their money seemed so compelling in the fourteenth century that even the city's inaccessibility to large ships posed few problems. Merchants were content to dock in the city's outports of Damme and Sluis and ferry their cargoes in small boats to the city's emporia.

No matter how favored by fortune, the government of Bruges spared neither effort nor expense in building up its business infrastructure. Even before the city had a proper town hall, it boasted two major commercial buildings (the old and new cloth halls), several municipal scales, and the huge man-powered crane for which Bruges was justly famous. Bruges was also the first city in the Low Countries to ban thatched roofs in the heart of the city in an effort to contain that curse of medieval towns, outbreaks of fire. The many impressive public works in support of business no doubt added to the city's luster, but its most important attraction was probably the web of human relationships that offered lodging, banking, brokering, and business contacts to the foreign merchant.

The cosmopolitanism of the men and women providing these services, and the harmonious manner in which they coordinated their efforts were crucial to the city's success as an international marketplace.[6] Cosmopolitanism among the business elite of Bruges was due to the extraordinary openness of the city to foreigners, particularly wealthy merchants able to acquire citizenship through purchase or marriage into the ranks of the upper bourgeoisie. Examples of transplanted foreigners include the Barbezans from Lucca, the Portinari from Florence, and the Adornes from Genoa. These last arrived in Bruges in 1340 and by the end of the century were important members of the elite of Bruges, owning an inn and an exchange bank. Today, direct descendants of the medieval Adornes still own the family chapel, now known as the Jerusalem church.

Another immigrant, this time from nearby Walloon Flanders, was Willem Ruweel, who acquired both a money-changing business and citizenship through marriage. Ruweel and his contemporary, Collard de Marke, have left a remarkably detailed record of the internal workings of business in Bruges in the 1360s, as a rich store of documentation was seized and preserved by the municipal government as a result of their bankruptcies. The data confirm that Flemish merchants still did not use bills of exchange in the fourteenth century, even though they were surely familiar with them. However, they show that money changers, together with innkeepers, provided an intricate and far-reaching system of book transfers that permitted those merchants with an account in Bruges to make payments for goods and services far beyond the city's walls. In effect, the Bruges money changers extended the giro transfer system described in Chapter 3 to foreign trade as well as local transactions. For example, Collard de Marke enabled his customers to draw upon their accounts in Bruges while visiting the Antwerp fair, either through drafts made on an Antwerp money changer or by dispatching his son to the fair.

Money changing as operated by Ruweel and de Marke seems to have been run not just for its own sake, but chiefly to provide working capital for investments. The use of customer deposits in this fashion amounts to banking with fractional reserves, an accepted modern banking practice, but regarded as illegal in most towns in medieval Europe until the fourteenth century, and even then hedged with restrictions where permitted.[7] This mechanism helped provide needed funds for investments in commercial real estate, partnerships with innkeepers, and public finance. But risks were high, and excessive exposure to such investments brought about the downfall of Ruweel, among others. Interestingly, the money-changing business survived Ruweel's bankruptcy because it was part of his wife's dowry and thus preserved from his creditors.

Prominent as were the money changers of fourteenth-century Bruges, they were dwarfed in importance by the innkeepers. Inns played a key role in the movement of goods along the overland trade routes of medieval Europe, and innkeepers provided not only lodging, but also warehousing, expert help with local governments, and even emergency financing. The late medieval inns of Bruges were unique in providing all these services plus brokerage, banking, and finance on an ongoing basis – in short, all the services necessary for doing business. Innkeepers included in their ranks prominent old families and the wealthy parvenus, such as the Adornes and Barbezans. They dominated the brokers' guild, for all innkeepers were brokers, employing other brokers without the means to own their own inns. Innkeepers also became increasingly powerful in local politics; many held the office of alderman (*schepen*), and innkeepers were often employed on diplomatic missions, particularly those who lodged Hanse merchants.

Critical to understanding the northern European trading system through Bruges in the late Middle Ages is the degree of cooperation between the money exchange and the inn. These two shared between them many banking functions in a cooperative, complementary manner, thereby forming an exchange network whose reach extended considerably beyond Bruges. Via this network, commodities, gold, silver, or petty coinage, letters of exchange and credit, as well as "bank" money held on deposit were circulated according to the needs of the customers. Thus, in his role as money changer, de Marke delivered to the inns of his customers at least twelve types of gold coins from places such as Castile, Venice, and England, as well as "black money" – the popular name for the mostly copper coins used for small purchases in the city. And because Bruges money changers and innkeepers had clearing accounts with each other, payment for those coins and other transactions could be made via book transfers.

Such an interlaced local system, coupled with contacts abroad and the constant travel of foreign merchants to and from Bruges, multiplied payment and credit possibilities. De Marke, for example, made use of a dense network of regional money changers and innkeepers from Ghent, Leuven, Douai, Tournai, Geraardsbergen, Valenciennes, and Antwerp to provide financial services to his customers. Truly long-distance transactions were also possible, such as payments made in Prussia by western knights on crusade, ransoms collected for prisoners held in Spain, as well as more typical business payments made in Paris and London. What is clear is that merchants used credit balances with Bruges innkeepers and money changers as currency, signing over their balances to a countryman bound for Bruges or ordering payment by letter or messenger, thus obviating the need for dispatch of coin or bullion. Another important development in negotiable credit instruments stemmed from the establishment of the Calais wool Staple in 1363, which channeled all exports of high quality wool through this port city, with English "Staplers" as the middlemen.[8] In practice, most of this wool was purchased in Calais by Flemish and Italian merchants for resale in Bruges, under terms of one-third cash down and the balance covered by letters obligatory held by the Staplers with full payment stipulated six to twelve months from date of sale. The Staplers in turn often exchanged these letters with other English merchants who made purchases using the unpaid sums stipulated in the letters as payment. Bruges money changers served as the clearinghouses for these transfers, which in effect allowed for the exchange of English wool for the myriad articles for sale in Bruges or elsewhere in the Low Countries, again without coins changing hands.

Bruges was certainly not unique in having innkeepers and money changers, for almost every medieval city had them, including some who cooperated in commercial networks. For example, the innkeepers of Ghent in the 1360s and 1370s seem to have served as deposit bankers for their customers, although no business records survive to verify this. In the southern French city of Montpellier, the innkeeper played a crucial role in the infrastructure of trade, as broker, guarantor of debts, and as an arranger of transport for his clients, although there is no evidence that he provided banking services there or anywhere else in the Mediterranean. Bruges's exceptionality was thus not so much a difference in kind but in the density of its network. This is important: as modern computer networks become powerful in proportion to the number of individual units they interlink, so did Bruges's commercial infrastructure, connecting the inns and exchanges of the densely urbanized hinterland of the Low Countries and northern France, become a powerhouse as it grew in size and compass.[9]

MERCHANT ADAPTATIONS — THE HANSE

Perhaps no other business-based organization shows the stresses and possibilities of late medieval trade better than the German Hanse. Similarly, no group is harder to define and analyze, for not only did the Hanse survive for half a millennium (from the mid twelfth to the mid seventeenth century), it manifested from its beginnings a power to metamorphose and evolve to take advantage of opportunities and minimize threats to its trade. In a sense, no matter how complex the "Cities of the German Hanse" (as they described themselves in 1358) became, they always preserved an image of themselves as a besieged merchant convoy, whose survival depended on mutual aid and solidarity. As a document of 1469 sought to explain to the English Privy Council, the German Hanse was neither company (*societas*), partnership (*collegium*), nor guild (*universitas*), but was a "federation (*confederatio*) of many cities, towns, and communities for the purpose of ensuring that business enterprises by land and sea should have a desired and favorable outcome and that there should be effective protection against pirates and highwaymen, so that their ambushes should not rob merchants of their goods and valuables."[10] The Hanse spokesmen were sly enough to omit mention that by the fourteenth and fifteenth centuries, a major raison' d'être for the federation was to protect against unfair taxation and harassment of its members by northern princes, as well as to agitate for and extort enhanced trading privileges. It had also evolved into a vastly larger organization, with around seventy cities belonging to the core, and perhaps another one hundred loosely or temporarily allied, including cities neither German nor part of the empire, such as Cracow and Stockholm.

Though often defined by what it was not, the German Hanse was an organization that sought to control the east-west Baltic trade, with Lübeck as the dominant partner. It was not until the thirteenth century that Cologne and other western cities joined the federation, making it a truly German Hanse. The group took advantage of shifts in the politics of trade in the West, securing a privileged position for its members in Flanders and England and establishing Bruges and London as the Hanse outposts in the West, each with a local trade and political structure known as a *kontor*. These two cities thus became the destinations and residences for Hanse merchants and merchandise, as well as centers of political and economic influence extending into their hinterlands and beyond. The eastern and northern counterparts of London and Bruges were the *kontors* of Novgorod and Bergen. Through the four posts flowed the furs, amber, and wax of Russia, the fish of Norway and Iceland, and the wool and cloth of England and Flanders.

The trade zone dominated by the Hanse has been likened to a "lesser northern counterpoint to Italian commerce in the Mediterranean," but there were important differences.[11] The preponderant trade goods tended to be low-value raw materials such as grain (mostly rye and barley from Prussia), forest products, and metals. With the increasing demand for imported foodstuffs during the later Middle Ages, beer, salt, and herring began to rival the more traditional trade items in value, further enhancing Lübeck's predominant position within the federation, in alliance with Bremen and Hamburg. This points up the other major difference between the two largest European trade zones, namely that by 1360 the German Hanse had a near-monopoly on both the carrying trade and trade in essential northern products. Not even Venice equaled this achievement in the Mediterranean.

However vigorously defended, Hanse predominance did not go unchallenged, nor did the sometimes rag-tag solidarity among Hanseatic cities remain unshaken. From the 1360s both the seafaring towns of the northern Netherlands and English merchantmen began to challenge the Hanse's Baltic monopoly. The Dutch, led by Amsterdam, contested the German hold on the herring and salt trades, perfecting a more efficient on-board curing process (to be discussed more fully in Chapter 8) and pioneering large-scale salt imports from the Bay of Bourgneuf in France. The English cut into the Hanse's shipping business with Prussia by offering attractive freight rates and aggressively priced English cloth as return cargo. Ultimately, both English and Dutch challenges proved irresistible, though not without the punctuation of a trade war between the Dutch and Lübeck's Wendish League in 1438, which split the Hanse into pro- and anti-Lübeck factions. Together with the Danish king, the Dutch exploited this chink and gained through the Treaty of Copenhagen in 1441 full trading rights in the Baltic. The English had already confirmed direct access for their cloth exports to Prussia through a treaty signed with the Teutonic Grand Master in 1410.

The key to the Hanse trading system was the so-called *Stapelzwang*, the requirement that all Hanse merchants buy and sell their goods at a staple, that is, an established place, in order to maintain maximum control over the flow of trade. For the most part these coincided with the *kontors*, of which Bruges was preeminent in the fourteenth and fifteenth centuries. Hanse officials ensured that their authority was not overridden by local functionaries and that Hanse merchants occupied a uniquely privileged position among foreign merchants residing in the Flemish city. Embargo and secession, the ultimate weapons of the Hanse, were employed against the Flemish in 1307–9, 1358–60, 1388–92, and 1436, and secured on each occasion greater rights for Hanse merchants in Bruges and elsewhere in Flanders. For example, they became the only customers assured of complete repayment of their deposits in case of the bankruptcy of a money changer or an innkeeper. In addition, the Count of Flanders suspended his right of salvage, granted Hanseatics exemptions from tolls and some taxes, and streamlined judicial procedures for them. This body of special privileges did much to give Hanse merchants a competitive edge in Flanders and elsewhere, aiding them in their long struggle with the Dutch.

THE TEXTILE INDUSTRY

The enterprises most vulnerable to this new environment of shrunken populations and rising labor costs were those in the textile industry. The markets in many parts of Europe for cheaper grades of cloth had already been in decline from early in the fourteenth century, due to the dislocations and depopulation caused by war, famine, and pestilence. Production capacity, already excessive at the time of the Black Death, increased even more, notwithstanding the probability that the market shrinkage was attenuated by the greater purchasing power of the survivors. Competition in the low to medium grades of cloth became fiercer than ever, especially with the entry of a significant new actor on the international scene. This was England, one of the most important suppliers of wool of all qualities, now enjoying a powerful price advantage as a result of the fiscal policies of its monarchs. Edward III had been piling on the duties on wool exports since the 1330s to finance his war with France. Part of this expense had been absorbed by the growers, but from 1363, with the establishment of the Calais Staple, the foreign buyers were burdened with the entire weight of the duty. From the 1340s onward, this levy averaged forty to fifty shillings per sack of 364 pounds, even more if the exporters were aliens, representing a huge percentage of raw wool cost for the lesser grades. Conversely, duty on the export of finished cloth was minimal, averaging only about three percent of the value of the product until 1373, when a still-modest "poundage" tax of five percent was added. The result was a steady surge of cloth exports, from miniscule quantities in 1350 to over 40,000 pieces per year by the end of the century.

The three great Flemish production centers – Ypres, Ghent, and Bruges – had long been in a protectionist mode, using all means at their disposal, including violence, to curb low-cost competition and counterfeiting in their immediate rural neighborhood. Their reaction to this new threat was to ban the import of English cloth and even its transshipment through Flemish ports. This policy promptly put the Flemish at odds with the Hanse and Genoese merchants who were important to Flemish international trade. Eventually, the Flemish yielded to the extent of permitting transshipment on condition that no English cloths were landed. In a second reaction to price competition, the Flemish producers accelerated their withdrawal from the cheaper end of the international market, while continuing to produce inferior grades for local and regional consumption. They thus bent all efforts toward ensuring the integrity of their top quality cloths, which still enjoyed a market that was growing and resistant to price competition. They continued to buy the majority of the best grades of English wool through the Calais Staple, pay the duty, and pass the cost along to their eager customers. The result was a business that was smaller, at least in unit volume but still profitable.

The enormous competitive pressure in the textile industry surprisingly did little to stimulate new or improved technology. Perhaps there was further penetration by some of the earlier labor-saving processes – such as carding, spinning wheels, broadlooms, and waterpowered fulling – but the only new medieval invention after the Black Death was the gig mill for nap raising, and its use was largely confined to England. On the contrary, there was strong resistance to the spread of all the medieval innovations, ostensibly on grounds of quality (genuinely so in the case of luxury cloths), but often in defense of particular interests. England, being the newest of the international competitors, appeared to be the most receptive to improvements in production processes. There, the cloth industry was mainly rural, with lower labor costs, access to flowing streams for fulling, and relative freedom from guild restrictions. But even in England, there was stiff resistance to the nap-raising mills when they began to make their appearance in the fifteenth century.

An interesting aspect of the English expansion is the symbiosis that began to develop between the new industry and Genoese shippers. The latter had long been stopping at English ports, leaving Mediterranean goods and collecting English wool for forwarding to Flanders and Italy.

After the 1350s, the rapidly growing cloth industry began to need increasing quantities of alum and dyes. After its last great war with Venice in 1381, Genoa regained full control over the alum mines of Phoacea in Asia Minor, and began building exceptionally large sailing ships to transport this bulk commodity. Although the main destination for the alum was the Low Countries, substantial quantities were dropped at Southampton. Another bulk cargo was woad from northern Italy, the most preferred dye of the Middle Ages, as it did not require a mordant and could be used as the base dye for a variety of other colors. These ships were wonderfully efficient for long, direct voyages, transporting the alum and woad for as little as eight percent of their purchase price in England. Southampton was also accessible to the new wool-producing area of the Cotswolds, where the Genoese picked up cargoes of fine-quality fibers for shipment to Flanders and elsewhere at very low freight cost. And finally, they carried substantial quantities of English cloth cheaply to new markets, such as Spain, that otherwise would have been beyond the reach of the English manufacturers.

The story of traditional manufacturers being forced to retreat to the high-quality end of the trade is repeated over and over in virtually all types of textiles for all parts of Europe.[12] Italian woolen fabricators faced competition in the international export markets from cheaper English cloths, and more importantly in their domestic markets from Italian cottons and blends. Cotton served an expanding market partly because of an increasing demand by all classes for lightweight undergarments, and also because of a general trend toward cheaper fabrics. In Florence, annual production of woolen cloth faded from the chronicler Villani's estimate of seventy to eighty thousand pieces in the 1330s to twenty to thirty thousand in the 1380s, and still further by the end of the century. Part of Florence's problem was the expansion and improved quality of low-cost rural production. The declining volume was partly offset by a much higher average unit value, but even at the luxury end, Italian woolens were facing competition in the form of a burgeoning local silk industry.

The introduction of the silk industry into Italy had begun in Lucca as early as the twelfth century with raw material supplied from the Levant. Its success prompted the spread of silk cultivation throughout Italy, including the planting of mulberry trees and breeding of silk-worms, vigorously encouraged by communes and princes. The expansion continued into the thirteenth and fourteenth centuries, much aided by the dissemination of a water-powered mill for twisting silk filament into thread, supplanting the costly and labor-intensive hand process. By the fifteenth century, imported raw material, except for the finest grades, was largely replaced by Italian. The great variety of qualities and prices of the local material enabled producers to offer a range of silks and combinations with other fibers to a much wider market, allowing the industry to continue growing despite the sharp decline in population.

Both cotton and silk were given a helping hand by a new cultural preference in the Mediterranean for darker colors, especially black. Traditionally, in that area, white had been the color of mourning, and people expressed their penance and grief by wearing unbleached, undyed garments. Starting among the nobility of Spain and Portugal in the fourteenth century and spreading into Italy via Naples, the use of black gradually became "official" for all classes for clothing and other furnishings of mourning. Cotton and silk (the latter by the affluent) were the preferred textiles for black, because of their lighter weight compared to woolens. And given the great mortality during the second half of the fourteenth century, demand was high.

The Italian cotton industry was largely devoted to the manufacture of fustian, a blend of cotton and linen. Beset by market shrinkage and problems of cost, it was already in decline when faced with new competitors from south Germany.[13] The center of this new industry was Swabia, where supplies of linen were available in the local markets. Wholesale merchants, such as the famous Fuggers of Augsburg, bought raw cotton in Venice and Milan, advanced credit to weavers in Ulm and other Swabian cities, and took charge of the finishing and eventual marketing of the finished product. The Swabian product was inferior to the Italian cottons that had long been sold in Germany and northern Europe but was much cheaper. It quickly captured a large share of the German market and by 1370 had made considerable headway in Italy's traditional markets for cottons and blends around Europe. Moreover, south German and Swiss merchants began to take over the marketing of quality Italian cottons throughout northern Europe. And by the early fifteenth century, German fustians had penetrated Italy itself, prompting a protectionist reaction. Here again, the traditional manufacturers found themselves unwilling or unable to meet the challenge of the upstart new producers and were driven to concentrate on the quality end of the market.

This brief and incomplete summary of events in the textile industry of the late Middle Ages highlights the reactions of various parts of the industry to changes in consumer preferences provoked by the introduction of new and cheaper alternatives. Except at the very top end of the quality spectrum, consumers appeared to prefer a lower price to slightly better quality or durability. The new sources of existing products, such as England for woolens, were able to reduce costs as the new fabricators gained experience and market share. The producers of fustians in Germany and cottons (at least initially) and silks in Italy showed a sensitivity to consumer demand that made them effective competitors over a wide range of product uses. Traditional industries in Flanders and Italy, faced with hard choices, usually opted for niche markets that they could hold through distinct product superiority, as in luxury cloths, or could control, as in local coarser grades. Clearly, the prizes in this new environment went to those entrepreneurs who were nimble, flexible, and sensitive to consumer preferences as never before. The losers gained only limited protection from the restrictions imposed by their guild organizations and even from the use of lower-cost rural production sources. These pressures of course provoked considerable labor unrest, in some cases leading to social upheaval. In Flanders, especially, the stresses and strains of the cloth industry were a constant accompaniment and frequent contributor to the county's turbulent politics.

SUPPLYING THE MILITARY

One "industry" that flourished throughout this period irrespective of market loss and market disruption was that of meeting the needs of the military. Although military demands separately affected many of the industries that are being discussed, it is nonetheless worthwhile to devote a segment specifically to this subject. War had become not only endemic throughout this period, but more importantly for business, it was being waged by larger and larger polities that had the means to acquire more and more of what Cicero once described as war's sinews – money. And as warfare became more sophisticated and widespread, its demands for supplies and weaponry impinged increasingly on the entire range of business endeavor. Business opportunities therefore abounded for those enterprises that could profit by serving the warring princes and communes.[14]

The construction industry benefited considerably from the demands of the military. The aftermath of the Black Death obviously had left a good deal of spare housing and church capacity, with the result that there was little construction activity for normal civilian requirements. There were, as usual, exceptions to this situation in various parts of Europe. In England, for example, cathedral building continued into the fifteenth century; and in Italy, the Low Countries, and south Germany, that same century saw much new building of grand edifices for personal and official use. But a great deal of new construction was for stronger walls surrounding castles and towns to withstand improved artillery, especially the use of iron cannon balls. Much work also resulted from the need to repair infrastructure, replace industrial facilities, and restore property devastated by war. And many ostensibly commercial projects, such as improved roads, canals, and bridges, were motivated by military objectives. Shipbuilding benefited especially, as fleets were built, leased to combatants, destroyed, and rebuilt.

The poor results of mining for precious metals in the first half of the fifteenth century were not from lack of trying. Governments desperately, if unsuccessfully, sought to squeeze more production out of worked-out mines as well as to encourage prospecting to generate cash for their campaigns. For example, in 1444 King Charles VII of France granted Jacques Coeur, France's treasurer and leading capitalist, the king's rights to ten percent of the output of the silver, lead, and copper extracted from a number of old mines near Lyon for a modest annual payment and a commitment to get them working again. Mining base metals was another matter. Iron ore and copper were in plentiful supply, and demand was brisk, fueled by persistent demand for their use in the fabrication of cannon, cannon balls, and plate armor, in addition to swords, knives, chain mail, crossbows, and helmets. The technological advances in mining and metallurgy described later in this chapter owed much to the encouragement of governments bent on pursuing their military ambitions.

Blacksmiths and metalworkers of all kinds were also much sought after and became increasingly specialized. Some shaped the iron when cold, using files, saws, drills, and rivets. Others concentrated on sword-smithing, locks and keys, or decorative work. Some who specialized further, especially in nonferrous metals, were called upon to fabricate the increasingly decorative breastplates and helmets of the nobility. Milan, from the thirteenth century an important center for the manufacture of arms and armor, prospered mightily. Leatherworkers, cobblers, clothing manufacturers, and artificers of all kinds found gainful employment filling government orders in cities throughout Europe.

Merchants, too, prospered from the arms trade. Francesco Datini got his start in that business in papal Avignon, which, ironically, was a major entrepôt for weaponry of all kinds. There he dealt in the metals and accessories for making arms, importing from various places – iron sheets for visors, wire for chain mail, tin studs for shields, blades and scabbards for swords. He also traded actively in ready-to-use equipment and harnesses for men and their horses. But one must not be beguiled into concluding that war for merchants, as for others, was anything more than the ill wind that sometimes blows some good. Datini could turn war to good account, but he and his managers and correspondents were always elated at any resumption of peace.

One aspect of military supply that merchants did learn to appreciate was the trend throughout continental Europe, from the second half of the fifteenth century onward, toward maintaining sizeable standing armies. This movement actually began late in the fourteenth century in Italy, as the major city-states expanded their territories and needed long-term contractual arrangements with their *condottieri* (contractor captains) to provide permanent forces to control their extended borders. In France, the monarchy had established a standing royal army in the mid fourteenth century and again during the final decades of the Hundred Years' War. But what was new was the maintenance of a sizeable and well-supplied permanent force during the forty years of relative peace following France's final victory over the English in 1453. The Italian states, Burgundy, and the Swiss also kept armies trained and ready. To businessmen, this meant a steady demand for clothing, weapons, and the usual accoutrements of war without the usual accompanying hazards.

MINING AND METALLURGY

Mining for precious metals was at a low ebb in the latter half of the fourteenth century, as the seams were playing out in the great silver mines of Freiberg and Kutná Hora in Bohemia, and in the lesser but still important ones of Iglesias in Sardinia. No new discoveries were on the horizon, and rising labor costs made the working of small mines impracticable. The situation deteriorated further in the first half of the fifteenth century, as silver production dropped to negligible proportions, especially after 1422, when Kutná Hora was shut down by the Hussite wars. Hungarian gold mines had been quite productive, but their output also fell. Then, in 1441, the Turks occupied mining areas in southern Serbia. All this contributed to the severe bullion shortage of the second third of the fifteenth century, giving governments even more urgent cause to encourage prospecting and to improve mining and smelting technology to get more out of existing properties. These efforts began to be rewarded in the 1460s.

In mining for precious metals, improved technology focused on powerful water- or horse-driven drainage pumps and more effective use of adits to make accessible formerly flooded mine shafts. And in smelting, the great advance was the rediscovery of the *seiger* liquation process practised by the Romans that finally succeeded in separating silver from argentiferous copper ores, releasing two very valuable metals from heretofore unworkable deposits. These advances made possible the reopening of the formerly great mines of Bohemia and Saxony, along with hundreds of smaller properties previously not considered worth exploiting. Intensive prospecting and better techniques resulted in significant new discoveries at Schwaz in the Tyrol and Schneeberg in Saxony that swiftly developed into high volume producers. And early in the sixteenth century, further rich finds in Bohemia and Saxony ensured steadily rising production until the 1530s, after which declining output in Europe began to be offset by the flow of precious metals from the New World.

In base metals, military demand continued apace, requiring continual increases in the production of copper and tin, and above all iron. Although there were no significant new developments in mining, operators became more proficient in using their equipment for extracting ores. In metallurgy, larger and larger smelters were built to meet the demand for iron. Using water-powered bellows, some smelters began to generate heat intense enough to melt the ore and create cast iron, leading to the blast furnace, the first firm example of which appeared in Liège in 1384. Here, the process of learning by doing was key to success, as repeated trials and errors were necessary to achieve the optimum mix of ingredients. As the blast furnaces increased in size, the use of water power became more vital for crushing ores and driving bellows. As a result, the location of smelting operations tended to be governed more by proximity to fast-moving water rather than to the mines. Also, the melting of the ore into cast iron permitted greater recovery of the iron and provided a convenient intermediate product from which forges could make wrought iron for a whole range of goods. And a new slitting mill turned out slender rods that made the job of making nails easier and cheaper. For all of Europe, it has been estimated that iron production had reached 60,000 tons annually by 1500.

The growing size and complexity of mining and smelting operations created demands for capital on an unprecedented scale. Financing was needed for more sophisticated and deeper tunnels and adits, numerous water wheels for a variety of purposes, ever larger blast furnaces, and the sheds and specialized furnaces for the silver separation process, the so-called *seigerhütten*. The sources of capital for these and other purposes will be discussed in Chapters 8 and 9.

Some of the output of iron mines and smelters was used by specialist toolmakers, who made tools such as the brace and bit and other equipment for masons and carpenters, requiring special skills. But the most by far went through the hands of the thousands of artisan blacksmiths scattered throughout Europe in towns, villages, and countryside for its conversion to end-use products. Operating mainly as individual entrepreneurs, blacksmiths shaped metal for plows and other farm implements, worked with wheelwrights in providing ironwork for carts, crafted armor, swords and other weaponry for the military, and manufactured a great variety of tools for urban tradesmen of all kinds. Some also specialized in fabricating and repairing the tower clocks that appeared in cities and towns across Europe. Blacksmiths were many, ubiquitous, prized, and despised, the last because of the noise, smoke, and stench of their operations, particularly as they began switching to coal from charcoal as a result of an increasing shortage of wood in the late fourteenth century.

The accomplishments of mining and smelting in the fifteenth century owed something to luck, but much more to the gradual accumulation of know-how over the Middle Ages. The legacy of "learning by doing" was improved focus and skill in prospecting, more efficient methods of exploiting both old and new discoveries, and lower-cost means of turning the raw metals into usable finished products.

SHIPBUILDING

Excess shipping capacity in the years immediately following the Black Death did not entirely inhibit the construction of new ships, and new designs did appear in the latter half of the fourteenth century, impelled by the need to service certain market niches competitively. In the north, builders merged two distinct ship types for carrying bulk cargo, the cog and the hulk, into a single design containing some of the best features of both, resulting in faster larger vessels with greater carrying capacity per unit of length. In the south, the great galleys that had been developed earlier by Venice and Genoa began to be used in the mid fourteenth century for regular runs to England and Flanders. These ships, broader and deeper than traditional galleys, relied mainly on large lateen sails, using oar power only when necessary. They were large enough to carry a substantial (up to 150 tons) and varied cargo of middling to high value, including cloth, wool, textile industry raw materials, wines, spices, and precious metals, but not bulk commodities. They were also used extensively as passenger ships for the pilgrim trade. Their large crews were expensive, but kept intruders at bay, virtually eliminating the cost of insurance, and their speed and reliability permitted profitable, regular scheduling.

The latter half of the fourteenth century saw three important developments in shipbuilding, even though their full effect was not manifested until early in the following century. The first was the increasing transfer of technologies and ideas between the north and the Mediterranean. Northern shipyards began to build galleys, and Mediterranean builders were finding cogs increasingly popular. The Genoese built cogs of unprecedented size, deploying them profitably, as we have seen, in transporting alum and woad to England and Flanders. And the Venetians ran semiannual convoys of large cogs to bring raw cotton from Syria to Venice for local cloth manufacture or for forwarding to Germany.

The second development was the acceleration of the government intervention noted on page 146. By 1400, the Venetian commune was operating great galleys as well as building them in its famous arsenal. Governments in France and Iberia likewise followed the Venetian example, establishing their own shipyards for building warships and other vessels of special interest to them. And all governments with maritime pretensions became increasingly involved in the recruiting of ever-scarcer seamen, especially galley rowers, a job which had become menial and of low status and for which unfree candidates had to be found.

The third trend was the growing emphasis on specialization. More ships of all sizes were aimed at certain market niches, with the objective of executing specific assignments at the lowest possible cost. Although this specialization did not become really obvious until the fifteenth century, the trend had already begun in the late fourteenth century, when new kinds of ships began to appear, from the huge Genoese cogs to the bewildering array of special-purpose coastal trampers and fishing vessels.

These three trends seemed to merge in the fifteenth century, as shipbuilders borrowed and copied design features, creating both versatile vessels usable almost anywhere and adaptations suitable for exploiting niche opportunities. Examples of the latter abounded, especially in the smaller boat category. The Portuguese, egged on by Henry the Navigator, designed the highly maneuverable caravel specifically for long voyages of exploration, with little carrying capacity and relatively large crews. Late in the century, they built much larger versions, still with good maneuverability and suitable for carrying cargo between Portugal and its island possessions in the Atlantic as well as the ports of West Africa. In the north, the Dutch were preeminent in design specialization for fishing boats. One type, the hoeker, had small holes in the hull, so that caught fish could be kept alive in a bath of sea water until the boat's return to port. But rightly the most famous of Dutch fishing boats was the herring buss, which was capable of making long voyages and maintained facilities for curing and packing the catch on board.[15]

The most important design development of the fifteenth century, however, was the three-masted full-rigged ship, described by Richard Unger as "the great invention."[16] First appearing in Atlantic ports of Iberia early in the fifteenth century, it was quickly picked up and adapted in the Mediterranean, where it was called a carrack. By mid-century, it had spread north to France, the Low Countries, England, and the German Hanse in the Baltic, with strong government encouragement everywhere. The versatile design boasted much-improved propulsion and control over earlier sailing ships and could be applied to a broad range of sizes. Because it was defensible, capable of carrying artillery, and adaptable to both bulk and high-value cargoes, it was useful for both war and commerce. Not surprisingly, therefore, it supplanted the great galley as the commercial vessel of choice for the runs from the Italian ports to northern Europe by the third quarter of the fifteenth century. The full-rigged ship, albeit with countless improvements, was not replaced as the prime sailing vessel of Europe until the arrival of the clipper ships of the nineteenth century.

The great strides in shipbuilding in this era, except for the period immediately following the Black Death, were a response to new opportunities rather than to adversities. One such opportunity was the shift away from land routes to water routes between the Mediterranean countries and northern Europe noted earlier, fostering more emphasis on designing ships adaptable both to Mediterranean and Atlantic conditions. Another was the need to satisfy the demand of princes for extensive maritime exploration and faster, more defensible vessels. But probably the most important was the opportunity created by continuous pressure to reduce the costs of moving goods − whether they be raw materials to producers or finished product to consumers.

We have seen in this chapter that the late fourteenth and early fifteenth centuries, far from being a period of stagnation and depression as characterized by many previous historians, was in fact one of significant constructive change. To be sure, the process was slow and uncertain; the diffusion of knowledge through "learning by doing" takes a great deal of time in an age of general illiteracy, frequent calamities, and disrupted communications. But though technology was slow to spread, the reaction of businessmen to new market opportunities was surprisingly swift. Through increased competition, greater sensitivity to consumer demand, and closer attention to costs, they made a wider variety of goods available to a wider range of consumers at lower prices. Governments were key contributors to this development, despite their often ill-judged policies. In sum, although the volume of production probably declined during this period, the volume per capita probably increased and the quality and variety of consumer goods unquestionably improved. Still more needed to be done in this direction, and costs were still too high. The perception of such needs and the design of a variety of approaches to meet them were soon to come.

8

THE FIFTEENTH CENTURY: REVOLUTIONARY RESULTS FROM OLD PROCESSES

———————— • ————————

The drive to reduce costs across Europe began gradually to acquire an aggressive rather than a reactive character after the more obvious and relatively easy responses to adversity had been made. Businessmen in the fifteenth century began to apply their learning-by-doing methodology to cost cutting in two directions, one to find ways of getting as close as possible to the source of their products, and the other to develop new forms of industrialization. Unlike the swift, theorized perceptions of modern business (downsizing, reengineering, reinventing, etc.) these developments were part of a slow, almost organic evolution, as businessmen followed the demands of the marketplace to their logical conclusion and sought ways to circumvent their traditional suppliers by identifying new ones or becoming producers themselves. This fifteenth-century development reflects the earliest stirrings across Europe of the drive toward vertical integration that so came to typify the strategy of nineteenth-century business leaders. Drawing closer to both producer and customer became the imperative of the late medieval businessman.

Although we have not stressed this point earlier, getting close to product sources was by no means a new idea in medieval Europe. European merchants, especially those of Venice and Genoa, had long perceived the virtues of this approach, establishing colonies throughout the Mediterranean and Black Seas, and securing trading privileges wherever they could, especially from a weakening Byzantine Empire. The strategy enabled them to obtain key raw materials and luxury manufactures at the lowest possible cost. Their outposts in the West gave them access to African gold, while those in the East provided gateways to the northern, central, and southern silk and spice routes, and directly to the markets of Persia and southern Russia. All this was immensely profitable, providing the sinews for the amazing and durable military power of Venice and Genoa.

European purchases in the East consisted of two broad categories of goods. The first included products of local cultivation or processing, such as cotton, sugar, silks, wheat, dyes, and semi-tropical fruits. Climatic conditions for the production of most of these goods were also present in the central and western parts of the Mediterranean, and the necessary skills to exploit them were acquired in due course. We have already seen that silk manufacture, followed by the cultivation of mulberry trees and the breeding of silkworms, spread to Italy and France. The growing of cotton extended to Sicily, Italy, and Spain, as did cultivation of sugarcane, fruits, and dye-producing plants. Thus, competition was available in the West for many of the items imported from the East, except to the extent to which quality differentials played a part, as in silks or Syrian cottons (both the raw material and finished fabrics). Also in this first category were certain minerals, especially alum, located by chance in the East and much in demand in the West. And here too, there was some competition from Western sources, which became significant after the discoveries of rich alum deposits in central Italy in the 1450s. By the latter part of the fifteenth century, therefore, trade in these indigenous goods was reasonably competitive and at least partially balanced by the flow of Western cheap and fine woolens and metal products to the East.

The second category of European import was of products originating in territories well beyond the eastern Mediterranean – pepper, ginger, cloves, and other exotic spices, as well as luxury manufactures such as fine silks and jewelry. This was probably the largest and certainly the most unbalanced part of East-West trade. As we have already noted in Chapter 3, certain of the European offerings, such as fine woolens and armor, were readily accepted in markets of the distant East, but their value fell far short of satisfying the Western appetite for spices. The gap had to be made up with precious metals, especially silver, always welcome in the territories of origin of spices and luxury goods – Persia, India, China, East Africa, and the East Indies – which, for simplicity over the next few pages, we will call the "Farther East."

NEW LIMITATIONS ON ACCESS TO EASTERN TRADE

Circumstances began to turn against the Venetian and Genoese trading patterns in the fourteenth and fifteenth centuries, steadily constricting their access to both categories of Eastern commerce. Their own ferocious rivalries and hugely wasteful wars on each other, as well as the continuing internecine struggles in Genoa, reduced the resources available to defend their colonies and trading interests. The collapse of the Mongol Empire in the mid to late fourteenth century followed by the depredations of Timurlane severely disrupted the northern trade routes, limiting the importance of the Black Sea ports of Caffa and Tana as gateways to the caravan routes to the East. At the same time, the expansion of the Ottoman Turks into Europe further squeezed access to the Black Sea, severely diminishing the importance of the Genoese colony at Pera opposite Constantinople, even before the capture of those cities by the Turks in 1453. To illustrate, the returns of taxes from Pera declined from Genoese £1.6 million in 1334 to £1.2 million in 1391, and to a mere £234,000 in 1423. The Turkish seizure of the alum mines at Phocaea in Asia Minor in 1455 was a further blow, even though initially the Genoese monopoly was merely transferred to the Venetians.

These events and the Mamluk conquest of Armenian Cilicia left the Italians largely dependent upon the Mamluk government for trade with Egypt and the Levant and access to spices and silks from the Farther East. Around the same time, trade between the Farther East and Egypt, which had long been in the hands of a powerful group of wholesalers called the Karimis, was taken over by the Mamluk sultan. His government had been facing the increasing cost of financing an aggressive foreign policy coincident with declining revenues from an economy suffering from depopulation. The sultan accordingly seized upon the direct control of trade as the prime means of restoring his fortunes and proceeded to wring as much profit as possible out of international business. He established state spice and sugar monopolies, which fixed the prices at which those items could be sold to Europeans. The Italian traders' difficulties were compounded in two further ways. First, the sultan proved to be an awkward business partner – arbitrary, suspicious, and prepared to use the considerable force at his command to press his negotiations. The second was the on-again, off-again papal prohibition against trading with the Mamluks, which, although not very effective, was nevertheless troublesome to the Christian traders.

As a result of these developments, the main source of alum was controlled by the Ottomans, whereas that of spices, aromatics, dyes, drugs, sugar, and cotton was dominated by the Mamluks.[1] By the mid fifteenth century, therefore, the vital elements of the Eastern trade had fallen into the hands of governments that were not only hostile, but also knowledgeable about the importance of the trade to the Europeans and how to extract the most from it. The decline in spice prices at Egyptian and

Levantine ports that occurred during the latter decades of the fifteenth century was caused entirely by an even sharper price drop in the Farther East, widening the gap in prices between the two sources. With Western demand continuing to increase, the attraction of circumventing the middlemen of Italy and the Middle East would become irresistible. The incentive to find new ways to cut costs was powerful, giving rise to two distinct approaches – direct dealing with the old sources and a search for new ones. New actors entered the fray with one or both of these objectives in mind.

The Catalans can hardly be said to be "new" entrants into the Eastern trading system. We have seen on page 83 that they had been important actors in the commerce of the western Mediterranean during the thirteenth century and had also sent their ships into the Atlantic. Catalan business in the East, however, began only late in that century and then on a small-scale and intermittent basis. But by the early fifteenth century the Catalans were hotly contesting Genoa's prominence in the East and proving just as aggressive as the Italians in fighting both Christians and Muslims for their share of the Levantine business. The activity of these doughty traders dropped off sharply in the latter half of the fifteenth century, and from the sixteenth century onward they ceased to be an important factor in Mediterranean commerce. During their heyday, the Catalans were motivated partly by their interest in getting goods cheaply to their home markets in Iberia and southern France; but for the most part, they saw themselves as maritime merchants, able competitors of the Genoese and Venetians for a profitable position in international trade for its own sake.

Other competitors entered into the commerce of the Mediterranean primarily to serve their markets better and more cost effectively. The Florentines had until the early fifteenth century concentrated on marketing and finance, leaving the transport of goods to others. Their venture into marine transport occurred shortly after their acquisition of Florence's archenemy, Pisa, in 1406. But the port there was silted up and useless for international traffic; it was not until 1421, with the purchase of Porto Pisano from Genoa, that Florence could become a sea power. The commune took charge: it financed and built as many as eleven great galleys and fifteen long galleys designed for the mixed luxury trade of the eastern Mediterranean and the wool and cloth commerce of the north and West. The city auctioned the ships for each voyage to private merchants, who for the first time were able to move their own merchandise in their own ships.[2] The Florentine fleet made frequent voyages to Catalonia, Sicily, the Levant, and occasionally to Flanders. But the anticipated advantages failed to materialize with any consistency in the face of fierce competition and the scarcity of competent crews, forcing the final abandonment of the project in 1480.

Merchants of southern France had long been active in Mediterranean trade, operating out of Montpellier, Aigues Mortes, and Marseilles, but only intermittently and never on a very large scale. From the 1430s, however, the famous French financier Jacques Coeur made France a serious contender. He travelled to the Levant, established excellent relations with the Mamluks, and soon became the main supplier of spices to southern France. In return, he shipped not only the usual cargoes of cloth, agricultural products, and coral, but also silver, copper, and other metals in substantial quantities. Such was his influence and diplomatic skill that he obtained the acquiescence of the papacy to his trade with the Muslims and of the King of Aragon to his competition with the Catalonians. His fall from favor in 1451 did not terminate the effect of his efforts; the four galleys that he had built continued to operate in the Eastern trade in the hands of others, and were later replaced by new ones built in the 1460s.[3] King Louis XI took an active interest in fostering Mediterranean trade, channeling the import of spices through French ports, carried in the "galleys of France." Controlling their own imports seemed to be the limit of French aspirations, as no attempt was made to establish colonies in the East or to become serious competitors of the Venetians.

The English came very late on the Mediterranean scene, even though English cloth of many kinds had been traded throughout all parts of that area since the latter half of the fourteenth century. The Venetians out of London and the Genoese out of Southampton carried virtually all of this merchandise throughout the fifteenth century, challenged only briefly in 1457 by a merchant from Bristol whose ships were captured by the Genoese near Malta. The most important English penetration occurred in the replacement of the Florentine galleys for the export of wool to Tuscany from the 1470s. This trade prospered to such an extent that by 1491 a staple for English wool was set up at Pisa, which was to be supplied exclusively by English ships. Unfortunately, this arrangement was scuttled by the French invasion of Italy in 1494 and the subsequent revolt of Pisa against Florence. Nonetheless, English shipping continued to fill the gaps left by the gradual withdrawal of Genoese and Venetian merchantmen from English waters between 1480 and 1530.

Although this invasion of the new competitors added significantly to Genoa's trading problems in the Mediterranean, its effect on Venice was trifling, as that city continued to dominate trade with Egypt and the Levant throughout the fifteenth century. While Genoa faded as a serious rival in this area, Venice maintained its role as the prime middleman by virtue of its role as entrepôt and its direct access to northern Europe through southern Germany. In addition, Venice supplanted the Genoese in Cyprus in 1489, turning that island's plantations into an important source of raw cotton after its production of sugar ceased being profitable as a result of competition from Madeira. The Genoese still traded in the Levant, where their main base was the island of Chios, still famous for its mastic, but even more valuable as a transshipment port for some of the spices acquired in Alexandria and Beirut, and especially for alum, that key ingredient used in the textile industry.

THE LOOSENING OF THE ALUM MONOPOLY

By far the greatest single source of good quality alum throughout the Middle Ages was the mines of Phocaea near Smyrna in Asia Minor. These had been under the control of the Genoese, except for brief intervals, since Benedetto Zaccaria acquired the monopoly late in the thirteenth century. Prior to the Fourth or "Chioggia" War with Venice (1378–81), a group of businessmen formed a peculiarly Genoese type of company, called a *maona*, to exploit the monopoly.[4] This organization managed the monopoly with great skill, adjusting production volume to optimize pricing and designing special bulk carriers to transport the material to northern Europe at low cost (see page 168). This highly profitable business was first threatened, then terminated by the Turks, who occupied the mines in 1455. The Ottomans awarded the management of the monopoly to the Venetians, whose term lasted only until 1463, when war broke out between Venice and Turkey.

Western Europe was soon in desperate need of this vital material. Alternative alum deposits existed in southern Italy and North Africa, but they were small and of poor quality. Western Christian importers suffered the double ignominy of not only having to pay stiff prices for the Turkish alum but also effectively funding the Turks' aggression against them. The situation was soon saved, however, by the discovery of a rich deposit of alum in 1460 at Tolfa in the papal states north of Rome. The Curia initially formed a partnership to take responsibility for marketing and regulating the supply of the commodity, but soon recognized its own ineptness at such a task and turned management over to the Medici

Bank, contenting itself with a handsome royalty. Although the papacy had stepped back from management, it actively pursued strategies to establish a monopoly position, despite the canon law condemnation of such practice. Papal actions included banning trade in Turkish alum and forming a cartel with one of the Christian producers. But the monopoly failed to hold, as the alum consumers found ways around the restrictions against Muslim suppliers, and Venice resumed business operating the Phocaea mines in 1481, after the end of its war with the Turks. And the Medici lost control of the alum trade after falling out with the papacy in 1476.

One further casualty from these events was Genoa. After its ouster from control of the Phocaea mines, the Genoese shipowners found limited uses for the huge specialized bulk carriers, which were too large for many harbors and uneconomical for mixed cargo tramping. Sailings to northern Europe were declining and tailed off sharply from the beginning of the fifteenth century. Modest amounts of Turkish alum continued to flow to customers around the Mediterranean and Atlantic coasts, and large ships were still useful for carrying cotton from the Levant, but most of this trade went to the Venetians. Genoese shippers had become trapped by their overinvestment in the large carriers, abdicating much local trade to foreigners, mainly Portuguese and Spanish, who often employed Genoese seamen. As the Genoese fleet owners adapted to the new realities, their mercantile activity shifted increasingly westward, both directly on their own account and indirectly on behalf of Portuguese and Spanish patrons.

THE PORTUGUESE:
EARLY EXPLORATIONS SOUTH INTO THE ATLANTIC

Although Portuguese merchants were not entirely absent from the Mediterranean in the fifteenth century, they were relatively minor players in that area. Their main sphere of interest lay in the Atlantic, especially to the south. They were not alone in these waters; Genoese mariner-businessmen had found profitable activity trading for gold on the Atlantic coast of Morocco as early as the thirteenth century, and in the fourteenth century had rediscovered the Canary Islands. And the Venetians and Catalans engaged in commerce in the same waters. But it was the persistent efforts of the Portuguese from the early fifteenth century, albeit greatly aided by individual Genoese, that solidly established a European presence along the coast and islands of West Africa. At first glance Portugal was an unlikely candidate for empire. Although politically united and stable by the fifteenth century, the kingdom had scanty natural resources, few merchants, a population of probably fewer than a million, and no great seafaring tradition. However, under the impetus of crusading fervor and wise rulers, the Portuguese succeeded as empire builders.

The initial African forays of the Portuguese were of a crusading nature, with Morocco and the port of Ceuta as prime targets. Some of the subsequent maritime expeditions to the south were also influenced by religious motives, so that the commercial rewards of the first twenty-five years or so of exploration were scanty. One important factor, however, was the determination of Prince Henry, romantically but inaccurately titled by nineteenth-century historians "the Navigator." Although no mariner himself, he vigorously promoted exploration, financing the discovery and colonization of Madeira in 1420 and of the Azores in 1427, as well as several of the early unrewarding voyages down the African coast. His influence gradually brought the pursuit of trade to prominence among those factors encouraging Portuguese exploration, although the residues of Holy War and Christian millennarianism long remained.

By midcentury, however, the commercial attractions of the area had become obvious – gold and slaves from Africa and a new low-cost source of sugar from the offshore islands. Moreover, the Portuguese received encouragement from three remarkable papal decrees in the 1450s that not only recognized Portuguese conquests, past and future, in Africa and "the Indies," but also prohibited other nations from infringing on their monopoly of discovery, conquest, and commerce in those ill-defined areas.[5] The Portuguese pushed their explorations, often with the help of Genoese captains and seamen, establishing a trading base on the mainland of Africa and seizing and colonizing the islands of Sao Tomé and Cape Verde in the 1470s (although they later lost the Canaries to the Spanish). By 1483, their ships had reached the mouth of the Congo River. The importance of these voyages lay not so much in the commerce that they generated, as valuable as that became, but in the knowledge they gathered of prevailing winds and ocean currents that made possible the spectacular discoveries toward the end of the fifteenth century. Those discoveries, of the New World and the route around the southern tip of Africa, were of course motivated by the twin objectives of securing direct access to the spices and fabled luxury goods of India and the Far East and promoting the Christian religion. This drive to circumvent the middlemen of the Near East and defeat the forces of a resurgent Islam was soon to be rewarded beyond the wildest dreams of anyone concerned.

RESURGENCE OF SLAVERY AND
THE EXPANSION OF THE SUGAR INDUSTRY

At this point, it is necessary to move to a much less attractive aspect of the westward and southward expansion of European business, the origins of the Atlantic slave trade. One of the lesser-noted aftereffects of the Black Death was the resurgence of slavery in the Mediterranean area. Although the traffic was not huge by later standards, it was substantial and steady, with reports of shiploads in the hundreds in the eastern Mediterranean and records of a dozen or so slaves regularly appearing on the manifests of mixed cargo ships in the West by 1400. Those destined for urban areas were mainly female, intended for domestic service to make up for the shortage of such help caused by the plagues. Enslaved domestic servants, often used as concubines, became fairly common in Italian cities, but the opposition of the church and public discomfort caused the practice to decline by the mid fifteenth century. Slavery did not reemerge at all in northwestern Europe, partly because of long-standing cultural objections, but also because agriculture there was not suitable for organization into labor intensive plantations.

In the Mediterranean, however, the enslavement of males for use in nonurban settings was persistent and significant throughout the fourteenth and fifteenth centuries. Large numbers of various origins were imported annually from the Black Sea port of Caffa and the Tunisian termini of trans-Saharan caravans to fill the ranks of the Mamluk armies and the depleted benches of Christian galleys operating in the eastern Mediterranean. Many more toiled as agricultural laborers on large estates in Crete, Majorca, and Aragon. Still others, including black slaves, had long been noted on rural estates in Muslim Spain, and Muslim slave traders continued to operate along the Moroccan coast after most of Iberia had been Christianized. The Genoese and Venetians dominated the flourishing Mediterranean slave trade and extended their reach into West Africa, where the Portuguese began to intrude aggressively following their voyages of discovery in that area. All this trade, although significant and very profitable, was quite modest compared with what was to come. The beginnings of really large-scale enslavement of West African black peoples for heavy agricultural work did not occur until the latter half of the fifteenth century; its driving force was the needs of the rapidly expanding sugar industry.

Sugar first appeared in Europe around the beginning of the twelfth century following the First Crusade. It was grown and milled in Egypt and Syria, and became a regular export item from those regions. Sugar was originally considered a spice and was valued not only as a sweetener, but also as a medicine, a condiment, a decorative material, a preservative, and for combinations of these attributes. Initially, it was very expensive and available only to the very wealthy in any quantity. Confections combining sugar with oil, crushed nuts, or vegetable gums made a pliable, edible substance that could be made into "subtleties," extremely elaborate shapes such as animals, buildings, and mythological figures. Presented at feasts, they could be admired, appreciated, and eaten, displaying the wealth and power of the host. But gradually, as the price began to decline in the fifteenth century, the use of sugar in its various liquid and crystalline forms began to trickle down to the less wealthy.

The problem with the cultivation of sugarcane is that it is highly water and labor intensive, requiring twelve months to ripen, and thus severely restricting the locations in which it can be successfully grown. And crushing the cane by medieval water- or animal-driven mills was laborious and inefficient. But the profitability of this luxury encouraged the spread of sugarcane cultivation wherever conditions permitted; Sicily and Spain became early producers, and when the Atlantic Islands of Madeira, Sao Tomé, and Cape Verde were rediscovered by the Portuguese, a significant new source of sugar production became available. Genoese entrepreneurs, with their nose for profit and experience in colonial management, slaving, and sugar production helped the Portuguese invaders establish colonies in these islands and create successful sugar plantations. By 1450, with the labor of shiploads of slaves from West Africa, the Atlantic island plantations had radically reduced the cost and increased the volume of sugar production, enabling the owners to reduce prices and displace the more expensive sources in Cyprus, Sicily, and much of Spain. Moreover, the lower costs translated by 1490 into prices reduced to one-third of their former level, bringing sugar within the reach of the larger market of the less affluent. In 1500, Madeira alone was producing in the neighborhood of 1,000 tons per year. At the same time, Antwerp's role as the principal refining center of northern Europe helped that city to attain its later prominence. The stage was thus being set in the late Middle Ages for the emergence of the colonial system of commodity mass production that was to have such an immense effect on the social and economic structure of the Western world for centuries to come.

THE INDUSTRIALIZATION OF FOOD SUPPLIES: TWO CASE STUDIES FROM THE NORTH

While in the south merchants and monarchs were collaborating to erect new trading and production networks spanning vast distances, those in the north were achieving success of a different but nonetheless impressive order in a more compact area. The goal of reduced cost and greater access was the same; but the complex relationships of business and government interests in north-western Europe resulted in two strikingly original examples of merging supplies and markets.

Fishing

Fish, as we have seen, was an important source of nutrition in medieval Europe. There had long been many varieties available to consumers from local streams and lakes, fishponds, nearby seacoasts, and long-distance fishing fleets. What was changing was the increasing sophistication of organization and regulation of the trade. At the local and regional levels, regulators were mostly concerned with overseeing the pricing, and above all the quality of fresh, salted, and smoked fish coming to market. A striking example of regulatory authority was the decree of the Paris commune that saltwater fish must reach retailers in Paris within thirty-five hours of landing in winter and twenty-four hours in summer. As the nearest saltwater port was 150 kilometers (approximately ninety miles) from the city, meeting this requirement entailed a frantic nonstop rush of jolting carts over bad roads in all kinds of weather. It appears that most deliveries were on time, but failure would have meant disaster for all concerned.

The catching and delivery of cured fish presented a different set of problems. We mentioned in Chapter 2 the "industrialization" of herring fishing along the Scania coast of the Baltic Sea. There, in the thirteenth century, shore-based German merchants received the catches of herring from the small boats of thousands of fishermen. They cured the fish, packed them, and distributed them throughout Germany, the Low Countries, and other parts of western Europe. The Germans closely regulated this lucrative business, especially the curing process itself, as keeping qualities and taste were vital to success. Volume was substantial, estimated at 10.5 million kilograms by the second half of the fourteenth century.

In the Low Countries, the cured herring market was dominated by Scania herring, which had to be imported through a staple port controlled by the comital government of Flanders. Flemish and Dutch fishermen brought in herring fresh, lightly salted, or smoked, along with a variety of other fish, but they became attracted to fishing for herring further north because the season began earlier and the fish were of better quality. By the fourteenth century they had devised larger nets and learned how to do full curing at sea, but were unable to exploit these advantages in the face of competition from the preferred Scania herring. Also, the government discouraged production of the sea-cured salted herring so that local fishermen would not be diverted from what the magistrates considered their more important function – bringing in fresh fish. As a result, most cured herring sold in the Low Countries came from the Baltic, and most fish exports were re-exports of the Scania product.

The emergence of the fabled Dutch fishing industry began in the early fifteenth century for three reasons. The first was that Dutch fishermen gradually learned to bring the quality of their sea-cured fish close to the Scania level. Second, the invention in Dutch shipyards of a specialized fishing vessel, the new deep-sea herring buss, permitted the production of greater volume at lower cost. Third, and most important, the supply of Scania fish became erratic due to war, boycotts, and a mysterious irregularity in the appearance of herring in the Baltic. All this prompted a change in government policy, which now encouraged the flow of capital to fund the new busses and the big nets. As a result, Dutch fishermen rapidly took over the supply of the large Low Countries market, and later began exporting to France and even to Germany. It was not really a big business, for the product, although nutritious, tasty, and cheaper than meat, was too expensive for mass consumption. But although the total production of cured herring from all sources does not appear to have increased versus the thirteenth century, there was an increase in per capita consumption, given the lower population. Thus, by the mid fifteenth century, Holland had the beginnings of a substantial new industry that, fuelled by population growth, was to become the huge and famous Dutch herring business of the seventeenth century.

Brewing

It has frequently been noted that beer in northwestern Europe and ale in England were consumed in prodigious quantities throughout the Middle Ages.[6] A byproduct of grain, especially barley, it was a thick liquid of varying alcohol content; it formed an important part of the diet of peasants and urban workers, and was cheerfully consumed by the aristocracy as well. In the countryside, women did most of the brewing for domestic consumption, while monasteries produced on a larger scale for their inmates and often for a wider market.[7] As urbanization spread, specialist commercial brewers began to emerge, using better equipment and making a superior product. By 1300, in Germany and the Low Countries brewing had become a thriving little industry with a local distribution network.

The key flavoring ingredient in the early brews was a mixture of dried herbs called *gruit*, the composition of which was a trade secret that varied by region and was tightly controlled and taxed by governments. But brewers in north Germany began in the twelfth and thirteenth centuries to replace *gruit* with hops, which resulted in a better tasting, better keeping, lower-cost product once they got the techniques and formulas right. The new product also travelled well, and as it gained popularity, the Germans began exporting it to Holland around 1300. Both local brewers and local governments in Holland resisted this invasion, the former for obvious competitive reasons and the latter because of the lost tax revenue. But the consumer triumphed, as the Dutch brewers learned the techniques and the municipalities found they could tax the hops in the same way as *gruit*. By the end of the fourteenth century, the cultivation of hops became an important feature of local agriculture, and the quality of Dutch beer became good enough to export on a substantial scale.

Commercial brewing was essentially an urban industry, even though home brewing persisted and rural production could at times compete seriously. By the fifteenth century, the size of the industry was such as to create a dichotomous relationship with the town and ducal governments. On the one hand, these authorities were increasingly dependent on the revenues from taxes on exports and home consumption of the finished product, as well as from taxes on ingredients. Together, these produced from thirty to fifty percent of the government revenues of many Dutch cities. On the other hand, the demands of this industry on grain resources were so huge that brewing production had to be regulated, especially in times of dearth, to ensure that adequate stocks of grain would be available for bread. Whatever its alcoholic allure, beer was a relatively poor source of nutrition, delivering only one-fourth the calories of bread made with the same quantity of grain.

By the late fifteenth century, business continued to increase, notwithstanding the fact that brewers in Flanders, Holland's best export market, had also learned the new techniques and had become worthy competitors. The commercializing process followed much the same pattern in each area, with a recognizably modern cast. First, the brewers achieved the desired quality and taste; then they sought economies of scale, first by increasing the size of each brew with larger kettles, and then by more intensive use of the equipment to increase the number of brews per kettle, and finally by consolidation of breweries. Because raw materials, primarily grain, constituted nearly seventy-five percent of the total product cost, economies were best achieved not so much by manufacturing scale as by seeking the optimum balance of ingredients at prevailing price levels and by managing transport costs. Finished product prices were strictly controlled, so that the juggling of grains (oats, wheat, rye, and barley) within the proportions established for taste and quality preferences (brews varied from town to town) required mathematical as well as management skill. And the tax system was so complex in application that examples for problems in school arithmetic were drawn from the beer business. Such intricacies required entrepreneurs capable of mastering both the complexities of production and the politics of taxation.

Given the variety of brews and regulations, it is not surprising that although production reached staggering totals in a number of brewing centers, the individual production units were quite small. For example, the beer production of Haarlem, a town of 11,000 people, was over twenty million litres in 1515, but this figure represented the output of over 100 breweries. There were no dominating organizations even after the enlargement and consolidations described above.[8] A second aspect is that here again we encounter the very slow trial-and-error development in each area, as the technology was slow to spread and habits slow to change. Nearly a century elapsed between the first imports of German beer into Holland and the establishment of local breweries capable of producing a product of equivalent quality. A third point is the huge and pervasive role of governments at all levels. Their determination to maintain tax revenues often held up development, as when the introduction of hops undermined the value of their secret *gruit* recipes. But once governments saw the advantages of taxing imports and exports of hopped beer, they became active in promoting the industry, establishing strict quality control standards and ensuring access to adequate sources of good water. And in England, where ale was long preferred over beer, the monarchy eventually went as far as to encourage the immigration of brewers and to protect them from the defenders of the ale producers.

The effects of surging beer consumption were apparent in the late medieval countryside. The fact that producing a litre of beer consumes a like quantity of grain, and that average yields were about 120 litres per acre, lead to the astonishing conclusion that ten percent of the land in Holland was devoted to raising grain for the brewing kettle. To satisfy the thirst of a city like Ghent alone would effectively require the entire production of a 75,000-acre grain field. Such demand helped promote more intensive land use and sustain the imports of grain from Poland even in a time of population loss. The attractive price, taste, and keeping qualities made hop beer a solid competitor to wine in northwestern Europe, seriously reducing imports of the latter. France and other wine producing regions remained loyal to wine in general, although beer became popular in Paris among the lower classes.

THE LATE MEDIEVAL REVIVAL OF FAIRS

The importance of the medieval fair has already been stressed late in Chapter 1: it formed one of the key institutional building blocks in the enormous growth of the European economy prior to the Black Death. Traditionally, the decline of the fair as an engine of business growth has been linked to the replacement of the Champagne fairs by Bruges as the meeting place par excellence for southern and northern merchants. Not only was the fair an economic relic of an earlier time, this view continues, but its renaissance after 1350 was an indicator of the distress and decline of the late medieval economy. However, as we have argued above, the demographic catastrophe of the Black Death led to economic development and increasing market specialization across Europe. Thus the widespread growth in numbers and importance of fairs after 1350, viewed through this lens, provides considerable support for the picture of an increasingly dynamic, flexible, and growing European economy.

In its externals, the late medieval fair differed little from those of earlier centuries: it was founded upon an annual (sometimes more frequent) grant of special privileges and/or tax exemptions for trade conducted in a specific locale over a period of from two to ten days. Often such fairs were associated with religious feast days or the anniversaries of local saints. In extent and complexity, however, the late medieval fair differed from its forebears both in the increase in numbers of fairs in most European regions (with the notable exception of England) and in the increasingly distinctive division of fairs into international (usually called "great"), regional, and local.

On both the top and bottom tiers of late medieval fairs there was notable expansion in the late fourteenth and into the fifteenth century. Particularly, the international fair saw renewal as increased overland traffic stimulated new and old commercial centers. New trade routes developed linking the Low Countries and Italy – albeit via routes skirting the battlefields of the Hundred Years' War – making the Rhine the commercial highway from south to north and stimulating the growth of fairs at Lyon, Geneva, and Besançon. The renewed flow of traffic also linked the "great" fairs of Frankfurt and the Low Countries, particularly Bruges and Antwerp, with the latter growing to dominate northern commercial and credit markets shortly after 1500.

The true measure of the role of the fair in the struggle to adapt to the new realities of fourteenth and fifteenth century Europe is given by the mid-tier, or regional fair. According to one recent historian, it was at this level of the economy that agricultural products from an increasingly specialized countryside were exchanged, fostering a "fusion" of numerous fairs into "complex, integrated networks spanning one or more agricultural regions."[9] And like the old Champagne fairs, these fairs were arranged sequentially throughout the calendar year, allowing merchants to travel from one to the next. Examples range from Spain, which had four distinct systems of interconnected fairs – Galicia and the Cantabrian mountains, Castile and Leon, New Castile and Estremadura, and Andalusia and Murcia – to southern Italy and Sicily with their own dense networks of regional fairs. In Sicily alone there were fifty new fair franchises granted between 1392 and 1499, four times the number granted before 1350. In the region of Naples, twenty-nine new fair franchises and 113 first occurrences of fairs mark the fifteenth century as approximately twice as active as the preceding century. Remarkably, given the association of late medieval fairs with economic backwardness, the urbanized regions of Europe provide similar examples of a renaissance of regional fairs. Lombardy showed a marked increase in fairs, particularly in the hill country at the foot of the Alps. France and the Low Countries show similar patterns of growth, arguing for a near universal growth in regional trade across all of late medieval Europe.

What accounts for this striking phenomenon? One cause certainly was the drive of businessmen to cut costs. A fair could reduce the overhead of bringing products to customers, because fixed costs were low (perhaps the rental of a bench and tent), and the flexibility of structure closely matched buyers and sellers. The more permanent and costly institutions of medieval cities could match neither the flexibility nor the lower cost of the fair. Moreover, the commercial advantage of the fair, particularly in uncertain times, was seconded by the efforts of princes to establish and encourage fairs in their territories. The reasons for such policies had to do both with potential revenues provided by a quickening in fair activity (so welcome to the frequently warring and impecunious princes) and with political calculation. The Flemish count, Louis of Male, for example, granted numerous fair privileges in the 1360s in an effort to weaken the monopolies of the "great" cities of Bruges, Ghent, and Ypres. His Burgundian successors continued this policy in the fifteenth century. Similar patterns occurred in Germany, Holland, and even as far east as Poland.

Yet another contributor to the growth of regional trade was the spread of improved road transport technology. Four-wheeled wagons equipped with the turning train and dished wheels became increasingly popular, as the devices added stability, maneuverability, and strength to these large vehicles. As a result, four-wheeled wagons became cost effective on the difficult roads of continental Europe for a broadening range of tasks. These vehicles became widely used in the thriving transport industry that arose in those regions of western Germany, especially Hesse, involved in the developing trade between Germany and Antwerp. Such was the association of Hesse and its drivers with these wagons that they became known as Hessian wagons, regardless of their actual origins.[10] And another fourteenth-century invention, the carriage suspended by straps or chains, gained wide acceptance by easing the agonies of travel among affluent merchants and their aristocratic clients.

Two new international fairs, those of Lyon and Geneva, symbolize the renewed importance both of overland trade routes and of the late medieval fair. Geneva sits at the western Alpine passes, which became after the thirteenth century the most heavily used route between Venice and southern Germany. By the fourteenth century, Geneva's fairs became important for the sale of south German and Swiss cloth, metals and weaponry, most of the latter produced in Milan. By the early fifteenth century, foreign merchants were using Geneva as a financial clearing house, settling their accounts and trading bills of exchange. Lyon succeeded as a fair both because of its geography and the official policy of the French crown. Situated at the confluence of two important rivers, Lyon commands a north-south route connecting the French Mediterranean with the French interior. Seeking to supplant Geneva in its role as financial center, Louis XI established the Lyon fair in 1463 and commanded his subjects to frequent it and not Geneva. The long-term success and international importance of Lyon were assured by the settlement there of Italian merchants, who brought banking and international trade to the city. After 1500, Lyon became synonymous with finance, rivaling Paris as the business powerhouse of early modern France.

Despite vast differences in size, location, and function, the fairs of the fifteenth and early sixteenth centuries were all to some degree the product of the late medieval imperative to reduce costs and streamline markets. As such they are examples of institutional change and adaptation in response to the challenges of the period, revealing a preference for more flexible, market-driven forms of exchange. Nothing is simpler than the merchant's tent and table, easily set up and taken down according to the vagaries of place, season, and demand. Undoubtedly, the opportunities fairs offered enabled many more merchants to bring goods to market, allowing integration and specialization in Europe's more backward areas, as well as innovation and economic rebirth in Europe's commercial heartland.

In the first part of this book, we criticized the propensity for historians to characterize the great super-companies of the early fourteenth century as "banks," when banking was only a part of their operations, and suggested "merchant-banks" (with a hyphen) as a term more aptly covering their main activities as both merchants and bankers. Applying the label "banker" to the Medici, Jacques Coeur, and the Augsburg entrepreneurs, among other fifteenth-century businessmen, is even more questionable. Of course, they too were bankers as well as merchants; but to an important extent, they were also industrialists. Perhaps they could be called "industrialist-bankers," but no single term is apt, or likely to be helpful. We will therefore focus on what differentiated them from their fourteenth-century antecedents – their willingness to venture upstream from marketing and finance by investing more of their capital and talent in production.

The Medici

In the introduction to the chapter "The Medici as Industrial Entrepreneurs" in his *The Rise and Decline of the Medici Bank*, Raymond de Roover noted, "It was an old tradition among Florentine families, . . . either to control or to manage a wool or silkshop in order to provide work for the 'poor'."[11] If the Medici were acting "true to this tradition," as de Roover says, then they did it in style, compared to, say, the Peruzzi Company's tiny interest in a small textile business a century earlier. The Medici were majority owners of two woolshops and one silkshop, all of which were significant operations. The company's investment in the three subsidiaries totaled 18,600 florins in 1451, representing nearly twenty-five percent of the company's total assets at that time. Profits too were substantial, amounting to 22,500 florins over the years 1441–51, about twelve percent of total company profits. Although not as lucrative in terms of investment return as other parts of the business, returns were reasonably good, especially for the silk manufacture, given the relatively lower risks involved. And these figures did not include profits made by the branches on marketing the products. The point here is that textile manufacturing was a continuing and important part of the business of the Medici Company.

Another departure from the norm for Florentine companies was represented by the Medici's ventures into mining. We have already mentioned that company's involvement in the alum monopoly following the discovery of major deposits at Tolfa, north of Rome. Although the Medici role here appears to have been mainly in distribution, the company also participated in an attempt to take direct control of an alum discovery near Volterra in Tuscany. Unfortunately, the mine was not up to expectations and was soon closed. Another foray into mining was Lorenzo the Magnificent's repeated attempts to gain control of the iron ore monopoly of Elba. He finally succeeded in 1489 by gaining a controlling interest in the company that mined the ore and sold it to ironmasters, who paid in cast iron or iron products as well as cash. The venture was reasonably profitable, but it did not make a lasting contribution as it began just a few years before the company's bankruptcy in 1494.

Jacques Coeur

We have seen Jacques Coeur in his role as international merchant-banker and as royal official. A third and very important facet to his career was that of producer. Coeur had the good fortune to be a merchant of Bourges at the apogee of English ascendency in France, when the court of the dauphin was forced into exile there. Having become supplier to the court from 1418 and master of the Bourges mint from 1427, he developed a close relationship with the dauphin, soon crowned King Charles VII. We have already noted the importance of this connection in advancing Coeur's trading interests in the Mediterranean, which he ran from Montpellier. His dual role as court supplier and Mediterranean merchant also gave him outlets for his industrial enterprises in paper, silk, and above all in mining.

As a trader in the Levant, Coeur recognized that he needed to supplement his eastbound cargoes of cloth, linen, agricultural products, and coral with silver, copper, and other metals so much in demand in that part of the world. As a mint-master, he was familiar with the prices of metals and the arbitrage opportunities inherent in the bimetallic ratios of gold and silver. His opportunity to exploit both sides of his expertise occurred in 1444, when he obtained the king's rights to ten percent of the output of silver, lead, and copper from some old mines near Lyon for an annual payment of 200 livres tournois. Coeur set about reactivating the mines and making them productive. The output he exported directly to the Levant in great quantities, for which he was able to acquire more of the luxury goods of interest to the royal court, thus completing the circle.

The Augsburgers

A mixture of skill and good fortune accounts for the success of another group of businessmen known collectively as the "Augsburgers" after their city of origin. The best known among them was Jacob Fugger, who will be discussed at greater length in the next chapter. Here we are concerned with the origins of their wealth, which lay in their early attraction to the mining and smelting industries. From small beginnings, the Augsburgers built a hugely important industry by the first quarter of the sixteenth century, far surpassing even Coeur's impressive mining and smelting operations.

The rise to prominence of the merchants of Swabian cities through their skill in organizing the highly successful fustian industry in the late fourteenth century was discussed on page 169. One of these cities, Augsburg, was then only of second rank, but enjoyed a double good fortune of location: being on the trade route between Venice and northern Europe and near the rich mining area of the Tyrol. By the mid fifteenth century, Augsburg merchants were experienced not only in the fustian business and in trading general merchandise, but also in buying and selling metals and ores. They were therefore well positioned to participate in the revival of silver mining that took place at that time through the discoveries at Schwaz in the Tyrol.

Wealth from manufacture and trade, plus proximity to the mines, brought the Augsburgers the lucrative investment opportunity of supplying the ore-rich but cash poor mine owners with badly needed capital to develop mining operations. Wisely leaving the mining and smelting of ore to the mine owners, the merchants stepped in with money and expertise, helping to organize the industrial processes and taking charge of the distribution, much as they had with the fustian industry. Traditionally, the medieval mining and smelting industry was small-scale and inefficient. This was still true in the fifteenth century, so there was much room for improvement. Merchants began in one of two ways, either advancing cash to small operators and receiving in turn their finished products, or taking the ore and setting up their own smelters. On a much larger scale, the grander merchants worked with the bureaucracies of the princes, who owned vast tracts encompassing numerous mines. Here the merchants competed for contracts which would enable them, for a large advance of cash, to acquire silver production at an

attractive fixed price per unit as the repayment of the loan. The earliest of these contracts was one for 35,000 gulden set in 1456 between
the Meuting Company of Augsburg and Duke Sigmund of the Tyrol.
In 1487 Sigmund gave the Fugger Company its start in minerals, when,
together with a Genoese firm, the Fuggers began lending him money
on the security of the duke's anticipated royalties from his mines. The
profits from these modest beginnings began the generation of cash that
gave rise to the prodigious investments in the mining industry during
the first quarter of the sixteenth century, a story to be dealt with in the
next chapter.

PAPER, PRINTING, AND PUBLISHING

The invention of movable type of the mid fifteenth century and the
extraordinarily rapid spread of the printing press throughout Europe is
well known, and will be dealt with only briefly here. The background
to this remarkable development and its business implications, however,
are perhaps less appreciated. For the forces that fuelled the demand for
printed intelligence continued to be hobbled until a plentiful and cheap
medium for the written word could be made available. Parchment was
fine for manuscripts, but it was prohibitively expensive (around six times
as expensive as paper in 1450) and not very suitable for printing technology; the ideal medium was paper.

The initial driving force behind the spread of the written word was
not only the much-cited burgeoning intellectual activity of the universities, but also the need of the growing government bureaucracies and
the larger business units to keep permanent records. We have said much
about the expansion of these organizations over the fourteenth and
fifteenth centuries. And governments not only grew, but greatly enlarged the scope of their responsibilities, spawning a host of increasingly
complex laws, whose implementation in turn required reams of detailed
regulations. Business too needed to keep many more records, partly as
a response to government regulations, but importantly, as we have so
often remarked, to improve controls. This combination is obviously
reflected in the voluminous books of account kept by the larger companies from the fourteenth century onward. And the use of paper for
that purpose was greatly increased by the seemingly extravagant length,
to a modern businessman, of the individual entries, which had to be
detailed to satisfy the legal requirements of most towns.[12]

Paper, like most of the innovations that came to medieval Europe,
first appeared in China and made its way through Muslim territories –
in this case, across North Africa to Muslim Sicily and Spain – by the

tenth century. Local production in Spain began about a century later and continued after the Christian recovery of most of that country. By the twelfth century, Italy had become a substantial importer of Muslim paper from Spain and North Africa, but soon it became a producer, developing its own production methods. By the end of the thirteenth century, the Italian product had achieved such a level of quality and price competitiveness that it dominated the markets of southern Europe, invaded the Muslim Mediterranean, and began inroads into northern Europe. French papermaking began in Champagne in the 1330s, spread rapidly to other parts of France, and before long France was exporting a quality product across western Europe. It was not until the late fourteenth century that paper production started in south Germany, but there too units quickly opened up in various towns in the area.

Papermaking technology successfully wedded processes and skills well known in medieval Europe – water-driven mills turning rollers fitted with spikes to shred rags and wood, molds and fine screens to collect the pulp, presses to squeeze water out of the sheets. After the introduction of sizing in the late thirteenth century, a product was available that could take ink without running. With improved methods of dyeing and the benefit of accumulated experience, production became increasingly cost effective. Thus, by the mid fifteenth century, paper was relatively inexpensive and in widespread use throughout most of Europe.

As a writing medium, paper was cheap and abundant enough to satisfy the demands of business and government by 1350, yet writing remained laborious handwork incapable of producing multiple copies except by recopying. University officials went some way toward solving this problem in book production by adapting the now familiar "putting-out" system – that is, by separating each text into quires (*pecia*) and distributing them among the university scribes for copying. The complete text was then deposited with the authorized university book dealers (called stationers), who rented it to students or copyists who copied part or all of the book. Despite early prohibitions against selling entire books, the demand was such in intellectual centers such as Paris and Florence that stationers became booksellers, and shops opened offering manuscripts to the general public. This business spread, abetted by the widening intellectual interests of the increasingly urban and literate population of the early fifteenth century. By mid century, books were also becoming a small but notable item of international trade; the manifests of several of the cargoes of Florentine galleys bound for western Mediterranean ports in the 1460s frequently included "cases of books," although there is no evidence to indicate whether the contents were handwritten or printed. In any case, the need for a faster, cheaper, and more reliable method of producing texts for large-scale distribution was so pressing that creative minds inevitably set to work to make their fortunes by solving the problem.

One technology that has often been credited as the forerunner of the printing press is the woodcut "block book." It is now well established, however, that the first appearance of block books actually occurred around the mid fifteenth century, the same time as the invention of movable-type printing. Each page of a block book was printed from a block of wood engraved with pictures or letters or both by means of a thin water-based ink. The method was crude but cheap and suitable for pamphlets, calendars, and thin books on religious or moralistic subjects, which were much in demand by the clergy as teaching tools for illiterate flocks. The printing of block books coexisted with movable type printing throughout the latter half of the fifteenth century, before dying out in the early years of the sixteenth. But woodcuts continued to have an important role in the printing of books where some imitation of the elegant illustrations, title pages, elaborate initials, and borders of the manuscript book were desired.

Much of the technology needed for typography was already at hand by the fifteenth century. Wine presses had been in use since ancient times, and the craft of engraving of letters and designs and the use of molds had been long practiced and had become highly developed throughout the Middle Ages. It is not surprising, therefore, that the early experimenters, including Johann Gutenberg, were goldsmiths, and that others were mint-masters. Here again, the innovators were craftsmen, not theoreticians, who by trial and error finally solved the problems of finding a suitable metal for type, making letters of the same body and height-to-paper but different widths, and formulating ink that would make a good impression without blotting. What was new and most unusual in the history of medieval technology was an invention, an identifiable breakthrough, that can be ascribed to an individual, Johann Gutenberg.[13] What was not so new was the problem of funding, for the equipment and materials needed for the experimentation required sizable repeated investment. But once discovered and taught to a few associates, the movable-type technique spread, despite many attempts to keep the process secret.

The rapid diffusion of the printing press is remarkable by most standards and truly astounding for medieval technology. From Mainz, the probable birthplace of the printing press, this new device quickly appeared in other German cities, notably Strasbourg and Cologne, and soon thereafter German printers set up shop in Rome and Venice. The Germans encountered severe resistance in Paris from the vested interests of some 6,000 copyists, scriveners, and illustrators who had made that city a center for disseminating manuscripts and who confiscated caseloads of books imported from Mainz. But they were no preindustrial Luddites, and after two professors established a press in the Sorbonne in 1470, other presses quickly followed. During the 1470s German printers fanned out across Europe, starting presses in Barcelona, Utrecht, Aalst, Bruges, Budapest, and Cracow. In England, exceptionally, the pioneer was William Caxton, a native, but he had acquired his experience in Bruges long before setting up his press in Westminster in 1476. Locals soon entered this new trade, especially in Italy, which became the leading exporter of books in the late fifteenth century. By the end of that century, there were no fewer than 252 locations where we know that printing had taken place; several of them, such as Venice, Lyon, and Augsburg, had scores of printers. The majority of these printers, of course, ran tiny operations turning out a few volumes and brief pamphlets. But others were substantial firms, capable of producing superb works in considerable quantity, proving that printing had become a significant and vigorously expanding industry.

The printing press introduced a problem with which medieval businessmen were unfamiliar – how to take advantage of the low marginal cost of each additional copy produced without being left with unsalable merchandise. Most production in medieval Europe was to order, and even in the textile industry, where international sales were mainly on consignment, the risk of holding an utterly worthless product was remote. A bolt of cloth, no matter how unfashionable the weave or color, could nearly always find a buyer at some price somewhere, but a book that nobody wants to read has no value. Because the profit on each additional volume sold is high, the temptation to print an excessive number of copies is strong. The early printers, seemingly aware of this problem, mitigated their risks by cautiously keeping to familiar formats and popular works. For the first decade or two, printed books simply replicated their manuscript versions, with the result that the type followed the style used in each main locality.[14] Thus printers in Germany employed the Gothic type, whereas those in Italy (also mostly German) used the "humanistic" or roman script favored there. It was not until the 1470s that a Frenchman, Nicolas Jenson, designed a type for the press with the paramount objectives of legibility and economy (Gothic was very wasteful of space).

What kind of texts were being published? The majority, of course, dealt with subjects and works for which there was a ready market. By the end of the fifteenth century, at least half of the editions printed were religious texts, mostly in Latin, starting with the famous Gutenberg

Bible. But there was also brisk demand for the Greek and Roman clas-
sics, especially Cicero's *Epistolae ad familiares* and Aristotle's *Politica*, books
on civil and canon law, and the famous Latin grammar of Aelius
Donatus. As the fifteenth century wore on, printed materials covered
the entire spectrum of human endeavor, including music, for the printing of which a special patent was granted by the city of Venice in 1498.

And who were the buyers? Not surprisingly, priests and monks were
important customers, as were university professors, students, lawyers, and
bureaucrats. But less predictably, the most important and fastest-growing
segment of the publishers' clientele was the educated reader with a
strong attachment to humanistic as well as religious subjects. A large
proportion of these readers were businessmen. As a result, in the late
fifteenth century concentrations of printing establishments were to be
found more in commercial centers such as Venice and Lyon than in religious and university cities, including even Rome and Paris.

Notwithstanding the precautions noted here, many printers found
themselves beguiled by early success into printing excessive quantities
of books and suffering the consequences. But the industry matured with
surprising rapidity, especially in Germany and Italy, where the top printers built sales organizations, took on financiers, and began to separate
the craft of printing from the business of publishing and marketing.
These larger firms were quick to advertise their wares, posting lists of
their publications and distributing promotional broadsides laced with
hyperbole. They gradually increased the number of copies per edition
from an average of around 150–200 in the 1470s to an average of
1,000–1,500 by the early 1500s. And they aggressively entered the export
trade, creating competition for the local printers, especially in England.
Thus, by the end of the fifteenth century, publishing had been transformed by the technological tinkering of a handful of Germans from a
plodding and restrictive collection of copyists to a new agile industry
preparing itself to meet the rising demand of an increasingly literate
public.

Voyage by voyage, mile by mile, innovation by innovation, European
businessmen of the fifteenth century succeeded in reaching the goal of
lowered costs. Such a massed deployment of learning-by-doing resulted
in progress in technology, industry, and transport undreamed of by their
business predecessors, while paradoxically leaving intact many merchant
traditions. By the end of the century, the organization of commercial
endeavors had so improved that businessmen undertook with confidence
ventures that would have been considered fantasies a hundred years
earlier. Equally significant were the unintended consequences: Europe's

commercial center of gravity began to shift westward and northward, not because of the final disappearance of the Byzantine Empire, as was formerly believed, but for a variety of other reasons. One was that European entrepreneurs had acquired the means to bypass the middlemen of the eastern Mediterranean in their quest for the luxuries of the East. Another was the revitalization of mining in central Europe. Still another was a significant improvement in overland transportation routes through Germany and France to the north. And finally, there were the growing resources of the larger political units in the West and north that attracted capital and enterprises of increasing size. The ships, the guns, the crews that sailed from Europe to appear in oceans and harbors across the world were the most visible symbol of the accumulated power of fifteenth-century Europe. The men − merchants, pirates, priests, saints and sinners − went (as one later declared) to serve God and King, and also to get rich. And it is perhaps in the formulation of this all-consuming ethic that European business had its greatest impact on world history.

9

SOURCES OF CAPITAL IN
THE LATE MIDDLE AGES

•

The burgeoning business activity described in the previous chapters required increasing amounts of investment in facilities, transport, infrastructure, and working capital, raising the questions of where the capital was coming from, how it was mobilized, and by whom. The answer to the "where" question is of course from agriculture and industry, the ultimate sources of wealth. As a result of the incremental improvements and diversifications we have discussed, farming and manufacturing were becoming increasingly market-oriented and cost effective, so that by the middle of the fifteenth century they were capable of producing healthy surpluses. Even the disruptions of recurring war and pestilence, serious as they were to the areas affected, could only temporarily impair the productivity of the economies in most parts of western Europe. And those calamities had a positive effect by stimulating the circulation of money – in economists' terms, by increasing the "velocity" of circulation.

The questions of who mobilized the capital and how are more difficult to deal with. The simple answer to the "who" is mainly governments, and to a lesser extent businessmen, sometimes working independently, more often in cooperation with governments, acting as their agents or even as members of their administrations. The "how," inseparable from the "who," does not have a simple answer, and its explanation will require a detailed analysis of the forces at play in various parts of Europe.

MOBILIZING CAPITAL:
THE KEY ROLE OF GOVERNMENTS

One of the notable developments of the fourteenth and fifteenth centuries was the growth in the size and efficiency of government bureaucracies throughout Europe and in their ability to extract cash flows from their economies. Formal departments emerged to manage functions of public service, as distinct from the monarch's household, in the areas of treasury, administration, and controllership. An important aspect of this evolution was the shift from reliance on "regalian" resources – such as the prince's own landholdings, feudal fees and rights, and intermittent "extraordinary" levies on wealth or agricultural production – to the exploitation of steadier, quicker sources of income. The latter included consumption taxes, income from monopolies, taxes on export-import trade, forced loans, and taxes on the assets of the general population. The mobilization of capital by governments was merely part of the collection of revenues for the whole range of government activities, including the costs of the administration required to manage the process.

The types and methods of extraction varied among the different polities of western Europe. In England, the king received a great new source of income beginning in 1275, when parliament granted him a tax on the export of wool and cloth. Then, from the mid fourteenth century, English monarchs began to receive a levy of "tunnage" on wine imports and "poundage" on exports and imports of general merchandise. The Italian cities had shifted from their earlier reliance on wealth taxes, reserving them mainly for emergencies, and began in the early fourteenth century to derive most of their revenue from consumption taxes (gabelles), supplemented by tolls and fees on goods passing through the commune. Flemish cities, likewise, came to rely on consumption taxes, especially on beer and wine. French kings used a different approach. For quick returns in emergencies, they were fond of debasing the coinage, which reaped huge profits from time to time. For regular income, they employed an internal sales tax and the salt monopoly, and from the fifteenth century onward, the *taille*, a direct tax on wealth imposed on the entire non-noble population, which became the principal source of revenue. Elsewhere, however, the princes and municipalities of Europe were looking increasingly to trade for a steady and relatively painless way to fund their day-to-day operations.

The problem faced by most fiscal administrations was that the flow of cash from the various tax systems rarely matched the needs of the realm, so that resort to borrowing was a frequent necessity. And because the credit rating of most royal administrations was abysmal, most loans were involuntary. Among the more obvious targets for forced loans were the merchants who were beholden to the rulers for the right to do business in the territory.[1] Usually, the loans were secured by the assignment of specific tax revenues or rights to farm them, with interest disguised as voluntary "gifts" or recognized "damages." In Germany, pledges of royal property (including, as we have seen, the output of their mines) were the usual security for royal loans. But although loans to princes were always risky, the more astute businessmen managed to obtain lucrative trading privileges as the price of their participation or to hedge their bets in other ways. Some formed syndicates to spread the risks; others played both sides of the game, acting both as bureaucrats and businessmen. The most famous of the latter was Jacques Coeur, who doubled as *argentier* or treasurer to King Charles VII of France between 1438 and 1451 while building his vast commercial enterprise. Much of his business, including the Mediterranean ventures described in Chapter 8, was intermingled with his activities as a royal officer. His most noted role was in mobilizing cash for the king, and his most spectacular achievement the huge loan that he raised for the reconquest of Normandy in 1450. Unfortunately, the "excessive" interest he allegedly charged on that loan apparently helped precipitate his downfall in the following year.

Loans to earlier medieval governments were in theory advances on anticipated tax revenues, to be repaid, hypothetically at least, as the taxes flowed in. In practice, however, assignments of government revenue were very difficult for creditors to cash in, as we have seen from our discussion of tallies in Chapter 3. And although these assignments were often traded, there was no organized market for such obligations, and the discounting was severe. Occasionally, monarchs borrowed on the strength of letters obligatory – a kind of promissory note – and these too were sometimes sold to others, again at a steep discount. Though such instruments were firm obligations of the crown, they were extremely difficult to redeem. In one case, the letters obligatory issued by Edward III of England to the Bardi Company in the 1330s were finally settled for a derisory sum in 1391, during the reign of Richard II. Cities too were not above sharp practises designed to hamstring their creditors. Bruges, for example, contracted a large debt with the Crespin family of Arras in the 1290s, which quickly fell into arrears. After decades of legal action, the city finally agreed to repay about a third of the original amount in 1330, but even this the city failed to do. Finally, in 1386, a disappointed descendant of the original creditors settled for a token payment of less than one percent of the original loan amount. In effect, therefore, a goodly portion of government "loans" constituted taxation in disguise, falling least heavily on those with the most power to obtain redemption.

The true laboratories of cash mobilization after 1300 were European cities. The crucial development here was the long-term public debt, distinct from either forced loans from citizens or farming of taxes, usually in the form of advances paid in anticipation of the collection of consumption taxes. In Italy, the practice of assessing forced loans (*prestanze*) on business and property owners was initially undisciplined and highly favorable to the business patriciates. Such loans, like the royal borrowings discussed above, were theoretically short-term in nature, but were serviced out of tax revenues that barely covered the interest. This system was unsustainable, and eventually the loans had to be commuted into shares in a funded public debt. The change occurred as early as the mid thirteenth century in Venice and Genoa and around the mid fourteenth century in Florence and other Italian cities.

The new form of debt, known as the *monte* because it was regarded literally as mountain-sized, consisted of shares issued by the commune, redeemable at its option, and paying a fixed low rate of interest. Throughout the remainder of the Middle Ages, the *monte* became the method of choice for raising money swiftly, and although redemptions did occur from time to time, balances reached truly mountainous proportions in many communes as a result of calamitous wars. In 1381, at the end of the war with Genoa, Venice, which usually had the means to keep its debt balance to a reasonable level, saw its *monte* rise to the equivalent of over 4.7 million gold florins, while that of Genoa exceeded 2.2 million. The shares were normally marketable at prices that varied with prevailing commercial interest rates and the relative fiscal strength of the commune. In the case of Venice, prices held remarkably steady, ranging between 80 and 95 percent of the original-issue value, so that the bonds remained a good secure investment until 1381, when the price crashed to 18 after a suspension of interest payments. The resumption of interest at the low rate of 4 percent gradually restored confidence in the bonds, which rose in value to 66 by 1402. On the other hand, the price of Florence's shares fell steadily with the growth of the debt, dropping below 20 by the middle of the fifteenth century.[2]

A variation on this type of debt was the *monte delle doti*, or dowry fund, which became a popular investment vehicle in Florence after its launching in 1425.[3] This fund united the desperate need of Florentine fathers to accumulate adequate funds for their daughters' dowries with the commune's desperate need for cash. Conceptually, the approach resembled a hybrid of a United States series E treasury bond and an insurance policy, whereby the investor deposited a modest fixed sum with the expectation of receiving a much larger amount after a fixed period of time for funding a specific dowry. In practice, the plan's payout system was rigid and hedged with the risk of forfeitures of interest and sometimes even principal if the beneficiary died or retired to a nunnery. As a result, the fund got off to a very slow start, but eventually, after bringing the risk-to-reward ratio into satisfactory balance, it became huge and closely linked to the public debt of the commune. It should be noted that dowries in themselves were a frequent source of capital to seed or maintain small businesses throughout Europe. We have already cited an instance in Bruges, and can add a more extreme example – that of Gregorio Dati, a Florentine businessman of the early fifteenth century, who married four times, each wife bringing a timely and substantial dowry to his faltering business.

North of the Alps and south of the Pyrenees, urban long-term debt followed still different routes. There, life or heritable annuities were the favored form of long-term debt creation. These instruments resemble annuities marketed by today's insurance companies whereby the investor purchases for a lump sum payment the right to receive a fixed return either for the term of his life only, or for his and one or even two generations of successors. A city was thus able to raise considerable ready money in return for encumbering future income in order to satisfy its annuity obligations. This became the favorite form of civic long-term debt in cities from northern France through Flanders, Brabant, the northern Low Countries, the German Rhineland, and down to Catalonia and Valencia. Only Bruges seems to have experimented briefly with a "*monte*-like" scheme, when in the early fourteenth century the city required the estates of orphans to be administered by a special city fund. In return for a capital contribution numbered in shares, the orphan received a fixed income until reaching his or her majority, when the principal could be reclaimed by the orphan.

Late medieval businessmen entered these new forms of capital creation at two points: either as purchasers of these investments or as creators and administrators of them. It should be remembered that medieval cities were ruled by the same men who ran their businesses, and there are myriad examples of an individual's civic service benefiting his business. By the fifteenth century, European princes had come to appreciate the financial abilities of some of their urban subjects: we have already seen the the role played by Jacques Coeur as financial broker to Charles VII of France. And in the Burgundian realm, the dukes made use of the financial talents of Dino Rapondi, a Lucchese who settled in Bruges in the early fifteenth century, and Peter Bladelin, a native of that city who became the financial wizard of Philip the Good (1419–1467). Both these men led the successful effort to harness the sale of annuities as a source of revenue for the duchy. These lessons were applied by later generations of financial advisors to Habsburg monarchs, who became the heirs of the Burgundians by 1500.

It is not our purpose here to discuss the intricacies of public finance in detail, but only to show the various ways in which states mobilized cash during the late Middle Ages. Not surprisingly, most of the great streams of revenue flowing to governments around Europe were deployed against the current expenses of the courts, their bureaucracies, and their struggles against their neighbors. But a portion was invested in capital projects, some in connection with wartime adventures. These were the funds driving the construction of ships, the search for improved and cheaper methods of mining and metallurgy, and the explorations for riches beyond the seas. Other government capital was invested directly in infrastructure designed to foster production and improved communication, examples of which we have seen in previous chapters.

BANKING AND THE USE OF FRACTIONAL RESERVES

Private funds also had a role to play in the increasing capitalization of industry in the fifteenth century. Most of those that did not originate from royal and ecclesiastical landholdings came from the accumulated after-tax profits of businessmen. A few of these, such as the "bankers" discussed in the previous chapter, embarked on their grander projects by pooling the funds of their smaller brethren in joint ventures. Relatively little cash was mobilized, however, through what we would call the normal banking system. As noted in Chapter 3, the use of fractional reserves did not become significant until the late Middle Ages, and even then the picture is confused and extremely varied across Europe. First, it must be remembered that the money changer/banker accepted two kinds of deposit. One was a long-term "time deposit" entrusted to the banker for a certain period and bearing interest. The rate of interest might be fixed in advance or be contingent on the profits of the borrower (called deposits *a discrezione* in Italy). Such investments were often intended to cover a specific anticipated liability, such as a dowry or a minor's estate. The other type was an unconditional deposit repayable on demand, bearing no interest. This usually took the form of specie entrusted to the bank to facilitate the transfer of funds to other merchants. Normally, the transfer orders were given orally. Written instructions, some of which seem roughly equivalent to modern checks, did occur in some centers from the fourteenth century onward, but there is little evidence to suggest that their use was widespread or more than a confirmation of oral instructions.

A bank that deals in both kinds of deposit is likely to have reserves that are less than 100 percent, because the banker of necessity must invest the long-term deposits in order to recover the interest paid to the depositors and return a profit. With sight deposits, however, the banker assumes a fiduciary role and must be in a position to redeem all deposits on demand. The temptation to tie up some deposits in long-term investments proved almost irresistible, threatening bankers with ruin if depositors' demands suddenly exceeded the supply of ready money. To guard against risks of this sort, most cities required banks to maintain a sizable sum as guarantee. In Flanders, those innkeepers who did brokerage (called hostelers) likewise had to post substantial bonds to protect the city against any claims of foreign customers upon bankrupt hostelers. And legislation designed to protect depositors could be very daunting. In Barcelona, for example, a law was passed in 1321 forcing failed bankers to be held for a year on bread and water until all accounts were satisfied; failing that, the consequences were extreme. In 1360, one such unfortunate, Francesc Castello, was beheaded in front of his bank.

The record for the use of fractional reserves across Europe is quite uneven. In the north, the only place for which we have hard evidence is Bruges, where, as we have seen in Chapter 7, money changers were using a large part of their deposits for investments. This kind of activity must have been fairly new, even though transfer banking in Bruges seems to have begun early in the fourteenth century. But this venture into modern-type banking did not survive beyond the mid fifteenth century, as the series of failures that it engendered provoked increasing restrictions on money-changing activity by the counts of Flanders. In England, the exchange of foreign coin for sterling was a royal monopoly from 1344, and all transfers were strictly controlled, so that transfer banking never got off the ground there during the Middle Ages. In short, the use of bank deposits as investment capital played a small and relatively short-lived role in the history of medieval finance.

In the south, Venice was on the leading edge and is regarded as the founder of giro banking. Although fractional reserves have been reported as early as 1321, overdrafts were forbidden by law, and it was not until the fifteenth century that the use of transfer deposits as a source of credit really took off. The driving force behind this development was the confusion and deterioration in Venetian coinage. But this frenzied activity came to a halt at the end of the fifteenth century, when three of the four big Rialto banks collapsed. The bank that survived, owned by the famous Pisani family, managed fairly well under a much more restrictive policy enforced by the government. But early in the sixteenth century, it was allowed to lend to the government to help finance its wars through anticipation of tax receipts (shades of England's Edward III and the Florentine bankers) and to invest in such risky projects as financing politicians and galley voyages. The Pisani bank eventually failed, after which banking in Venice became increasingly conservative.

The data are also mixed elsewhere in the south. Tuscan merchants had less need for a giro system, as they usually accomplished transfers effectively by setting off transactions among themselves, rather than through banks. There were, however, numerous money changers who kept deposits, and some of the larger merchant-banks, such as the Cerchi and Strozzi of Florence, occasionally invested some of them, but the amounts were small relative to scale of their total business. Moreover, the number of such banks dropped from seventy-one at the end of the fourteenth century to only eight by 1516. The Genoese, of course, were among the first practitioners of money changing and deposit/transfer banking, and did get into fractional reserves by permitting overdrafts by some of their customers. And although they occasionally provided funds for international ventures, they seem not to have been reckless in the use of their reserves, as there are no records of the kind of spectacular failures that occurred in other cities. This is likely due to the fact that Genoese investors preferred to lend their money directly to commercial ventures rather than to utilize banks.

Barcelona was another important deposit-banking center, but with such a severe record of fraud and failure that rigorous policing by the government was frequently required. The city is more noted, however, for establishing Europe's first public bank, the *Taula de Canvi de Barcelona*, in 1401. Formed because of the disorder in private banking, the *Taula*, guaranteed by the municipality, acted as fiscal agent of Barcelona and Catalonia, accepted deposits from citizens, and lent money to the city. It competed with private banks, but did not displace them and often accepted their deposits. The *Taula* engaged in a broad range of activities – some very risky – over the centuries, but survived until it was absorbed into the Bank of Spain in 1853. Genoa's more famous public bank, the Bank of Saint George, expanded rapidly after its establishment in 1408, but the government's attempt to use it to support a ruinous monetary policy was a failure, and the bank was dissolved in 1444.[4]

The experiments in deposit banking and fractional reserves in the fourteenth and fifteenth centuries appear at first glance to be forerunners of modern banking systems. The techniques used were similar, and the process worked fairly well for a time, but the similarities between medieval and modern banking are more apparent than real; medieval technology, communications, and legal environment were inadequate to sustain the management of the credit risks involved. Moreover, because money supply was based on precious metals, without the flexibility provided by negotiable credit instruments, specie shortages could lock up the economy, as owners of scarce cash determinedly held onto what they had. Commercial cities were thus subject to wrenching cycles during which the extension of credit ran out of control, resulting in panicky collapses. The system accordingly stuttered and stalled, and governments in turn reacted to protect themselves by applying severe restrictions. What medieval commerce lacked above all was a bank of last resort; the public bank of Barcelona was an interesting start in this direction, but it was not a model for the modern central bank. There was therefore no continuity between the medieval experiments and the eventually successful financial systems developed centuries later.

NEW DEVELOPMENTS IN COMMERCIAL CREDIT
AND EXCHANGE

Expanded use of credit instruments in Northern Europe

The bill of exchange, always popular with its Italian originators, came to enjoy increasing acceptance among other businessmen, especially those engaged in trading at the reviving regional and international fairs. By the end of the fifteenth century this device had found its way among merchants throughout most of Europe, including even those of the Hanse. But it remained primarily a means of transferring capital and only secondarily a credit instrument, so that the preponderance of settlements continued to be made by bank transfer. Thus, although there are examples of endorsed bills of exchange dating as far back as the late fourteenth century, their value as such was constrained by their limited negotiability. Such bills were assigned by a letter to others as a means of paying debts, but the original drawee always remained responsible for the debt. True negotiability did not occur until the beneficiary assigning the bill became the new principal, with full liability, without which there was no way to build up a system of circulating credit. Such negotiability occurred first in the Low Countries (see below) and slowly spread to other parts of Europe during the sixteenth century through the international clearing houses created at the great fairs of Geneva, Lyon, Besançon, Genoa, and other cities.

In the meantime, a much more effective short-term credit instrument, the promissory note made out to bearer, was independently developed and perfected in the trade axis of London to Antwerp. This device was a written promise to pay a certain sum at a certain time, which passed from holder to holder as a means of paying debt. It had been used in the wool trade from before 1400, but mostly between and among English merchants who could rely on English courts to enforce their rights.[5] These bearer notes became increasingly popular in Antwerp and achieved official recognition in 1507, when the magistrates of that city established explicitly that the holder of an endorsed note, no matter how many times it had changed hands, had the same legal right as the original noteholder. This ruling was confirmed for all the Low Countries by imperial decree in 1537. Around the same time, bills of exchange in Antwerp began to include the notation "or to bearer of this letter," thus taking on the characteristics of promissory notes; by 1541 they had achieved juridically the same status as promissory notes.

A further development began at this time that was to have immense ramifications for modern credit markets. The notes and bills that we have been describing circulated at face value, but as business boomed and the need for cash became urgent, holders of these instruments became frustrated at increasing delays in obtaining payment. As a result, the idea of discounting notes and bills became accepted, with the first example of discounting a promissory note dating from 1536. This practice, along with the concept of lending at interest, was formally permitted by imperial decree in 1540. As a result, financiers with surplus cash began buying matured notes and bills at a discount as investments. The discounting of unmatured instruments, the modern form, did not take hold until the second half of the sixteenth century, beyond the purview of this book.

The Antwerp Bourse

Another medieval innovation, a market for trading commercial paper, was a very early harbinger of what would become a hugely important institution for raising capital. The origins of the institution we now call the stock exchange lay in Bruges in the fifteenth century. Indeed, the very name by which such an exchange is known in several European languages – Bourse – recalls the square and family inn where merchants first gathered for the purpose of exchange.[6] But we must guard against an anachronistic leap in exaggerating the modernity of such embryonic exchanges, for no medieval exchange dealt in "shares" of companies; rather it was bills of exchange or merchandise that changed hands. And it was not in Bruges that the final architectural embodiment of the "Bourse" occurred, but in that emerging urban giant, Antwerp, which already by 1450 was beginning to rival Bruges as the great merchant city of the European north.

The history of the Antwerp Bourse shows many common character-istics to that of Bruges: long before there was a building, there was the custom of merchants meeting at a stipulated place and time. Naturally, such meeting places were to be found in the neighborhoods with the densest concentrations of resident merchants. In Antwerp this was the area near the central marketplace known as the "Engelse wijk" – the English ghetto. This was not only a place of residence but also a busy trading neighborhood, particularly during the fairs of Antwerp around 1400. The location of a "Bourse" remains shadowy throughout this period, and it is likely that the name was attached to several houses; a member of the Bruges family, de Beurse, was an owner of such a house on the "Zilversmidstraat" in 1411. It was not until 1485 that a request was made of the magistrates of Antwerp by a group of resident foreign merchants that they be allowed to form a "common body" or society and a general "Borse."

A great deal of confusion has arisen over this request, with many his-torians making the mistake of calling it the foundation document of the Antwerp Bourse. In fact, the request was for recognition of a confra-ternity – quite common in that era – with a general "purse" or fund collected from the membership to promote and protect the interests of the group. Though far from founding an "exchange" in the modern sense, this document does signal the social ties that were beginning to coalesce into permanent associations among merchants. And crucial to such organizations was the transaction of business among their members, underlining the point that the exchanges, long before they were build-ings and institutions, existed as social ties among merchants.

Merchant custom did finally settle on both a locale and a building by 1515 with the so-called "Oude Bourse," which had the essential traits of an open square surrounded on all four sides by a covered gallery. Here merchants, both foreign and local, gathered to exchange bills and currencies; or to quote a slightly later document, they "could gather in order to deal and negotiate with regards to their business and trading." As Antwerp became not only the preferred point of exchange for English cloth on the continent, but the exchange point of Portuguese and south German trade, the Bourse became thronged with merchants from all corners of Europe. The Bourse came of age as a true capital market when Charles of Ghent, the future emperor Charles V, approached the Antwerp colonies of foreign merchants, particularly the

Augsburger merchant-banker Fugger, for the money necessary to enable him to purchase the imperial crown. After 1520, the Habsburgs regularly sold short-term state bonds on the Antwerp exchange.

The final constitutional age of the Antwerp capital market occurred in the great rush of development and growth in the city after 1500. Not only did the population of the city more than triple between 1480 and 1568, but the volume of business transacted in the old commercial neighborhood surrounding the Old Bourse grew to a point far exceeding the capabilities of its commercial buildings and squares. Acutely aware of the challenges of growth, the Antwerp magistrates commissioned architects and planners to lay out new neighborhoods outside the old city center, and the needs of commerce were among those considered. Thus in 1531, the "New Bourse," a building designed and constructed with the requirements of an exchange in mind, and situated in a planned neighborhood with broad, straight streets, was completed. Not only was this a revolution in architectural design, it signaled a further step in the evolution of the medieval to the modern exchange. For henceforth, the exchange was to be located some distance from the harbor, warehouses, and other collection points of trading goods, underlining the fact that bills of exchange, bonds, and other abstract financial instruments were the true business negotiated at the Bourse.

CONSUMER CREDIT

While on the subject of banking and credit, it is useful to digress briefly to the subject of consumer credit. Very little change took place in the dispensing of such credit during the late Middle Ages. It was managed mostly by small-scale pawnbrokers for the poorer clients and occasionally by larger merchant-banks for aristocratic customers who had fallen on hard times or had simply outspent their resources. Jews remained active in this field in Germany, Italy, and Iberia, but had been expelled from both France and England around the turn of the fourteenth century, replaced largely by Italians, the so-called lombards, many of whom actually came from the Piedmont and Tuscany. Some of the emigrant Italians belonged to substantial family organizations. And notwithstanding the migration of Jewish pawnbrokers into Italy from Germany after the pogroms of the Black Death, Christian Italians continued to be active in the trade.

What change there was in consumer lending occurred in the attempts to curb the rate of interest. Typically, pawnbroker interest was extremely high, with weekly rates that compounded to annual charges surpassing fifty percent. Church doctrine continued to condemn as usury interest at any level on consumer loans. Most municipalities, recognizing that abolishing the practice would not relieve the need of the desperate poor, licensed pawnbrokers in an attempt to exercise some control over the rates. The church explicitly condemned this approach at the Council of Vienne in 1311–12, but many towns continued to issue licenses both to Jews and to Christians. The church did, however, take some positive steps to help alleviate the plight of the poor. In the Spanish bishoprics of Burgos, Palencia, and Calahorra, the *Arcas de Limosas* were established around 1431 to lend money interest-free, with personal property taken as security. And it was a branch of the Franciscans that came up in the mid fifteenth century with the idea of supplanting the usurious pawn-broker with the famous public nonprofit pawn banks that became known as the *monti di pietà*. With the pope's approval, these banks were established in cities and towns throughout Italy and were permitted to offer loans at interest of five percent per annum. They did not succeed in displacing the Jews as intended, because they were much less flexi-ble in their terms and in the quality of collateral they demanded. But they provided a wedge for church recognition that the condemnation of usury might apply only to excessive interest, rather than to any inter-est. Similar institutions appeared in Flanders and the Low Countries at the end of the fifteenth century, and by the middle of the sixteenth century, cities in those areas began to become directly involved in this type of lending. The *monti* themselves developed different, often politi-cally motivated characteristics in each locality, and some became very large and diversified. The best-known of them is the *monte dei paschi di Siena*, founded in 1472, which survives to this day under government ownership as the fourth-largest bank in Italy, with 22,000 employees.

AVAILABILITY OF CAPITAL TO MEET BUSINESS NEEDS

This analysis of capital sources seems to suggest that only a limited portion of the total capital generated in the economies of late medieval Europe was available to businessmen. And referring back to the table in Chapter 6 (page 141), overall money supply during the period 1280–1500 appears to have been on the low side, ranging from "vari-able" to "famine." Certainly there was nothing in any of the broad eco-nomic indicators, such as they were, that pointed to a period of significant capital growth. And yet we have seen the development of new or expanded industries across Europe in agriculture, fishing, brewing, mining, metallurgy, shipbuilding, marine and road transporta-tion, armaments, publishing, and even in textiles. And clearly, western

Europe was vastly more powerful economically in 1500 than it was in 1380. How do we account for this anomaly?

The work of Richard Goldthwaite provides one answer. In an intriguing book, Goldthwaite inquired into the sources of wealth in Renaissance Italy between 1300 and 1600, asking why so much of it was invested so conspicuously in art and architecture.[7] Much of the money, he found, was business profit acquired through the efforts of traders, financiers, and manufacturers, this at a time when Italians were losing pride of place in eastern trade. Apparently declining trade in the East was more than made up by increasing business to the north and west. And even the much noted supplanting of eastern Mediterranean trade by western and Atlantic trade may have been more relative than real. In particular, the Italian role as international financiers and transmitters of specie remained intact in the East and increased in the West with new opportunities in Iberia and the Low Countries. Their manufacturing base expanded vigorously in military supplies, glass, and luxury goods and continued to grow even in textiles, despite the setbacks from German and English competition mentioned in Chapter 7. At the same time, the small city-states were consolidating into important regional economies dominated by Milan, Florence, Venice, Rome, and Naples, all of which were growing luxury goods markets.

The second important reason for the accumulation of capital in Italy, paradoxically, was the redistribution of wealth caused by war and pestilence, raising the demand for luxury goods and weaponry, both of which were Italian specialties. Moreover, even the waves of invasions by German, French, and Spanish forces, although destructive, brought considerable business, as the invaders poured in cash from their countries and later the New World to advance their political ambitions. And one must not overlook the papacy, that most efficient generator of cash, which directed considerable resources, even during the Avignon period, toward building its temporal power base in Italy.

Abundant cash was not matched by equally numerous places to direct it, however. Only a limited amount was invested in business fixed assets and inventory. Considerably more, as we have seen, was loaned to municipalities for a variety of purposes. But there is evidence of a continuing surplus in the steady and heavy investment in land that persistently drove up land prices. And further evidence appears in the steady decline of interest rates, from a range of seven to ten percent in the fourteenth century to as low as four percent in the sixteenth (but not for loans to profligate princes, for which rates were often twelve percent or more). And there was still plenty of money left over to finance the glorious works of architecture and art that are the most enduring results of a lavish consumption of luxuries. Thus the merchant's counting house provided much of Renaissance culture's substance, though little of its inspiration.

Although Italy is a special case in many ways, it is not unique. Other parts of Europe may not have enjoyed Italy's surpluses, but certain territories, especially the Low Countries, southern Germany, and even France, clearly generated enough capital to meet whatever demands were made by the new industries. And in the case of the Low Countries, there was money enough to finance a boom in the fine arts, from music to sculpture. This brings home once again the undisputed physical evidence that agriculture and industry were impressive generators of surplus throughout the High Middle Ages. During the relatively peaceful years of the twelfth and thirteenth centuries, western Europe was able to pour substantial amounts of capital into the expansion of frontiers and creation of infrastructure described in Chapter 1 and still have enough left over to finance the prodigious surge of nonproductive construction of churches, city walls, and castles that so characterized the period. And in the war-torn and pestilence-ridden fourteenth and fifteenth centuries, when much less capital was spent on monumental construction, much more was devoted to trade-enhancing infrastructure – port facilities, bridges, canals, locks, and weirs – and to productive facilities. The inescapable conclusion is that the economy of western Europe was much richer and more powerful in 1500 than it was 200 years earlier.

Not all areas shared equally in the generation and constructive use of capital. France's productivity had been hampered by the ravages of English invaders and freebooters alike, but began to recover in the second quarter of the fifteenth century and grew rapidly in the second half. By the end of the fifteenth century, the French kingdom had become a major economic power. England, however, was the laggard of western Europe, slow in picking up the new technologies and too long addicted to the war-like excesses of her kings. In mining and metallurgy, papermaking, and printing, England was not competitive with continental producers; and their herring fishermen, although productive, never approached the same scale of activity as the Dutch. The English not only wasted assets in their long war with France, they also failed to adapt to the changing technology of warfare, notably the use of artillery. In brief, England of the late fifteenth century was stuck in the High Middle Ages, still focused upon an old industry, woolen textiles, and still building great cathedrals. Only in maritime transport was England beginning to catch up to its continental rivals, a development that would make itself felt early in the sixteenth century.

COLLABORATION OF BUSINESS AND GOVERNMENT IN THE MARITIME EXPLORATIONS OF THE LATE MIDDLE AGES

From the first, interest in overseas exploration was mixed and tentative at best. The early ventures along the West African coast were conducted mainly by Genoese and Portuguese marine entrepreneurs, but as results proved meager, they increasingly required the encouragement and financial support of Henry the Navigator. The important financiers were also reluctant to put their money into such high-risk projects. Christopher Columbus's unsuccessful attempts to secure financing for his first transatlantic voyage and Jacob Fugger's refusal in 1493 to invest in Vasco da Gama's journey to the Indies are typical examples. But once a project showed viability and profit, even with high risk, businessmen became eager to participate. At that point, however, the ventures were usually politicized, and the royal governments involved wanted the spoils mainly for themselves. Eventually, the governments would find that they lacked the administrative competence to manage the commercial complexities and would license monopoly rights to individuals or companies in exchange for annual fees. In effect, they followed the pattern of the Genoese and Venetian colonizers in the eastern Mediterranean and Black Seas, allowing merchant control and direction while reserving sovereignty and a royal share of the profits for the state.

Portugal

Although the fifteenth-century explorations of the African coast and south Atlantic were carried out in the name of the Portuguese crown, the necessary financial resources were provided by Genoese and Portuguese businessmen, who, unwilling to risk money directly in these ventures, were prepared to lend to the royal sponsors. Prince Henry the Navigator, despite some commercial success in his endeavors, died deeply in debt. The fantastic journeys of Bartholomeu Dias and Vasco da Gama of the late 1480s and 1490s were also government projects, and the ships' officers were not merchants but aristocrats. The objective of da Gama's voyage of 1497–9 to India and the East Indies was commercial, in the sense that he sought to tap into the sources of the spice trade, but the methods employed were related more to intimidation and conquest than to trade. Despite the arrogance and mismanagement of opportunities displayed in this venture and despite the losses in men and ships, the survivors returned to Lisbon with a sufficiently impressive cargo of spices to ignite the further interest of royalty and commercially oriented aristocrats. The expeditions that rapidly followed were well armed and provided immense profits from wholesale looting as well as from trade. The attitude of these aristocratic invaders is elegantly summed up by a historian: "They had no wish to become growers of pepper or ginger. But the diversion from infidel control of so lucrative a commerce was, like the taking of tribute and loot, an occupation suitable for Christian gentlemen."[8]

The Portuguese monarchy swiftly established its authority, organizing colonies and military outposts and claiming rights to the sea lanes, along with trade in spices, gold, and slaves. It formalized the royal monopoly in 1505 by channeling all import and export trade through a newly created organization, the *Casa da India*. The *Casa* also directed the flow of spices to the factor of the Portuguese crown in Antwerp, which had exclusive selling rights in the north. But the complexities of managing this trade and the overseas colonies were beyond the competence of this tiny monarchy, and soon all of the goods were sold to Portuguese and foreign merchants. And the European financiers, initially little involved in Portugal's Eastern commerce, became very active. By the late 1500s, beyond the period covered in this book, most of that business, including the control of the Eastern outposts, passed into private hands via the sale of licenses. Here we see a repeat of the experience of Genoa, which ultimately leased most of its overseas possessions to private groups. Scammell characterizes such action as a "universal expedient," where communications are poor, administrations are weak, and ready cash is preferred to distant future prospects.[9]

Spain

Spanish activity in the Atlantic was circumscribed throughout most of the fifteenth century by the diversion of resources to the final expulsion of the Muslims from Granada and to the pursuit of royal ambitions in Italy. Nevertheless, Catalan mariners had been early seekers of African gold, and Castilians launched numerous expeditions after 1450 in competition with the Portuguese and with the backing or approval of the crown, notwithstanding the papal prohibitions of midcentury. The most notable of Spain's incursions was into the Canary Islands, which by dint of persistent effort finally came under Spanish authority in 1493.

The full achievement of Spanish explorations and conquests in the Americas lies outside our period, but the organization and financing of the early expeditions laid the groundwork for later success. As is well known, Christopher Columbus shopped around the courts of Spain,

France, England, and again Spain between 1486 and 1492 before finding backers for his first voyage. And it was made possible only because the crown was not obliged to contribute funds; the financial support came from a royal official and a number of Columbus's Genoese compatriots. The second voyage, however, was large, ambitious, and very much a royal venture, with objectives of trade, gold, and Christian conversion that swiftly evolved to conquest and colonization. After Columbus's fall from favor on his return in 1496, the crown revoked his monopoly and granted licenses to other expeditions led by Spanish aristocrats and gentry, who used their own funds and loans from merchants.

The denizen investors, primarily the Genoese in Seville, kept well clear of direct involvement in the early voyages of exploration, other than those of Columbus. Those and later expeditions by Sebastian Cabot and Hernan De Soto to which the Genoese contributed were largely unrewarding and confirmed the Genoese preference for investing in missions of trade rather than conquest. Accordingly, they quickly responded to the opportunities presented by the needs of the burgeoning settlements. As early as the first decade of the sixteenth century, the Genoese of Seville were dominating the business of providing sea loans at huge rates of interest to traders and shipbuilders, accepting the risks inherent in the sea loan business described earlier (page 61). They also engaged directly in trade with the nascent settlements, providing both necessities and luxuries at a great profit.

Likewise, the Spanish monarchy, once it had recognized the potential of the early discoveries, became determined to make the most of the opportunities presented. But rather than follow the more or less decentralized model that the Portuguese drew from Genoese experience in the Mediterranean, the Spanish adopted the more tightly controlled centralized style of the Venetian rule over its colonies in the Levant. Thus the Spanish crown not only required that all discoveries and conquests be made in its name, but quickly exerted its authority over all administrative and commercial activities in the new empire. It created regulations governing emigration, the establishment of towns, extraction of minerals, licensing of monopolies, and the taking of tribute; and it sold licenses permitting exemptions from certain of the regulations. It controlled nominations to ecclesiastical appointments, and circumscribed the independence of the conquistadores, replacing eventually even the most successful leaders with government officials of more certain loyalty. All these actions were designed to maximize royal control and royal profit. And although none of the ships trading in the Americas was state-owned, their destinations, at least at the European end, were strictly limited to Seville and Cadiz, ensuring government oversight of all trade with the colonies. To be sure, there were numerous cracks in this elaborate bureaucratic edifice, but overall, the system was remarkably effective.

THE FUGGER PHENOMENON

While busily working to organize its new American possessions, the Spanish kingdom, still very much embroiled in Italy, became increasingly involved in central and northern Europe. Joanna of Castile, one of the daughters of Ferdinand and Isabella, married the son of the Habsburg Emperor Maximilian I and gave birth to a son, who became Charles I of Spain on the death of Ferdinand in 1516. As grandson of Maximilian, Charles was a prime candidate to succeed him as Holy Roman Emperor on Maximilian's death in 1519. However, Charles found himself in a bitter contest with Francis I of France for the votes of the seven electors. The Spanish kingdom had not yet begun to gather the wealth of the Americas in any quantity, and its still-penurious ruler had to seek the assistance of private financiers. His first reaction was to tap foreign merchants established in Spain – the Genoese, and the German Welser Company – but the competition of the French was such that the combined resources of these firms were insufficient to gain the prize. Charles finally turned to Jacob Fugger, who, having long been financier to the Habsburgs, was able to mobilize pledges of over 500,000 golden gulden. Thus Charles was elected King of Germany and Emperor Charles V of the sprawling Habsburg possessions in Austria, Germany, the Low Countries, and the Franche-Comté, as well as of Spain and the Americas.

Who was Jacob Fugger? He was an Augsburger, as noted in Chapter 8, whose family got its start as weavers in that city around 1380. Certain members formed a business partnership that gradually moved into trading on the Augsburg-Venice axis, importing raw cotton for the manufacture of fustians and exporting metals and other German goods. By the time that Jacob appeared on the scene, the family partnership was strictly limited to family members, excluding both outsiders and non-performing relatives. The partnership was well established, buying and selling a wide range of goods, locally and internationally, and already involved in advancing credit to Austrian archdukes, the papacy, and the emperor. Jacob began his apprenticeship in Venice, where he was exposed to Venetian business and accounting systems, and returned to Germany to work with his older brothers in an increasingly successful partnership during the 1480s and 1490s. He steadily assumed leadership, and when his last brother died in 1510 he took absolute control, which he maintained until his own death in 1525.

Superficially, Fugger's large-scale lending to the emperor suggests a return to the pattern of the fourteenth-century super-companies, a notion reinforced by his long and fruitful relationship with the papacy and the princes of central Europe. In fact, the Genoese of Spain were much closer to the super-company model, providing loans and services to the monarchy in return for privileges. Fugger was different in that he expected specific repayment, and insisted on adequate security, even to the extent of writing to Charles V in 1523 gently but firmly reminding the emperor of his debts, an unheard-of impertinence. Eventually he obtained as a partial repayment the income from leases to three Spanish religious orders that owned extensive agricultural properties and a highly productive mercury mine.

Mining was another feature of Fugger's business that distinguished him from his fourteenth-century forebears. The family business originally entered the metals trade through accepting mine output as security for loans to princes. It was reluctant to invest in mining itself, as too risky and capital intensive, but gradually entered the industry through building smelters to process the ores owed by producers to whom the company had advanced funds. The company plunged deeply into mining and smelting in the Tyrol and in Hungary, where around 1495 it formed a joint venture with a gifted Hungarian engineer and inventor, Johann Thurzo, to operate copper and silver mines, rolling mills, and smelters. This important departure from the Fugger policy of "no outsiders" was necessitated by the fact that as foreigners in Hungary they could only function there as partners of a native; even so, two marriages between the families were arranged to forge a strong personal link between the two companies. The Hungarian venture became a substantial industrial enterprise of several hundred workers, enjoying a near-monopoly of Hungarian mining and metals, including iron, lead, and zinc, in addition to silver and copper. The business was long-lasting and immensely profitable, providing much of the sinew for Jacob Fugger's funding of Charles V's successful candidacy.

Aside from its great mining interests, the Fugger Company was an important wholesaler and trader with connections from Antwerp to Venice, as well as a leading, if cautious, financier of princes and businesses throughout central and northern Europe. As chief papal banker in Germany and Scandinavia, the company enjoyed the monopoly of transferring funds from the sale of indulgences, arousing the hostility of Martin Luther and others. But until late in Jacob Fugger's life, when he had to look to Spain for recovery of part of his huge loans to Charles

V, the company did little business in that country and its colonies, which were to become so important to his successors. And, unlike other south German enterprises, the company stayed clear of the speculative Portuguese spice trade in Lisbon and Antwerp, despite its extensive business in the latter city. Similarly, the Fuggers sensibly avoided serious engagement in France, in this instance because of their strong Habsburg connections. But Jacob Fugger was innovative as well as shrewd; we have already noted in our discussion of the Antwerp Bourse that he initiated a bond issue to help redeem his pledges, thus setting a pattern for the marketing of government debt.

The Fugger Company gives the overall impression of a transitional business organization. In one sense, it can be regarded as a prototype of the nineteenth-century industrial operation, because of its focus on mining and metallurgy involving heavy capital investment and the management of complex manufacturing processes. In another, it was among the first of the new breed of financiers who began to mobilize credit for governments by floating bonds for investors rather than by direct lending. In yet another, it was similar to its immediate medieval predecessor, the Medici Company, driven by the unique business and political will of its principal architect (Cosimo in the case of the Medici), but doomed to decline in the hands of less gifted successors, even when they showed considerable talent. Such was Anton, Jacob's nephew, who took charge of a business in 1525 valued at over two million golden gulden and continued to develop it successfully for a time, but ultimately presided over its decline. The firm, weighed down by ever-increasing involvement in credit to the Habsburgs, was greatly weakened by the time of Anton's death in 1560, and gradually slid toward extinction in the seventeenth century.

The importance of the Fuggers and many other, lesser, but still large organizations in south Germany lay in their ability to create substantial concentrations of capital out of their rulers' insatiable demands for cash. Typically, such companies got their start in textiles and trading, the profits from which provided the funds to invest in mineral extraction and production. The aristocratic owners of the deposits lacked the means to exploit them, giving the opportunity to businessmen to do the job for them under contract. This marriage of convenience worked extremely well for both parties. The businessmen accumulated wealth on a grand scale that enabled them to fund ever-larger projects, while the owner/rulers obtained a rich stream of income to fuel their political ambitions. But the latter were never content to live within their means and demanded loans of ever-increasing size from their business associates, who were reluctant to refuse for fear of losing their favored positions.

The existence of the very large firms continued to be precarious through the end of the Middle Ages and beyond. But in a sense, the rise and fall of such firms as the Fuggers was incidental to the overall success of European governments and business in raising and deploying capital in productive new ventures. There was nothing inevitable or altruistic about the cooperation of business and government, driven as it was by greed, opportunism, and crusading and missionary Christianity. But however mixed the motives, the results brought not only voyages of discovery and conquest, but financial innovations like the Bourse, negotiable credit instruments, funded state debt, and experiments in a wide array of banking techniques. For the most part, business in late medieval Europe continued to be carried on by a myriad of relatively small-scale operators who, alone or in concert with others, provided the skills and utilized the capital for economies that were beginning to enjoy vigorous growth. And it was the diverse and improvisatory genius of the largely anonymous that would be the most valuable legacy of medieval business.

IO

A NEW AGE FOR BUSINESS

•

One of the victims of recent historical writing has been faith in the enduring dividing lines of European history. A century ago the labels and concepts "Middle Ages," "Renaissance," and "Reformation" stood as firm markers of historical change and steady evolution to the "modern" world. This is no longer the case, and for business it never was: there is no easily recognized "early modern" era in business history, for many of the techniques of organization and management remain those inherited from the late Middle Ages. It is a near certainty, for example, that a partner in the Peruzzi company of 1300 would have felt quite comfortable in the counting house of the Fugger company in 1520. Yet, with the sixteenth century's growing population and its widening trade with Africa, Asia, and the New World, with the Atlantic beginning at first to equal then surpass the Mediterranean as the heart of the European economy, can we not notice a transition to something more recognizably "modern"? And transition it was, an almost seamless evolution, not a "revolution," as business expanded in scope and complexity but not in method. In this final chapter we will examine some examples of how this transition played out.

DEMOGRAPHIC RECOVERY

The central fact of the second half of this study is the "Great Dying" of the mid fourteenth century, which if it did not inaugurate, certainly continued the assaults of recurrent war, pestilence, and famine on Europe's people. Not only did plague strike down the traditional victims of infectious disease, the young and the aged, but, as so many contemporaries remarked, it struck down young and mature adults, both women of childbearing age and men in the prime of productivity. Thus after the massive mortalities of ca.1347–90, Europe entered a prolonged period of demographic stagnation, whose effects on the economy were only partly ameliorated by the higher percentage of people living in cities. The numbers are startling: in 1340 there were roughly 74 million Europeans; in 1400 there were 52 million, and there was little change for two more generations. The effects of the demographic decline on business were anything but uniform, and we have seen that late medieval businessmen adapted to the challenge in a variety of ways. But inarguably, if Europe were to enjoy another era of sustained economic growth, such as that of ca. 1000–1300, there would have to be an end to the people shortage.

The cycle of demographic stagnation was indeed broken around 1450, for reasons that remain mysterious, inaugurating a sustained period of population expansion. The tempo of growth varied widely from region to region: in England, for example, although growth was modest before 1510, the country's population nearly doubled in the next century. In the Netherlands the great age of growth occurred in the first half of the sixteenth century, before the dislocations of the Dutch revolt caused a decline. Tuscany had a spurt of explosive growth between 1490 and 1552, with southern Italy not far behind, boasting a doubling of population between 1505 and 1595.[1] Two trends must be stressed within the pattern of general growth, however, for they have significance for the evolution of business. First, by and large, population growth was greater in the areas we have been have been calling "north" and "northwest" (Scandinavia, British Isles, Low Countries, Germany, and most of France) than in the Mediterranean region (Italy, Iberia, and southern France). The best available statistics for the period 1500–1550 show an increase from about 36 million to 42.5 million, or 18 percent for the "north" and from 18.3 to 20 million, or only 11 percent, for the Mediterranean. The greatest growth rates occurred in Germany and the northern Netherlands, but, despite lagging somewhat behind its northern and eastern neighbors, France continued to contain slightly over a quarter of Europe's people throughout the sixteenth century.

The second trend is the persistence of the late medieval pattern of increased urbanization across Europe in this era of demographic upsurge. Although it is estimated that ten percent of Europeans lived in cities in 1500, some twelve percent resided there in 1600, with Italy at seventeen percent and the Low Countries at twenty-five percent. Striking in this repopulating of Europe's cities is that population grew fastest in Europe's largest cities – Venice, Rome, and to a lesser extent Florence in the south; Antwerp, London, and Paris in the north. In the north, at least, such growth could literally create boom towns like Antwerp, whose population doubled from 1450 to 1550. This trend resulted in the remarkable statistic that whereas in 1500 the total number of residents of smaller cities (population 5,000–40,000) exceeded those in larger cities by four to one, by 1600 the disproportion had shrunk to two to one. Thus Europe's largest cities were both population and (as we shall see) business dynamos across the sixteenth century.

<h2 style="text-align:center">THE GREAT INFLATION</h2>

Besides demographic recovery and increased urbanization, the other central business fact of the sixteenth century was inflation. Population certainly played a role in this, yet historians have traditionally cited the influx of silver from the New World as the cause. However, it has been correctly pointed out in recent research that inflation began well before significant quantities of New World silver reached Europe around 1540. Inflation thus had more complex origins than simply an increase in the supply of money and people.

Measuring inflation is a notoriously difficult problem in any era, including our own, for it involves a calculation of many variables: not only bullion supply and coinage fineness, but also the speed at which money changes hands (its velocity) and the prices of a "representative" basket of commodities over time. The supply of bullion in Europe was significantly increased by the boom in central European silver mining of the late fifteenth century described in Chapter 7. The result was an estimated 90,000 kg of annual production by the 1520s – a five-fold increase over the mid fifteenth century's annual totals and a level that would not be equaled by New World silver imports until the 1560s. Concurrent with the new silver stream was the Portuguese success in direct imports of African gold, which amounted to around 40,000 kg annually before 1540, worth an estimated 520,000 kg of silver. The impact of a vastly increased bullion supply was multiplied by the continuation of widespread coinage debasements by European rulers. And last but not least was the growth in credit mechanisms detailed in Chapter 9, which simultaneously increased money supply and exchange velocity. The European money market of the sixteenth century was a dizzying and dynamic spectacle for any businessman in search of profit.

Late medieval Europe was no stranger to bouts of severe inflation resulting from crop failures, wars, coinage debasement, and the like. But these were largely episodic in nature and local or regional in scope. The sixteenth-century developments, especially the increased population and urbanization of Europe, were of a structural nature, giving rise to a substantial and sustained inflation over a very long term. In the two European regions in which relatively complete records of commodity prices survive, England and the Netherlands, the increase in grain prices from 1510–1519 to 1630–39 was 670 percent; in livestock it was 355 percent; industrial goods, 204 percent; and the composite index increased by 490 percent across the period.[2] Inflation, of course, has both its winners and losers; but its persistence and its significance, as in the sixteenth century, make any long-term business strategy very difficult.

MARKET DEVELOPMENTS

Spices and metals

By 1550 there was a near global market in gold and silver bullion as Europeans began and continued to exploit both New and Old World resources. Was the same true of other precious commodities, spices for example? The spice trade had grown and developed along with the European economy since the days of the first crusades, to the enormous enrichment of both the Levant and the chief Italian merchant cities. The century between 1450 and 1550 witnessed tumultuous change in the prices of both ginger and pepper, the two most important spices consumed in Europe. Through the smoke screen of fluctuations, there is a definite drift lower in the price of pepper and a steep decline in the price of ginger in the second half of the fifteenth century. By 1500, pepper prices in the markets of the Levant and Egypt had dropped by a quarter and ginger prices by half; and prices for cloves, frankincense, dyes, and other aromata showed similar declines. Meanwhile, prices in the markets at Venice remained essentially stable; the widening profit margins and quickening demand encouraged the Portuguese drive down the coast of Africa and then eastward to the shores of India. Portuguese ships already by the 1480s were returning with loads of African malaguetta pepper, a type inferior to the Far Eastern varieties, yet considerably cheaper. This no doubt brought the spice to a whole new clientele across Europe, further spurring demand.

The role of Portugal in the expansion of the spice trade into a global, European-dominated business was crucial, although it should be noted that the Portuguese refrained from undercutting the Venetians, keeping their prices high. But spices were not the only spur to the inexorable drive of Portuguese trade, which was originally based on West African gold, slaves, sugar, pepper, and ivory. These commodities were obtained by peaceful trading along a string of Portuguese forts extending south

along the coast of Africa and ultimately reaching the shores of southern Asia. Gold surpassed spices in Portuguese commerce for several
decades after 1440, and slave labor grew in value as sugar plantations
continued to expand in Madeira, the Azores, and several African islands.
By 1501 the Portuguese had thus knit together a far-flung trading
network in the above commodities through its spice staple in Antwerp,
allowing trade for south German copper and silver, the two most important commodities that were exchanged for Asian spices. In effect, the
Antwerp staple closed an enormous trade circle encompassing both
Europe and Asia even before the rise of Atlantic-American trade.

Textiles

The quantity and variety of trade goods of all kinds in the marketplaces
of western Europe continued to increase, reflecting growing demand
and greater availability. Nevertheless, textiles remained the mainstay
among manufactured products offered for sale. The market and production developments in that industry during the fourteenth and fifteenth
centuries continued to play out along the same lines as described in
Chapter 7. The "new boys" became clearly dominant in their chosen
fields – the English for woolen cloth, the south Germans for fustians,
and the Italians for silk – but competitors old and new were determined
to gain positions in any way they could.

   In wool, the English government enhanced the ascendancy of its
clothmakers over those of the Low Countries from 1430 by ending
the practice of allowing wool purchasers to buy on credit, mandating
payment in full in English coin. The cost effect of this change and the
entrenched monopoly of wool export through Calais nearly crippled
the cloth industry of Flanders and Brabant. In order to survive, some
traditional producers were forced to look elsewhere for wool supplies.
Some created a separate manufacture utilizing inferior Irish, native, or
other non-English wools, while at the same time struggling to maintain
their traditional industry using exclusively high-quality English wools.
Others, such as Ypres and its satellite producers Langemark, Comines
and Poperinghe, flatly refused to change for fear of damaging their
reputation for quality, thus condemning themselves to decline. Further inroads on English wool dominance began around 1450, when, as
a result of experiments in sheep breeding and flock management,
Spanish merino sheep began to supply Italian and northern clothmakers with wool equal in quality to the best English Cotswold and
Marcher fibers. But although Bruges became the staple site for Spanish
wool imports to the north, a deep-seated prejudice against Spanish wool

resulted in slow, grudging acceptance among the traditional cloth centers of Flanders, Brabant, and Holland.

Much of the finer cloth produced in England was exported to Antwerp and elsewhere in an unfinished state. Antwerp, in fact, became not only the most important point of sale of English cloth, but the site of a significant fulling, dyeing, and finishing industry with English cloth as its raw material.[3] This consignment of cloth to Antwerp had the added advantage of allowing the eventual cloth purchaser to influence the final dyeing and finishing of the cloth to match local preferences. All this looks very much like a replay of the practices of the early fourteenth-century Florentine processors of the Calimala guild, who likewise imported Flemish cloths as "grey goods," finished them to suit southern preferences, and exported them throughout the Mediterranean. And likewise, the English cloth converted in Antwerp also was re-exported, in this instance as the chief trade good in the holds of the increasingly aggressive English merchantmen as they tried to establish trading outposts in the Baltic and force their way into direct trade with the Mediterranean. By the end of the fifteenth century, some seventy to seventy-five percent of England's annual exports of 130,000 cloths flowed through Antwerp or other Brabantine markets. English cloth was thus both a cause and an effect of expanding trade in the European north from 1460–1550.

At the low end of the trade, where the competition from English cloth was fiercest, the smaller fringe cloth villages of Flanders responded to the "English challenge" by developing a cloth type made entirely of non-English wools with a simple worsted weave and minimal finishing. These cheap fabrics, known as "say," flowed via the fairs of Antwerp to markets in Italy and Spain in substantial volume. Another successful adaptation was the development of low-cost light fabrics in south Flanders using a new type of long-fiber wool and different weaving and finishing techniques. This distinctly new product line became the direct forerunner of the seventeenth- and eighteenth-century worsted industry based in the same region.[4]

Another important change in the textile market was a shift in taste originating among European elites, away from traditional woolens in favor of silks. As early as the 1490s, a report on the decline of the traditional industry in Rouen declared that "the great lords have been accustomed to dress themselves in silk cloth; and now both the lords and others of lesser estate are wearing silk."[5] The same change of fashion occurred in Burgundy, where a sumptuary law of 1497 blamed the taste for silk for the "great decline and unsuitability of the drapery of our country." Demand for silks, beginning in the upper reaches of society, trickled down to the lesser nobility and wealthier members of the urban patriciate. Response from the textile industry came in two forms. The first was the spread of silk manufactures northward from Italy, so that by the end of our period Cologne, among other centers, had a well-developed silk industry. The second was the start-up of an industry in imitation silks, an offshoot of the light draperies. Many of these were produced in Italy to resemble silk, though composed of linen, wool, or a wool/linen blend. These were the taffetas, the damasks, and other similar fabrics that with silks would remain the choice of the affluent in Europe well into the seventeenth century.

The south German ascendancy in the manufacture of fustians discussed on page 169 continued apace. Already by the mid fifteenth century, Augsburg, Saint Gallen, Constance, Nordlingen, and the Danube cities of Regensburg, Vienna, and many others, had become important production centers. Large quantities of this cloth were traded with the Italians to the south, with nearly equal quantities shipped north to Antwerp, where Hanse Germans and English merchants were ready customers. By the sixteenth century, the flourishing fustian market attracted the interest of the great Jacob Fugger himself, who established a fustian weaving operation in the small town of Weissenhorn, outside Ulm. The business was continued by his nephew Anton, who in 1535 had 30,000 gulden invested in the operation, from which he expected an annual profit of 2,000 gulden. Thus fustians represented a relatively modest profit center for the Fuggers, perhaps a counterbalance to riskier but potentially more profitable ventures elsewhere.

ANTWERP: COMMERCIAL AND FINANCIAL HUB OF "NEW AGE" EUROPE

South German metals, Portuguese spices, English cloth, international finance, inflation – all were elements of the new business pattern of the late fifteenth and sixteenth centuries, which clearly mark the period off from its predecessor. But it is distorting to speak of these elements separately, in isolation from one another, for in reality the tempo of change owed much to the collision and combination of these forces. No place showed this new age for business with more force and clarity than the city on the Scheldt estuary perched between Flanders and Brabant, Antwerp. By 1500 not only was it the staple for Portuguese spices, the chief market for German metal, the key entrepôt for English cloth; but also its commercial exchanges, particularly its famous Bourse, orchestrated the gathering force of European business expansion, directing it in unimagined new directions.

Thirteenth- and fourteenth-century Antwerp gave little hint of this great future, for the city was very much in the shadow of the great Flemish cities. In fact, in 1356 the Flemish count, Louis of Male, reportedly at the urging of merchants of Bruges, invaded Brabant and occupied Antwerp, which remained subject to Flanders until 1406. This Flemish aggression, however, is perhaps the clearest indication of awareness of Antwerp's growing role as a merchant city. Accidents of nature also benefited the city. In 1375–76 and again in 1404 a series of floods and winter storms struck the coast of Flanders and Brabant causing enormous destruction, and then construction – for the scouring action of the great tides allowed large seagoing vessels to reach the port of Antwerp for the first time. This further reinforced the city's position as the crossroads of a series of important overland trading routes. Equally important to this good fortune of Antwerp were the growing difficulties experienced by Bruges in maintaining access to the sea. Centuries of inexorable silting of the Zwin, the channel linking the city to the sea, had already resulted in the founding of two outports, Damme and Sluis. By the mid fifteenth century, only Sluis continued to function as a harbor capable of receiving large ships; from there most cargo was offloaded onto smaller boats to begin the ten-kilometer trip to the markets of Bruges.

The growth in trade after 1460, coupled with the increasing difficulty of reaching Bruges, in effect caused a shift of some oceanborne trade to other ports in the vicinity of Bruges along the Walcheren coast. Thus the entire region of the Scheldt delta came to play a cooperative and symbiotic role in accommodating shipping and serving as the connecting point for overland and riverborne trade. But slowly and unmistakably, commercial preponderance shifted to Antwerp, linking that city to the important Rhine and Baltic cities of the German Hanse and, by extension, to those of southern Germany and Italy.[6] Thus road and river traffic were crucial to the health and development of Antwerp, as were the city's storage and trading facilities.

Perhaps the most important force favoring Antwerp over Bruges came to be the politics of the ruling Burgundian dukes. This family, descended from the French royal house, had over the course of several generations built upon the foundation of Burgundy and Flanders to unify the duchies and counties of Brabant, Gelders, Holland, and others. The ambitious centralizing policies of the Burgundian dukes, especially those of Maximilian of Habsburg, husband of Margaret, heiress of Burgundy, caused a series of uprisings in Bruges leading to general civil war between 1483 and 1492. Maximilian himself was even imprisoned in Bruges by rebels in early 1488, a result of the poisoned atmosphere caused in part by his order to all foreign merchants in Bruges to depart the city for Antwerp in 1484. These actions, coupled with blockades of the Zwin and crushing war indemnities upon the return of peace, caused many merchants to leave Bruges for good. Antwerp, on the other hand, enjoyed Maximilian's favor because it remained loyal to him, and the city also offered the attraction of a thriving series of fairs and a more flexible and less confining guild and social structure than did rebellious Bruges.

Rivalry between Bruges and Antwerp should not be exaggerated, however, for throughout the fifteenth and even into the sixteenth century there was also a great deal of complementarity. Bruges remained the chief consignment point for English wool shipped from Calais; it remained as well the principal point of sale for cloth produced in west Flanders and northern France; and, as mentioned above, Bruges also became the staple for Spanish wool sales in the north. But Antwerp by 1500 had attracted to its markets the increasingly dynamic sectors of the European economic expansion: in the words of one historian, "the ascendancy of Antwerp rested upon the tripod formed by English woolen cloth, Portuguese-Asian spices, and south German copper and silver."[7] It was the presence of these commodities and the residence of foreign merchants who came to buy and sell them, reinforced by superior warehousing and trading facilities provided by the city, that thrust Antwerp into a dominant role in the early modern economy.

The crush of expanding trade posed its own problems, however, particularly as the exchange of German silver and Portuguese spices necessitated financial structures more varied and supple than ever before. By 1500 it was apparent that the chief exchange and finance mechanisms of fourteenth- and fifteenth-century Bruges, those provided by money changers and innkeepers, were no longer capable of the breadth of scale required by the new trading opportunities. What developed, chiefly in and around the Bourse, was a system of negotiable credit instruments, together with the legal and business safeguards and guarantees described in the previous chapter.

The more fluid and long-term nature of these new credit developments in the Antwerp market in turn encouraged syndicates of merchants to form and pool their capital. This money was made available to finance trading ventures, either short- or medium-term, with each partner taking a share of profit or loss. In practice this meant that a smaller group of active partners would collect money from a larger group of passive or "silent" partners, use it to accomplish the planned business, and then settle up and divide the profits. Such a decentralized and variable group might exist only for the length of one trading expedition, or it might continue across several or dozens of trading ventures. This form of organization (or perhaps organized disorganization) had several advantages: it spread risk among a number of merchants; it kept costs low because staff and brokers were hired only when needed and only for long enough to accomplish the business; and last but not least, it attracted many more investors from more sectors of society, increasing the pool of investment capital. If all this has a familiar ring, it should: these sixteenth-century arrangements have an uncanny resemblance to the systems developed centuries before by the businessmen of two other great port cities, Genoa and Venice, discussed in Chapter 3.

A few other features of the Antwerp financial market deserve comment. The sale of rents, annuities, and government bonds remained an important source of capital, particularly for financing industry and warfare. For example, the capacity expansion of Antwerp brewer Gilbert van Schoonbeke cited in note 8 in Chapter 8 was financed partly by selling annuities worth 200,200 gulden, or three-quarters of the needed sum. These annuities paid out at a specified rate for the lifetime of their holders without giving them any direct share in the profit or loss of the business. Schoonbeke himself put up the remaining 71,100 gulden while retaining complete control of the firm. The famous Plantijn printing company, on the other hand, was ninety percent financed by nine investors in 1560; only ten percent was held by Christoffel Plantijn himself.[8] Meanwhile, state finance on the Antwerp market reached truly monumental proportions by the mid sixteenth century. The English crown alone had borrowed more than 503,000 gulden by 1546; Maria of Hungary, protector of the Low Countries, borrowed some 184,434 gulden; the king of Portugal issued obligations for 37,512 gulden. These debts should properly be understood as loans to support royal consumption – particularly that sport of kings, war.

The final innovation of the Antwerp market was the development of the beginnings of a commodity market associated with the so-called "English exchange," based on English wool and cloth and supplemented by lead, dye-stuffs and other lesser commodities. Around 1550, the magistrates of Antwerp chose a new location for the "English house" remote from the port facilities of the old city, thereby for the first time removing the goods themselves from the vicinity of trading. Traditionally, commodities were inspected by the potential buyer, usually in the company of both the owner and a broker, who had arranged for the buyer and seller to meet. Only after such inspection would the deal-making commence. But with the new "English Bourse," as it came to be called, buyers and sellers dealt in contracts of purchase, well away from the warehouses where the goods themselves were stored. This trading removed from trade goods was made possible by the increasing standardization of manufactures as certified by seals, or "trade marks," thus eliminating the need for laborious piece-by-piece inspection. Thereby "trading" took another step toward the abstraction of the commodities market of today, where pork bellies are bought and sold by brokers who have never set foot on a slaughterhouse floor.

REGIONAL DEVELOPMENTS

Decline of the Hanse

The commercial and industrial alignments in the cloth industry, the gradually won supremacy of Antwerp over Bruges, and the new trade directions pursued by the Portuguese contributed to the patterns of trade in the Baltic. The German Hanse had risen to clear dominance in the fourteenth century, favoring Bruges with the western monopoly of their commerce; but the federation by the mid fifteenth century was facing determined competition from the cities of the northern Netherlands, headed by Amsterdam. Unlike the scattered and loosely unified members of the Hanse, the Dutch could tap into a dynamic pastoral-agrarian economy whose surplus could easily be transported along the numerous inland waterways that interlaced the country. This resource, combined with that from a thriving and innovative fishing industry, particularly in herring, gave the Dutch steady and rich sources of capital to deploy. Much of it came to be invested in shipping, thanks in part to the Hanse's demand for cargo space and the increasing Dutch skill in the construction and piloting of sailing vessels. So successful were the Dutch in competing for shipping tonnage that by 1544 Lübeck, one of the chief cities of the Hanse, admitted Dutch supremacy in the Treaty of Speyer. This supremacy was underlined by the Danish Sund tolls of 1557 (collected from all ships passing between the North and Baltic Seas), which showed that sixty percent of the cargoes conveyed from the Baltic to the west in that year were carried in the holds of Dutch merchant ships. Although the financial and commercial hegemony of Amsterdam was achieved outside of the chronological limits of this book, its foundations were clearly apparent well before the seventeenth century.

France

Lyon was but one manifestation of a business revival that swept across France in the decades following the end of the Hundred Years' War in

1453 and became a mighty surge during the sixteenth century. This rapid growth, almost exponential in some areas, was most pronounced in the Atlantic seaports and in towns to the north, such as Rouen, Troyes, and Orléans, but above all in Paris.[9] The recovery of the textile industry in northern France was mirrored in Paris, where specialist workshops such as Gobelin and Canaye dyed and finished great quantities of cloths brought in from other centers. Always a major market, Paris was becoming an increasingly important industrial and financial center under the watchful eyes of the crown. At last, the business of France was beginning to do justice to the resources of this fertile and populous country.

Italy

The cities of northern Italy continued to be great business centers, despite the fact that most were losing position relative to the rapidly growing towns of the north. Genoa, in particular, suffered contraction, as one by one its quasi-independent satellites fell to Turks, Mamluks, Venetians, and others, with the last survivor, the once hugely profitable complex at Chios, succumbing in 1566. But these losses were more than offset by the substantial gains in Spain, where the Genoese of Seville not only financed and exploited many of Spain's ventures in the New World, but also began to finance the monarchy itself. And Venice at the end of the fifteenth century was at the peak of its powers, dubbed then by a French ambassador "the most triumphant city." It continued to dominate trade in the eastern Mediterranean and had gradually acquired a significant hinterland in northeast Italy, enabling it to secure the trading routes through the Alps to the burgeoning markets of southern Germany and onward to northern Europe. To be sure, Venice was under continuing political and economic pressure from the the growing power of the Ottoman Empire and the nation-states of France and Spain, but it remained a first-class business center through the end of our period.

The vitality of business throughout Italy owed much to increased manufacturing as well as trade. The eastern Mediterranean, still a vital source of spices notwithstanding the Portuguese inroads in the Far East, was even more importantly a supplier of raw materials – cotton, silk, and dyes for the textile industries, and soda for glass and soap. The finished products fabricated from these materials, as well as woolens, found ready markets throughout Europe, as did the wide range of military hardware produced in northern Italy. There was also much business to be had within Italy itself in the expanding regional economies surrounding Florence, Venice, and Milan, and in the growing luxury goods markets of Rome and Naples. And these same cities and many others experienced the continuing boom in the construction and decoration of palaces, churches, and civic buildings for which they became famous. Finally, although there were no longer firms of the international stature of the Medici after its decline and fall late in the fifteenth century, Italian businessmen continued to expand their roles as international financiers and transmitters of specie to the East. The decline of Italy's importance in the business of Europe lay in the future.

Spain

In Chapter 4 we noted that the effect of the *reconquista* was to divide Iberia into three trading zones – north Castile and Portugal, Andalusia and the southwest coast, and Aragon/Catalonia. During the High Middle Ages, by far the most commercially active of the three was Aragon/Catalonia, centered in the busy seaport of Barcelona. The late Middle Ages, however, witnessed the dynamic growth of Atlantic trade in all directions from the seaports of Spain and Portugal and the bustling commercial center of Seville. And trade grew not only as a result of the overseas explorations, but also because of Spain's new export commodity, merino wool.

Business on the Mediterranean side of Iberia, although falling behind the Atlantic area in relative terms, continued to grow, especially in Valencia and the more southerly ports. We have already commented on the aggressive trading of the Catalan merchants in the fifteenth century. But Barcelona's importance as a commercial and manufacturing center entered absolute decline as that century wore on. First, its cotton manufacturing industry fell victim to the price and quality advantages of Italian and German fustians; the number of workshops dropped from a peak of 300 to ten or fewer by the early fifteenth century, and despite later import bans, the industry never recovered. Second, its vibrant Jewish community was effectively driven out around 1400. Then, after 1425, Barcelona lost the economic advantages of being the seat of government of the region, as the Aragonese court moved to Naples. And finally, by mid-century, the city was riven with factional strife between international merchants and protectionist artisans, leading to the disastrous Catalonian civil war of 1462–72. Barcelona only partially recovered from these setbacks and by the early sixteenth century was viewed as a charming, but not very enterprising, city of 30,000 inhabitants.

ACCOUNTING AND FINANCIAL CONTROLS IN A CHANGING ENVIRONMENT

The growth in the complexity of business and the sophistication of financial instruments was not accompanied by any significant improvement in the techniques of accounting. The exuberant trading in the markets of Antwerp and elsewhere in the north at this time was largely managed on an individual-venture basis that did not lend itself to elaborate control systems. Nevertheless, the advanced accounting concepts of the Italians, including double-entry bookkeeping, had reached Antwerp in the fifteenth century and had become, as we have seen, widely practiced among the great companies of southern Germany. Yet many historians have not been prepared to recognize the appearance of "true" double-entry accounting until what they regard as the defining document, the treatise of Luca Paciolo, was written in 1494.[10] Because of the importance ascribed to this work, it is worthwhile to pause and consider it in some detail.

Paciolo was not a business practitioner but a prestigious academician. A protegé of Leon Battista Alberti, he studied mathematics, architecture, geometry, and their practical applications, including business accounting. He was patronized by the rich and famous, including several popes, taught at universities throughout Italy, and collaborated with Leonardo da Vinci. His publications included a number of learned manuscripts, the most enduring of which is the *Summa di Arithmetica, Geometria, Proportioni et Proportionalità*, which appeared in 1494. The *Summa* consists of five treatises – on arithmetic and algebra, the use of arithmetic and algebra in trade and reckoning, bookkeeping, money and exchange, and pure and applied geometry. This surprising mélange of the theoretical and practical in one collection suggests not only a wide-ranging intellect but also a comfortable relationship between business and university in Italy at this time.

Paciolo's treatise on bookkeeping was the first of its kind. He did not claim to "invent" accounting, but simply documented what he considered to be the best of the many systems practiced in Italy, namely the Venetian method. The work is by no means an exercise in theory. It is a practical cookbook for businessmen that outlines procedures step by step, laced with entertaining aphorisms on the conduct of affairs, such as "he who does business without knowing all about it, sees his money go like flies." His Franciscan background is revealed in biblical references and in the use of the Holy Cross as the identifying symbol of the original ledger. And his analysis includes the pious exclamations common in medieval accounts; when discussing the trial balance, for example, he comments, "if the loss exceeds the profit (may God protect each of us who is a really good Christian from such a state of affairs)."

The treatise discloses a business world that is still very personal. In fact, its ultimate objective is to provide a periodic record of the subject's total net worth. The opening chapters instruct the merchant to list in the capital account all his cash, jewelry, property, and even items of clothing, and to run accounts for household expenses alongside, although separately from, those for business expenses. Paciolo then gives guidance on setting up and making entries in the journal and ledger, creating a partnership account, translating currencies into a standard unit of account, establishing profit centers for specific trading transactions, dealing with brokers, government officials, and banks, and constructing a trial balance. He finishes his essay with a useful summary of all his instructions.

Paciolo's book, as a start-up guide for aspiring entrepreneurs, is a useful description of small-business bookkeeping in Italy at the close of the fifteenth century. But it is not an indicator of the state of the art of accounting as practiced by the larger firms, being incomplete in many respects. For example, it makes no reference to accruals or depreciation, concepts well known to businessmen for some time. Paciolo's presentation would have been regarded by professional accountants and managers as simplistic. In particular, his insistence on recording the details of every transaction in a memorandum book before entering them in a journal was seen as an unnecessarily time-consuming step; it was eliminated by later writers. Nevertheless, the treatise is extremely important, not so much for its content as for the intellectual imprimatur that it awarded to business and accounting practice. Translated into several languages, it greatly aided the dissemination of Italian accounting principles throughout Europe.

For the larger firms, the continued emphasis throughout the fifteenth century on the improved management controls described as "merchant adaptations" in Chapter 7 is best illustrated by the experience of the Medici Company. Its accounting and financial controls were vastly superior to those of the Bardi and Peruzzi of the previous century and surpassed even those of the meticulous Datini. The Medici head office demanded and received regular, timely financial statements in sufficient detail to enable Raymond de Roover, centuries later, to prepare the incisive analyses that we have found so enlightening. These statements, submitted annually for branches in Italy, biennially for those "beyond the Alps," were scrutinized item-by-item by the general manager in the presence of the branch manager. Of special interest in these reviews was the identification and segregation of doubtful accounts. Bad debts were transferred to a separate ledger and charged to profit and loss; other accounts of a questionable nature but of lesser concern were not charged to profit and loss, but nevertheless were segregated into a "doubtful" category. In many ways, the Medici and other Florentine books have a rather modern look about them: they included tax returns, fixed asset and depreciation accounts, and a variety of systems for apportioning expense. Indeed, the famous Florentine tax surveys (*catastos*) of the fifteenth century presumed the existence of taxpayers' sophisticated accounting techniques and the availability of supporting financial statements. Although Paciolo selected the Venetian system as his standard, Tuscany provided more appropriate models for the larger firms, perhaps because, as B. S. Yamey suggests, the prominence of the partnership form of organization there made regular reckonings habitual.[11]

Curiously, de Roover in his majesterial study *The Rise and Decline of the Medici Bank* credited the company's longevity more to its corporate structure than to its system of controls. The Medici Bank was organized as a holding company, exercising control through majority ownership of each of its subsidiary operations; whereas the fourteenth-century Bardi Company, for example, was a single corporate entity wholly owning all of its branches. The holding company form of organization, de Roover reasoned, protected the Medici from repeating the Bardi experience – collapse of the entire company caused by the failure of one or more parts of the business.[12] We have seen in Chapter 5, however, that the bankruptcy of the super-companies owed much more to the general deterioration of the international grain trade managed from Florence than to the greatly overstated losses in England. The corporate structure argument has some merit, but its structure was of less importance to the company's survival than the efficacy of its control systems. It is no coincidence that the Medici collapse occurred after a lengthy downward spiral of less attentive management and weakening controls – ironically in 1494, the year that Paciolo published his treatise.

Outside of Italy, the great companies of south Germany, with their strong links to Venice, were early and apt students of the Italian bookkeeping systems. Accounting formed an extremely important part of Jacob Fugger's apprenticeship in Venice, while his chief accountant Matthaus Schwarz studied under masters in Milan and Genoa as well as in Venice. Jacob, like Datini a century earlier, was a fanatic about control and included in his frequent visits to his branches exhaustive examinations of accounts and balances. He also took the Medici system an important step further by dispatching auditors to check inventories and the quality of the accounts receivable. The organization of his reporting systems and his thorough knowledge of them gave Fugger the grasp of detail he needed to execute the transactions, big and small, that built the company.

We opened this section with the suggestion that the techniques of accounting had not kept pace with the growth in the complexity and velocity of business transactions that was occurring in the busy trading cities of the north. Certainly, control systems, as we have seen, had greatly improved, but their efficacy still depended upon intense discipline on the part of the owner-managers. Moreover, the systems were best suited to the more traditional manufacturing and marketing enterprises. The frenetic pace of business on the Antwerp Bourse permitted no more than a cursory measure of control venture by venture, with little opportunity for thoughtful analysis and risk management. The result was, of course, frequent error and undetected fraud that brought down enterprises, large and small, and weakened even the giants, such as the mighty Fugger Company. Indeed, control techniques could be said to lag behind innovations in trading techniques even to this day.

RELIGION, REFORMATION, AND BUSINESS

One of the stubborn remnants of the former low regard for the Middle Ages among historians is the belief that the moral and theological teachings of the church retarded and hampered business. Further, it is argued that only the Reformation freed businessmen to pursue a rational policy of capital accumulation and concentration sufficient to qualify as "capitalist" in nature. The great name associated with this school of thought is the German sociologist Max Weber, who in his *Protestant Ethic and the Spirit of Capitalism* linked the two in what he regarded as the new economic age that dawned in the mid sixteenth century. Weber's ideas are explicitly antithetical to our central argument, that the "spirit of capitalism" was alive and thriving throughout most of the Middle Ages.

In our section The Doctrine of Usury and Business Adaptations to It in Chapter 3, we outlined the efforts of God-fearing businessmen and church authorities to reconcile the practical need to generate capital for production and trade with the moral problem of charging for the use of money. We also noted the tensions within the church between doctrinaire theologians and pragmatic administrators in establishing the principles for determining what practices should or should not be condemned as usurious. Recognizing the necessity of trade and traders to the proper functioning of human society, the church increasingly accepted the notions of unpredictability of gain and compensation for losses or "damages" as legitimate practices. And in addition to using bills of exchange and other devices, businessmen in the thriving commercial centers of Italy and southern Germany only thinly disguised the imposition of a modest charge for the time value of money. It is therefore important to stress that the church before 1550 was neither prohibitionist with regard to business, nor was it an adherent of laissez faire; rather it stood in a kind of productive tension with the more unbridled forces of entrepreneurism.

An excellent example of the developing relationship between church and business can be found in the debate over the so-called "triple contract," or as it was known in Germany the "five-percent contract." The essence of the question involved a new form of partnership, developed around 1460, in which three transactions take place: first, a contract of partnership in a particular venture; second, a contract of insurance of the principal, by which insurance is given through assignment of the future probable gain from the partnership; and last, a third contract selling (at discount) the future uncertain gain for a lesser certain gain.[13] The question was whether this removal of risk from a commercial dealing also removed the exemption from usury prohibition enjoyed by business partnerships. Critics saw in such innovations a cloak for loans at interest, because even the partnership's nickname – "five-percent contract" – referred to the net return to the capitalist partner. Defense of the contract came strongly and from a surprising source, the University of Ingolstadt, near the growing financial and commercial city of Augsburg. There a young theologian named John Eck, in 1514, spoke out loudly in defense of the partnership contract. He attracted the notice and financial support of the Fuggers, allowing him to travel in July 1515 to Bologna, the great seat of both canon and civil jurisprudence in Europe, to dispute the point in public. After a five-hour exercise in learned argument, Eck was widely considered to have won the day. This minor episode in the career of the great opponent of Luther and adherent of orthodoxy in the future Reformation debate underlines the latitude possible for innovative business practice among even orthodox theologians. The resolution of this case caused the leading historian of medieval usury doctrines to conclude: "the moralists' acceptance of the [triple] contract meant the practical exclusion of the old usury theory from business finance."[14] Although this may be an exaggeration, it is important to note that the acceptance was made by the Catholic Church, and that the chief figures of the Reformation, notably Luther and Zwingli, changed nothing in this received tradition.

Business, however, was especially useful in disseminating the Reformation message. Printing and publishing in the sixteenth century grew enormously, spurred by growing population and literacy and by the increasing use of the vernacular that printing itself generated. The industry continued to be concentrated in the same centers of intellectual, government, and business activity as before; but one important "new boy" was Wittenberg, where printers moved in and enriched themselves by satisfying the demand for Martin Luther's immensely popular tracts and his German translation of the New Testament.[15] Erasmus of Rotterdam was the other best-selling author of this period, but by far the greatest volume of publication was in standard religious and classical works.

Anyone who has read thus far in this book will have found the other part of Weber's argument – that there were no examples of great accumulation and concentration of business wealth before the Reformation – to be equally false. In addition to the many great companies that we have discussed, dating from the thirteenth century onward, we could add several more, such as the Veckinchusen of Lübeck and the Grosse Ravensburger Gesellschaft of Ravensburg. The Fuggers alone in 1546 possessed the equivalent of 13,000 kg of gold as their combined capital, a sum easily exceeding that at the command of any crowned head of Europe. Clearly, the "capitalist spirit" – a dedicated and rational pursuit of profit as a principal goal – is a medieval, not a modern development.

Was there then a new age of business by 1550? Our analysis leads to a qualified yes. Certainly in terms of breadth and depth of opportunity, the sixteenth century presented the businessman with far more than did previous centuries. Direct trade with the Orient, the lure of the New World, and increasing trade across Europe are only a few of the changes that must be noted. Concomitant with increases in scale and complexity of business were the changes and refinements in what we have called the "tools of business" – business organization, accounting and management techniques, finance and transport. The sixteenth century brought nothing radically new here, but refinements, elaboration, and above all the spread of business knowledge allowed larger numbers of businessmen to make the leap into the new markets of the age. Most striking of all, perhaps, is the extent of cooperation between businessmen and the strengthened state governments of early modern Europe. From Portuguese princes, to kings and queens of England and Spain, even to Habsburg emperors, businessmen found allies in exploiting the opportunities offered by exploration and trade. Examples abound: Genoese seamen sailed west to the New World while in the employ of the king and queen of Spain; in England the crown granted important monopoly rights to the merchant adventurers; the English monarchy also made abundant use of the Antwerp credit market; and the Fuggers of Augsburg extended their loan of an imperial sum to enable Charles I of Spain to become emperor. All these are signs of the marriage of two of the most successful organizational forms of the West – the company and the state. By 1550, these two were prepared to encompass and subdue the world.

As is so often the case in business, success breeds success. The boom in the size and efficiency of the credit markets, particularly in Antwerp, Lyon, Augsburg, and Venice, contributed to the steady erosion of interest rates in the century from 1450 to 1550, bringing the cost of borrowed money to around five percent or less. Shipping rates also plunged as the resurgent European states gained control of their coastal waters and surrounding oceans. In the Mediterranean alone, the rates fell twenty-five percent during the sixteenth century. Encouraging and reinforcing the fall in these tariffs were the technological innovations that led to the full-rigged, heavily armed carrack and eventually the Dutch "flute" ship, matched in ground transport by the Hessian wagon – the very design that would one day carry American settlers, themselves descendants of European peasants, westward onto the Great Plains of North America.

CONCLUSIONS

The stark portrait of the vital statistics of the European economy figures prominently in most traditional histories of medieval Europe. The image is a graph of the population and gross product data revealing the shapely, still-rising curves of the thirteenth century, followed by a period of flattening in the early fourteenth, and then an ugly, precipitous drop during the latter half of that century. The downward slope continues, although more slowly, until the middle of the fifteenth century, when a hesitant, gradual upturn occurs and steepens, angled for the rapid growth of the sixteenth century. Though more comely, the picture of the economy in 1500 is still not as healthy as that of two centuries earlier.

This macroeconomic overview has the advantage of broad perspective, rather like viewing the earth from an aircraft flying at 35,000 feet. Our closer (or lower altitude) look at the economy of the late Middle Ages in Chapter 6 (see page 141) is also helpful in giving recognition to the shorter-term variations in economic activity, which occur in approximate thirty year spans. But business is done at ground level, the work of infantry, not air force, so our conclusions offer nuance and depth to an overly quantitative view of the period. There is no disputing the macroeconomic data cited above, depicting the European economy of the early sixteenth century finally struggling back to something approaching the level achieved two hundred years earlier. Yet our journey through the business landscape of medieval Europe tells a very different story, one of an economy that had become vastly more productive than suggested by the numbers alone. Taking this into account allows for a solution to the riddle of how Europe managed to seize the opportunities offered by exploration and technical advance while still mired in what some have called the depression of the late Middle Ages.

Two main threads of continuity run throughout our book. First and foremost is the fact that the elite, both as private persons and as representatives of lay and ecclesiastical institutions, supplied most of the force and direction of economic development. Their dietary preferences shaped the evolution of agriculture; their desires for luxury foods, apparel, and symbols of prestige laid the foundations for international commerce; their control of resources determined how surpluses were to be used – whether for military adventures, for monuments of pride and faith, or for productive infrastructure. Driven by compulsion, cooperation, and competition, businessmen contrived to meet the desires of the elite, and with considerable success. Many prospered in the process, and participated in swelling and revitalizing the ranks of the elite. Mass markets there were, to be sure – as in textiles and basic foodstuffs – and these became increasingly important as the Middle Ages wore on, but they were not yet the driving force that determined the direction of commerce.

Businessmen met the power of the elite in yet another form, that of governments and their growing bureaucracies. These did their utmost to control the flow of commerce and to extract as much revenue as possible from it. In the course of time, medieval governments became increasingly successful in this endeavor, often thanks to the businessmen-turned-bureaucrats in their service. In addition, we have seen that government was interested not only in wringing cash out of business, but also in regulating commercial activity, sometimes for the protection of the state, but often for the common good.

Second only to the desires of the rich in shaping business history was the sheer force of inventiveness that created the devices of business and trade. Ideas were drawn from many sources, both indigenous and imported, and were adapted successfully to a vast variety of uses. As great borrowers, European entrepreneurs adopted and improved upon inventions originating in the Far Eastern and Islamic cultures, as well as those inherited from Rome. Examples include not only "industrial" applications, such as farm equipment, textile machinery, mills for grinding, fulling, or operating bellows, navigation instruments, and paper making, but also imported cultivated products such as cotton, sugar, and silk. Also appropriated were ideas about business tools, including *commenda* contracts, sea loans, and marine insurance.

To the two most famous indigenous inventions of our period, the windmill and the printing press, must be added innovations in business organization. Guilds are one example on a local level: although not entirely original in concept, European guilds provided discipline of the production process, while at the same time promoting public order. On a broader level, businesses achieved a rich diversity of organization, from individual proprietorships acting on their own or in association with fellow citizens, to the mighty multiple partnerships of the super-companies, to the even larger quasi-governmental Genoese trading companies (*maone*), to the great commercial federations of the Hanse. And these businesses originated the tools suitable for the advancement of their commerce and for control of their operations. The bill of exchange and double-entry accounting respectively were only the most famous of such tools.

Too easily lost from view in traditional histories are two additional conclusions that can be drawn from this study. The first is that by the end of the great expansion in the mid fourteenth century, European entrepreneurs had accumulated a vast store of knowledge. They had learned how to build complex structures, how to cultivate a great variety of edible and inedible crops, how to manufacture quality goods in quantity and transport them over long distances by land and sea, and how to organize and control their operations under a wide range of circumstances. The second is the remarkable retention of that knowledge despite the travails of the latter half of the fourteenth century. Even more important, the learning did not stop. On the contrary, the age's very adversities unleashed a wave of adaptive response and recombinant inventiveness. Whereas during the High Middle Ages the business imperative was to provide increasing quantities of food, clothing, and shelter for a growing population, after the Black Death the driving force was the need to cut costs. This in turn spurred pursuit of knowledge of a practical sort to solve new problems of organization, logistics, and technology. Some knowledge from an earlier age was discarded: size per se was no longer an asset, the overland trading routes through France were no longer viable, and mining and transport technologies were no longer up to the demands made on them. Other experiments were abandoned after outliving their usefulness, as in the case of Bruges money changers of the fifteenth century.

The history of late medieval business is neither a collection of biographies nor a contest for who came closest to "modernity." It is rather a story of building on and adapting the old knowledge, while groping toward new knowledge through experimentation and the slow transmission of successes. Even the mature textile industry underwent significant change, as new lower-cost producers penetrated old markets (as in English woolens) or excelled in expanding the newer blends (as in German fustians). But the victims defended themselves against low-cost competition by concentrating on niche markets ranging from inexpensive says to luxury woolens. They and the manufacturers of cottons and silks not only developed profitable business, but also expanded their markets by offering more affordable apparel of a wider range. Thus both struggling and new industries contributed to a greatly enlarged market.

The most dramatic result of fifteenth-century experimentation occurred in the transport and metals industries, where the interplay of new information was most pronounced. In marine transport, as Richard Unger has noted, increasing contact among shipyards in the north and south permitted the knowledge of new ship designs to circulate freely, leading simultaneously to the proliferation of special purpose vessels and the rapid acceptance of the general purpose full-rigged sailing ship.[1] In metals, the urgent demands of ambitious rulers compelled innovations in weaponry that quickly spread around Europe, overcoming all attempts at secrecy.

Given the evidence of progress in the late Middle Ages, the great expansion of the sixteenth century should have come as no surprise. The early modern period, so often treated as a clean break from medieval Europe, is clearly no more than an almost seamless extension of it. Improved communication, better understanding of the physical world, more efficient dissemination of information and knowledge through the printing press, and recognition of intellectual property rights were all firmly in place at the end of the fifteenth century. And the medieval business legacy also included the rediscovery of the immense profit opportunities in slave-based plantation monocultures that were to have such serious long-term consequences. Whether for good or ill, the tools and techniques of medieval business lay in readiness for the repopulating Europe of the early modern era.

The vibrant European economy of the thirteenth century has rightly impressed most modern historians. But it was the seemingly stagnant and even retrograde fifteenth century that produced the intelligence, vision, and resources to mount the exploration and eventual domination of a large part of the world – a feat patently beyond the means of the Europeans of 1300. To be sure, the course of the late Middle Ages was a bumpy one. But historians seem to have concentrated their attention overmuch on the bumps – the famines, the plagues, the dynastic struggles, the currency crises – and perhaps too little on the undeniable progress of the journey.

NOTES

1 Georges Duby, *History Continues* (Chicago, 1994), 61.
2 Massimo Montanari, *The Culture of Food* (Oxford, 1993), 7.
3 *Ibid.*, 16–17.
4 Werner Rösener, *Peasants in the Middle Ages* (Urbana and Chicago, 1994), 101. Elsewhere, records about the rations of Peterborough Abbey in Northamptonshire, England, from 1294, provide a good illustration of the medieval peasant's diet. Of the 5,867 to 6,035 calories consumed by the average servant daily, 5,440 came from brown wheat bread, 317 from oatmeal, 10–162 from peas and beans, 44–60 from cheese, and 56 from butter. See *The Agrarian History of England and Wales*, v. 2, H. E. Hallam, ed. (Cambridge, 1988), 829.
5 England alone, according to the Domesday survey of 1086, boasted more than 6,000 watermills, or approximately one per 350 people, assuming a population of two million.
6 A useful summary of post-Roman and Medieval Italy can be found in J. K. Hyde's *Society and Politics in Medieval Italy* (London, 1973).
7 Florence and its environs provide a good example of the close integration of town and country in Italy. See Johan Plesner, *L'émigration de la campagne à la ville libre de Florence au XIIIe siècle*, trans. F. Gleizal from Danish to French (Copenhagen, 1934).
8 Marc Bloch, *Caractères originaux de l'histoire rurale française*, translated into English by Janet Sondheimer as *French Rural History, an Essay on Its Basic Characteristics*, foreword by Bruce Lyon (London, 1966).
9 R. H. Britnell, *The Commercialisation of English Society, 1000–1500* (Cambridge, 1993), 12–13.
10 Three of the nine laws enacted in the first year of the reign of Lombard

King Aistulf (750 A.D.) relate to merchants, some of whom were described as "great and powerful."

11 R. H. Britnell, *Commercialisation*, 10, puts it this way: "The development of formal markets in medieval England as in the rest of western Europe was inseparable from the exercise of power and the creation of law."

12 This process will be discussed more fully in Chapter 4.

13 See Peter Spufford, *Money and Its Use in Medieval Europe* (Cambridge, 1988), 74–7.

CHAPTER 2

1 We make no claim to originality in the use of the term "tools of trade." We do, however, believe it useful to point out that our sense of the term is much broader than that, for example, found in Harry Miskimmin's *The Economy of Early Renaissance Europe, 1300–1460* (Englewood Cliffs, NJ, 1969). Here the phrase relates to systems of organization, rather than to the financial devices such as bills of exchange, etc., that merchants used to facilitate trade. Those we call "traders tools" (see Chapter 3).

2 Italy was at the top of the list, estimated at 99 percent, with the United States not far behind at 95 percent, according to a survey reported in *The Economist* of March 2, 1996, pp. 57–8. For those who might think that these were all tiny businesses, *The Economist* in another article (October 5, 1996) reported that family businesses accounted for 40 percent of the Gross Domestic Product and 66 percent of the work force in the United States, and 65 percent of the GDP and 75 percent of the work force in Germany.

3 Much of the material for this section was drawn from Steven A. Epstein's *Wage Labor and Guilds in Medieval Europe* (Chapel Hill and London, 1991).

4 Municipal interventions in the food trades will be discussed further on pages 54 in Chapter 3 and 133 in Chapter 6.

5 For a useful collection of documentary sources and analysis of women's work, see P. J. P. Goldberg, *Women in England c. 1275–1525* (Manchester and New York, 1995).

6 More will be said about the role of guilds and merchants in politics in Chapters 3 and 4.

7 Quality of cordage was of crucial importance. Originally, master spinners were required to do all work in their homes or workshops and to mark their products with a distinctly colored thread. Later, much of their work was concentrated in a communal warehouse called the tana, located next to the arsenal.

8 For more information on the workings of the construction industry in Florence and elsewhere, see Richard A. Goldthwaite, *The Building of Renaissance Florence* (Baltimore and London, 1980), Part II.

9 Jean Gimpel, *The Medieval Machine* (New York, 1976), chap. 6.

10 The company that operated the Stora Kopparberg mines in Sweden celebrated its seven hundredth anniversary in 1988.

11 James Masschaele, "Transport Costs in Medieval England," *Economic History Review* 46, 2 (1993): 266–79.

12 Francesco Pegolotti, *La pratica della mercatura* (Cambridge, MA, 1936), 256–8.

13 Frederic C. Lane, *Venice, A Maritime Republic* (Baltimore and London, 1973), 119.

CHAPTER 3

1 This argument appears in the opening pages of de Roover's *Money, Banking and Credit in Medieval Bruges* (Cambridge, MA, 1948) and elsewhere in his works.

2 As were the long-standing arrangements in Islamic societies; see Abraham L. Udovitch in "Bankers without Banks: The Islamic World" in *The Dawn of Modern Banking* (New Haven and London, 1979), 253–73. Udovitch emphasizes the crucial importance of social-personal relationships in Islamic trade.

3 There is evidence that Flemish and Hanse traders did make limited use of the bill of exchange until restricted from doing so after the formal political organization of the German Hanse in 1370. But they also began to keep deposits with innkeepers and banks, which, by the late fourteenth century, they used to similar effect, as will be discussed in Chapter 8.

4 See Gerald Day, *Genoa's Response to Byzantium, 1154–1204* (Urbana and Chicago, 1988), chap. 5.

5 Francesco Pegolotti, *La pratica*, 293–7. For the complete list in English, see R. S. Lopez and I. W. Raymond, *Medieval Trade in the Mediterranean* (New York, 1955), 108–14. The list was compiled between 1310 and 1340.

6 For an excellent, well-documented article on this subject, see H. Krueger, "The Genoese Travelling Merchant in the Twelfth Century," *Journal of European Economic History* 22 (Fall 1993): 251–83.

7 Richard A. Goldthwaite, "Local Banking in Renaissance Florence," *Journal of European Economic History* 14 (1985): 5–55. This subject will be treated in some detail in Chapter 9.

8 See A. Udovitch, "Bankers without Banks," 263, 269.29

9 It should be noted in this context that most goods in international trade moved on consignment, and could not be used to underpin credit instruments. More will be said about consignment in the section on international commerce in Chapter 6.

10 Some of those systems will be described in Chapter 4 and others in Chapter 9.

11 For a good recent review on this subject, see W. T. Baxter, "The Tally and the Checker-board," in *Accounting History*, R. H. Parker and B. S. Yamey, eds. (Oxford, 1994); and for details of the administrative processes of the English bureaucracy, see E. B. Fryde, "Materials for the Study of Edward III's Credit Operations, 1327–48," *Bulletin of the Institute of Historical Research* 22 (1949) and 23 (1950).

12 John F. McGovern, "The Rise of New Economic Attitudes – Economic

Humanism, Economic Nationalism – During the Later Middle Ages and Renaissance, A. D. 1200–1550," *Traditio* 26 (1970): 217–53, provides a wide-ranging review of the writings of scholastics, jurists, and businessmen on private property, pricing, and profits in the Middle Ages.

13 Raymond de Roover, *The Rise and Decline of the Medici Bank* (Cambridge, MA, 1968), 116–20, reports one loss and gains ranging from 7.7 percent to 28.8 percent in fifty-seven transactions between 1437 and 1465.

CHAPTER 4

1 Gerald Day, *Genoa's Response to Byzantium*, 5–7.
2 R. H. Britnell, *Commercialisation*, 85.
3 Stephen P. Bensch, *Barcelona and Its Rulers, 1096–1291* (Cambridge and New York, 1995), 5.
4 Canto XV, lines 3–5.
5 Susan Reynolds, *Kingdoms and Communities in Western Europe* (Oxford, 1984), 174
6 Robert Bartlett, *The Making of Europe* (Princeton, 1993), 192.
7 Readers seeking a concise account of the rise of the Italian communes can see J. K. Hyde, *Society and Politics in Medieval Italy*.
8 For example, see the case of Benedetto Zaccaria at the beginning of Chapter 5.
9 Doria stayed on considerably longer, but many of his crewmen mutinied and returned to Genoa because of Doria's failure to pay their wages. See Jonathan Sumption, *The Hundred Years' War* (Philadelphia, 1990), 265.
10 The most notable of these, the Fondaco dei Tedeschi, was reserved exclusively for German merchants. For what is still the best overview of Venetian history and institutions, see F. C. Lane's *Venice*.
11 Although Siena was a Ghibelline city, its biggest company, the Bonsignori, was a long-serving banker to the papacy.
12 John F. McGovern, "The Rise of New Economic Attitudes in Canon and Civil Law, A.D. 1200–1550," *The Jurist* (1972): 39–50.
13 The mixed make-up of local and foreign jurors in English merchant law courts was formalized in the "carta mercatoria" of Edward I in 1303. Legal decisions stemming from cases in these courts became important in the late Middle Ages; an example appears in footnote 5, Chapter 9.

CHAPTER 5

1 For further information on this man and his business, see E. B. Fryde, *William de la Pole, Merchant and King's Banker* (London, 1988).
2 The Bardi Company's logo was a heraldic diamond shape, and that of the Peruzzi was three golden pears on a blue background.
3 Robert L. Reynolds, "Origin of Modern Business Enterprise: Medieval

Italy," *Journal of Economic History* 12 (1952): 360.

4 An idea of the complexity and practical nature of the problems students likely encountered can be gleaned from *Merchant Cultures in Fourteenth-Century Venice: The Zibaldone da Canal*, trans. John E. Dotson (Binghamton, NY, 1994).

5 Although common, this system was not universally applied, as there is evidence that the Alberti Company, a contemporary of the Peruzzi, reported inventories as a separate asset.

6 Individuals or companies could bid for the right to collect gabelles on certain items for a specific period. The difference between what the winner paid the commune and what he collected was his profit or loss. During the depression of the late 1330s, so many farms lost money that bidding ceased for a time.

7 As an example, the Bardi and especially the Peruzzi helped finance the Knights Hospitalers' conquest of Rhodes in 1309 and provided much-needed cash for its defense in the years immediately following.

8 The Medici Company will be discussed in Chapters 9 and 10.

CHAPTER 6

1 For example, in 1336 Catherine de Norwich expended only 37 percent on bread and ale and 47 percent on meat and fish. Christopher Dyer, *Standards of Living in the Middle Ages* (Cambridge, 1989), 56.

2 Eliyahu Ashtor, *Levant Trade in the Middle Ages* (Princeton, 1983), 236, 277–8.

3 See, for example, John Day, *The Medieval Market Economy* (Oxford, 1987); Frederic C. Lane and Reinhold C. Mueller, *Money and Banking in Medieval and Renaissance Europe* (Baltimore, 1985); John H. Munro, "Patterns of Trade, Money, and Credit," in *Handbook of European History 1400–1600*, vol. 1 (Leiden and New York, 1994), 147–95; Peter Spufford, *Money and Its Use in Medieval Europe* (Cambridge, 1988).

4 See Chapter 3 for a discussion of the role of precious metals in the "imbalance" of trade with the East.

5 See the section on International Commerce at the end of this chapter.

6 Oresme, a renowned scholar from the University of Paris, argued among other things that debasement was harmful and that only the "community," not the prince, could debase the coinage, and then only in an emergency. The "community" in France at that time was deemed to be the nobility.

7 See Spufford, *Money and Its Use*, for a useful statistical analysis and commentary on this subject in his chapter "The Scourge of Debasement," 289–318.

8 John Hatcher, "England in the Aftermath of the Black Death," *Past & Present* 144 (1994): 1–35.

9 The sources cited at the beginning of the section on money supply earlier in this chapter also deal extensively with late medieval price data.

10 Steven A. Epstein, *Wage Labor and Guilds*, chap. 5.
11 The Jacquerie is named after the "Jacques" or peasants. The Ciompi were the washers and carders, the lowest wage earners in the textile industry, so called because of the characteristic clumping sound made by their wooden shoes in the wash houses and sheds.
12 Even where "proletarian" trades, such as weavers and dyers in Flanders, had powerful guilds, they were controlled by wealthy, politically powerful men who had little in common with the average workman. And other industrial workers, such as fullers, were entirely excluded from government.
13 Raymond de Roover provides a useful description and two good examples of consignment sales in *Medici Bank*, 143–7.
14 But happen it did. E. Ashtor, *Levant Trade*, 445, cites several cases where merchandise was returned from Alexandria because of lack of buyers during an economic downturn.
16 For example, Gregorio Dati, a Florentine merchant, reported in his diary that he was set upon at sea in September 1393 by a galley and was robbed of considerable personal and company property; but he did recover some of it later, albeit with great difficulty and at great expense.

CHAPTER 7

1 One example is the famous *La pratica della mercatura* compiled in the 1340s by Francesco Pegolotti, the top salaried employee of the Bardi Company of Florence. A copy of this handbook, filled with sage advice as well as details about business practices, weights and measures, coinage, etc., in markets all over Europe and the Near East, was owned and revered by branch managers of the Datini Company some fifty years later.
2 Although business people continued to be preponderantly male in the fourteenth century, women were becoming increasingly involved, especially in Flanders, as will be shown later in this chapter.
3 As noted in Chapter 3, the working day had been divided into canonical segments, the length of which varied by seasons.
4 An important exception to the lack of documentation was Venice, where the arsenal encouraged shipbuilders to prepare written treatises on their systems. See Richard Unger, *The Ship in the Medieval Economy* (London, 1980), 192.
5 Benjamin Z. Kedar, *Merchants in Crisis: Genoese and Venetian Men of Affairs and the Fourteenth-Century Depression* (New Haven & London, 1976).
6 Note that in Bruges, unlike in Italy, there are numerous examples of women actively engaged in international commerce. For example, the wife of Willem Ruweel not only brought to her marriage a money-changing office, but also ran the day-to-day operations.
7 Indeed, the role of money changers in Bruges declined in the fifteenth and sixteenth centuries due to repeated failures and increasingly hostile govern-

ment policy. The whole subject of transfer banking and fractional reserves in the late Middle Ages will be treated in more detail in Chapter 9.

8 A staple was an administrative center established by a government in a town through which all exports or imports of a specified commodity were required to flow. Calais, conquered by the English in 1347, was a convenient offshore gateway to the nearby Low Countries.

9 The importance of dense networking will be highlighted again in Chapters 9 and 10 in discussing the origins of the Bourse and the rise of Antwerp.

10 Philippe Dollinger, *The German Hansa* (Stanford, 1970), 412.

11 J. H. Munro, "Patterns of Trade, Money, and Credit," in *Handbook of European History*, v. 1, 160.

12 Florence was an exception. When its businessmen began manufacturing fine cloth from top-grade English wool in the 1320s, they were motivated not so much by pressure on the cheaper end of the trade as by the need to meet market demand for luxury cloths left unsatisfied because of interruptions of supply from Flanders due to wars and embargoes. For the "flight to quality" in general, see John H. Munro, "The Origin of the English 'New Draperies': The Resurrection of an Old Flemish Industry, 1270–1570," in *The New Draperies in the Low Countries and England, 1300–1800*, ed. N. B. Harte (Oxford, 1997).

13 See Maureen Mazzaoui, *The Italian Cotton Industry in the Later Middle Ages, 1100–1600* (Cambridge, 1981), 138–153, for a succinct review of this and related developments.

14 We will not discuss agriculture here, despite its importance, because supplying forces with victuals was so often involuntary and unprofitable. For this, and for a general picture of the organization and funding of major campaigns in that period, an excellent reference is J. H. Hewitt's *The Organization of War Under Edward III, 1338–62* (Manchester and New York, 1966). This book provides a lucid account of the assembling of troops and mobilizing of ships, weapons, supplies, and victuals for Edward III's invasions of France in the early years of the Hundred Years' War.

15 The operation of this remarkable boat will be discussed more fully in the section on fishing in Chapter 8.

16 Richard Unger, *The Ship*, chap. 5.

CHAPTER 8

1 We have already noted that the term "spices" covered a huge range of products, many of which would not be considered spices today. At this time, however, the spice trade can be said to have been dominated by pepper, with ginger an important but distant second in value.

2 The auction procedure used until 1461 is of interest. It lasted about an hour, timed by a burning candle; the highest bid before the candle went out was the winner, resulting in a wild scramble in the last few seconds. This method

was used centuries later in the London docks for certain cargoes landed by the East India Company.

3 More will be said about Jacques Coeur later in this chapter.

4 The Genoese used this type of company to run certain of their overseas establishments. These had their own armed forces and acted not unlike the English and Dutch East India Companies of the seventeenth century.

5 An important motivation for the later circumnavigation of Africa was the quest for the mythical Christian kingdom of Prester John.

6 Early consumption data are difficult to obtain, but we know that Edward I provided one gallon a day per man for his troops, about the same rate of consumption of ale that has been estimated for English monasteries in the thirteenth century.

7 In England, brewing was still a small-scale operation into the fourteenth century, performed mainly by women in their homes both for domestic consumption and for sale. Women were so predominant in brewing in England that the word "brewster" was coined to denote a female brewer. But the role of women declined in the late Middle Ages as brewing became increasingly commercialized under the control of men. See Judith M. Bennett, *Ale, Beer, and Brewsters in England: Women's Work in a Changing World, 1300–1600* (New York, 1996).

8 But Brabant did boast at least one very large brewery in the 1550s. In Antwerp, an enterprising brewer, Gilbert van Schoonbeke, built an integrated system of breweries involving the investment of some 271,000 florins.

9 S. R. Epstein, "Regional Fairs, Institutional Innovation, and Economic Growth in Late Medieval Europe," *The Economic History Review* 47 (August 1994): 466.

10 William J. Wright, "The Nature of Early Capitalism," in *Germany: A New Social and Economic History, 1450–1630*, ed. Bob Scribner (London, 1996), 182.

11 Raymond de Roover, *Medici Bank*, 167.

12 Here is a typically worded entry from the Peruzzi accounts of the fourteenth century: "Giovanni, son of the late messer Guido di messer Filippo di Peruzzi owes us as at January 9, 1335 libr.71 s.16 d.6 florentine. We post this debt in the tenth red book in [page] CXLIII. The said money was taken [in the fiscal year] from July 1335 to July 1336 for his personal clothing and footwear expense, along with 8 golden florins that he spent when he went to Lombardy with messer Simone de' Peruzzi who went as ambassador to messer Mastino. [The apparent inconsistency in the date of the debt stems from the fact that the Florentine year began on March 25; in our terms, the debt was recorded January 9, 1336.]

13 Although there is no unassailable proof that Gutenberg was the original inventor, and some controversy remains, the evidence in his favor is very strong and generally accepted.

14 Many of the finest early printed works were printed on vellum, despite the high cost and technical problems, to demonstrate to the skeptical that printed works could be as elegant as manuscripts.

CHAPTER 9

1 Other targets were magnates, royal officials, and even municipalities. Louis XI of France exempted the city of Lyon from the *taille* in 1462, in return for which he expected and got a stream of large subsidies and loans.

2 In 1460, the Medici Company reported holding shares in the *monte* with a nominal value of 105,950 florins but a market value of 18,358 florins.

3 Anthony Molho, *Marriage Alliance in Late Medieval Florence* (Cambridge, MA, 1994), discusses the dowry fund in considerable detail.

4 The Bank of Saint George (*Banco di San Giorgio*) is sometimes confused with the *Officio di San Giorgio*, a powerful private financial institution that had its own ships and fighting men. It was the *Officio* to which the Genoese government leased its Black Sea colonies after the fall of Constantinople in 1453.

5 Legal decisions stemming from court cases could be important, as in the 1436 pronouncement of the London mayor's court in the case known as *Burton v. Davy*. This case established that the bearer of a transferable bill of exchange enjoyed equal legal standing with the original payee mentioned in the bill and thus could sue for nonpayment in the law-merchant court. This precedent helped pave the way for truly negotiable bills of exchange in the following century.

6 This new kind of market had its origins in the dense interconnectedness of fifteenth-century Bruges business life described in Chapter 7 in the section on Flemish adaptations. It began with the meeting of merchants to exchange information in the commercial district of the city, which extended from the central square into another square named for an inn owned originally by the van der Beurse family. By the mid fourteenth century, the family owned a complex of three houses, often called collectively "Ter Beurse," which became the name, first used in 1453, of the gathering of merchants who dealt in bills of exchange.

7 Richard A. Goldthwaite, *Wealth and the Demand for Art in Italy, 1300–1600* (Baltimore and London, 1993).

8 G. V. Scammell, *The World Encompassed: The First European Maritime Empires c. 800–1650* (Berkeley and Los Angeles, 1981), 269.

9 *Ibid.*, 190–1, 264–5.

CHAPTER 10

1 Most of the data in this section come from Jan de Vries, "Population," in *Handbook of European History*, 1–50.

2 John H. Munro, "Patterns of Trade, Money, and Credit," in *Handbook of European History*, 173.

3 Note that on page 167 in Chapter 7 we saw that the sale of English cloth and even its transshipment had been banned throughout Flanders.

4 Patrick Chorley, "The Draperies légères of Lille, Arras, Tournai, Valenciennes:

New Materials for New Markets?" *Drapery Production in the Late Medieval Low Countries: Markets and Strategies for Survival* (Louvain, 1993), 152–3.

5 *Ibid.*, 163, fn. 35.

6 It is noteworthy that by the sixteenth century, German merchants in Antwerp were competing successfully with Venice in providing pepper and textiles for the thriving cities of south Germany.

7 John H. Munro, "Patterns of Trade, Money, and Credit," 165.

8 This company was a very large exporter of books, with customers throughout Europe.

9 For example, R. H. Bautier, in *The Economic Development of Medieval Europe* (London, 1971), 237–8, cites the number of permits granted to unaffiliated merchants to trade on the Seine: they rose from 48 in 1453 to 188 in 1462 to 891 in 1533. Increases of the same order occurred in ship traffic at Bordeaux.

10 His last name is often also reported as Pacioli, but we will use the version preferred by Gene P. Brown and Kenneth S. Johnson in *Paciolo on Accounting* (New York, 1963), which provides a useful introduction along with a translation of Paciolo's accounting *Summa.*

11 B. S. Yamey, "Balancing and Closing the Ledger – Italian Practice, 1300–1600," in *Accounting History: Some British Contributions*, R. H. Parker and B. S. Yamey, eds. (Oxford, 1994), 264.

12 The "true" holding-company structure, with the Medici Company as majority shareholder in each of its subsidiaries, ended in 1455 after the death of Giovanni Benci, the company's general manager. Thereafter, the Medici principals maintained legal dominance through majority ownership as individuals in each of the branches. The effect on control, however, was much the same.

13 John Thomas Noonan, *The Scholastic Analysis of Usury* (Cambridge, MA, 1957), 209.

14 *Ibid.*, 229.

15 For example, his treatise *An den Christlichen Adel deutscher Nation* sold 4,000 copies within five days of its publication in 1520. His New Testament translation appeared in fourteen authorized editions and sixty-six pirated editions within two years of its first publication in 1522. See Colin Clair, *European Printing*, 123.

CONCLUSIONS

1 Richard Unger, *The Ship*, chap. 5.

FURTHER READING

INTRODUCTION

Very few books have been completely devoted to medieval business or medieval businessmen. Beyond Raymond de Roover's *Medici Bank*, Armando Sapori"s *Crisi dei Bardi e dei Peruzzi*, Iris Origo's *Merchant of Prato*, E. B. Fryde's *William de la Pole*, Edwin Hunt's *Medieval Super-companies*, Michel Mollat's *Jacques Coeur*, and several books on the Fugger family, the list is very short indeed. Most of this literature deals with certain exceptional individuals or organizations and, although helpful, provides only a limited view of business in medieval Europe. Far more useful as sources for our book are those works on a variety of other subjects that also tell much about what businessmen did. Many outstanding volumes in their special fields, such as Frederic Lane's *Venice, A Maritime Republic*, Stephen Bensch's *Barcelona and Its Rulers*, Eliyahu Ashtor's *Levant Trade*, Colin Clair's *History of European Printing*, Maureen Mazzaoui's *Italian Cotton Industry*, and Richard Unger's *Ship in the Medieval Economy*, probe deeply into the objectives, organization, and activities of businessmen while telling the stories of city-states, industries, and technologies. It is therefore difficult, perhaps even inappropriate, to attempt a lengthy annotated bibliography that describes and evaluates an array of publications in terms of their relevance to our book. We believe that the reader will be better served by an outline, chapter by chapter, identifying some of the more useful publications we have explored in researching our book, with just a few elaborating notes where special comment is warranted or the title does not adequately convey the work's content.

GENERAL

Auty, Robert, et. al., eds. *Lexikon des Mittelalters*. Munich and Zurich: Artemis-Verlag, 1977. This is the most up-to-date and complete dictionary treatment of the Middle Ages.

Fryde, E. B. *Studies in Medieval Trade and Finance*. London: Hambledon Press, 1983. Contains reprints of sixteen articles on a variety of economic, government, and business subjects of the High and late Middle Ages published between 1951 and 1979.

Lane, Frederic C. *Venice, A Maritime Republic*. Baltimore: Johns Hopkins University Press, 1973.

Lopez, Robert S. *The Commercial Revolution of the Middle Ages, 950–1350*. Cambridge: Cambridge University Press, 1976.

———. and Irving W. Raymond. *Medieval Trade in the Mediterranean World*. New York: Columbia University Press, 1955.

Pirenne, Henri. *Economic and Social History of Medieval Europe*. Translated by I. E. Clegg. London: K. Paul, Trench, Trubner & Co., Ltd., 1936.

Postan, M. M. and Edward Miller, eds. *Cambridge Economic History of Europe*, Vol. 2, *Trade and Industry in the Middle Ages*. 2nd edition. Cambridge: Cambridge University Press, 1988. Little changed from the first edition of 1952, but contains industry analyses of textiles, mining, metallurgy, and construction that are still useful.

———. and E. E. Rich, eds. *Cambridge Economic History of Europe*, Vol. 3, *Economic Organization and Policies in the Middle Ages*. Cambridge: Cambridge University Press, 1963.

Scammell, G. V. *The First European Maritime Empires, c. 800–1650*. Berkeley and Los Angeles: University of California Press, 1981. Contains excellent long essays on "empires" relevant to our period – the Hanse, Venice, Genoa, Portugal, Spain – and their interrelationships.

Spufford, Peter. *Money and its Use in Medieval Europe*. Cambridge: Cambridge University Press, 1988. Deals extensively with mining as well as minting and monetary issues.

Strayer, Joseph R., ed. *Dictionary of the Middle Ages*. New York: Scribner, 1988. Contains entries of varying quality, some of which are detailed and very good; all include bibliographies.

CHAPTER 1: ECONOMICS, CULTURE, AND GEOGRAPHY OF EARLY MEDIEVAL TRADE

Abulafia, David. *The Two Italies*. Cambridge: Cambridge University Press, 1977. Deals mainly with the twelfth century, but provides useful background information on the early trading cities of north Italy, especially Genoa, and their commerce in the south.

Britnell, R. H. *The Commercialisation of English Society, 1000–1500*. Cambridge: Cambridge University Press, 1993.

Duby, Georges. *The Early Growth of the European Economy*. Ithaca, NY: Cornell University Press, 1974.

———. *History Continues*. Chicago: University of Chicago Press, 1994.

Hallam, H. E., ed. *The Agrarian History of England*. Cambridge: Cambridge University Press, 1988.

Montanari, Massimo. *The Culture of Food*. Oxford: Blackwell, 1993.

Raftis, James A. *Peasant Economic Development within the English Manorial System*. Montreal: McGill-Queens University Press, 1996.

Reynolds, Susan. *Kingdoms and Communities in Western Europe, 900–1300*. Oxford: Clarendon Press, 1984.

Rösener, Werner. *Peasants in the Middle Ages*. Urbana and Chicago: University of Illinois Press, 1994.

CHAPTER 2: TOOLS OF TRADE: BUSINESS ORGANIZATION

Byrne, Eugene H. *Genoese Shipping in the Twelfth and Thirteenth Centuries*. Cambridge, MA: Medieval Academy of America, 1930.

Epstein, Steven A. *Wage Labor and Guilds in Medieval Europe*. Chapel Hill and London: University of North Carolina Press, 1991. Covers thoroughly a wide range of guild activity in northern and southern Europe from Roman and early medieval times until the mid fourteenth century.

Gimpel, Jean. *The Cathedral Builders*. Translated by Teresa Vaugh. New York: Grove Press, 1983.

Goldberg, P. J. P., translator and editor. *Women in England c. 1275–1525*. Manchester and New York: Manchester University Press, 1995.

Goldthwaite, Richard A. *The Building of Renaissance Florence*. Baltimore: Johns Hopkins University Press, 1980. Despite its narrow geographical focus, this book is instructive as a guide to the medieval construction industry and organization.

Harte, N. B. and K. G. Ponting, eds. *Cloth and Clothing in Medieval Europe: Essays in Memory of Professor E. M. Carus-Wilson*. London: Heineman, 1983.

Masschaele, James. "Transport Costs in Medieval England." *Economic History Review* 46 (1993): 266–79.

Mazzaoui, Maureen F. *The Italian Cotton Industry in the Later Middle Ages, 1100–1600*. Cambridge: Cambridge University Press, 1981.

Munro, John H. *Textiles, Towns, and Trade*. Aldershot: Variorum, 1994. A collection of wide-ranging articles on medieval textile technology and commerce.

Pegolotti, Francesco B. *La pratica della mercatura*. Edited by Allan Evans. Cambridge, MA: The Medieval Academy of America, 1936.

Unger, Richard W. *The Ship in the Medieval Economy, 600–1600*. London: Croom Helm; Montreal: McGill-Queen's University Press, 1980. Discusses extensively the design, construction, and uses of ships in northern Europe and the Mediterranean, along with the motivating economic forces.

CHAPTER 3: TRADERS AND THEIR TOOLS

De Roover, Raymond. "The Commercial Revolution of the 13th Century." *Bulletin of the Business Historical Society* 16 (1942): 34–9. Reprinted in *Enterprise and Secular Change.* Edited by F. C. Lane and J. C. Riemersma. Homewood, IL: Richard D. Irwin, 1953.

——. *Money, Banking and Credit in Medieval Bruges.* Cambridge, MA: Medieval Academy of America, 1948.

——. "New Interpretations of the History of Banking." *Journal of World History* 2 (1954): 38–76.

——. "The Development of Accounting Prior to Lucca Pacioli According to the Account-Books of Medieval Merchants." In *Studies in the History of Accounting,* edited by A. C. Littleton and B. S. Yamey, 114–74. Homewood, IL: Richard D. Irwin, Inc., 1956.

——. *The Rise and Fall of the Medici Bank, 1397–1494.* New York: W. W. Norton & Co., 1966.

Edwards, J. R. *A History of Financial Accounting.* London: Routledge, 1989.

Noonan, John Thomas. *The Scholastic Analysis of Usury.* Cambridge, MA: Harvard University Press, 1957.

Parker, R. H. and B. S. Yamey, eds. *Accounting History; Some British Contributions.* Oxford: Clarendon Press, 1994.

Reyerson, Kathryn L. *Business, Banking and Finance in Medieval Montpellier.* Toronto: Pontifical Institute of Medieval Studies, 1985.

Udovitch, Abraham L. "Bankers without Banks: Banking and Society in the Islamic World of the Middle Ages." In *The Dawn of Modern Banking,* selected papers delivered at a conference held at UCLA, September 23–5, 1977. New Haven, CT: Yale University Press, 1979.

CHAPTER 4: THE POLITICS OF BUSINESS

Bensch, Stephen B. *Barcelona and its Rulers, 1096–1291.* Cambridge and New York: Cambridge University Press, 1995.

Brundage, James A. *Medieval Canon Law.* New York: Longman, 1995.

Constable, Olivia Remie. *Trade and Traders in Muslim Spain.* New York: Cambridge University Press, 1994. A lucid account of the wrenching transformation of business life in Spain as the *reconquista* changed the direction of trade and industry.

Hyde, John K. *Society and Politics in Medieval Italy.* London: MacMillan Press, 1973. Traces the social and economic evolutions in Italy from the late Roman period to 1350.

Kaeuper, Richard W. *Bankers to the Crown: The Riccardi of Lucca and Edward I.* Princeton: Princeton University Press, 1973.

Nicholas, David. *The Metamorphosis of a Medieval City: Ghent in the Age of the Arteveldes, 1302–1390.* Lincoln, NE: University of Nebraska Press, 1987.

Reynolds, Susan. *Kingdoms and Communities in Western Europe.* (Cited under Chapter 1.)

Richard, Jean. *Saint Louis.* Translated by J. Birrell. Cambridge: Cambridge University Press, 1983.

CHAPTER 5: BUSINESS GETS BIGGER:
THE SUPER-COMPANY PHENOMENON

Abulafia, David. "Southern Italy and the Florentine Economy, 1265–1370." *Economic History Review* 33 (1981): 377–88. Reprinted in *Italy, Sicily and the Mediterranean, 1100–1400*. London: Variorum Reprints, 1987.

Brucker, Gene A. *Renaissance Florence*. New York: John Wiley & Sons, 1969.

Campbell, Bruce M. S., ed. *Before the Black Death: Studies in the 'Crisis' of the Early Fourteenth Century*. Manchester: Manchester University Press, 1991. This collection of articles deals primarily with the "crisis" in England, but includes John H. Munro's analysis of the adverse changes in transaction costs in the textile trades of northwest Europe.

Dotson, John E., translation and introduction. *Merchant Culture in the Fourteenth Century: The Zibaldone da Canal*. Binghamton, NY: Medieval & Renaissance Texts & Studies, 1994.

Edwards, J. R. *A History of Financial Accounting*. (Cited under Chapter 3.)

Fryde, E. B. *William de la Pole*. London: The Hambledon Press, 1988.

Hunt, Edwin S. *The Medieval Super-companies: A Study of the Peruzzi Company of Florence*. Cambridge: Cambridge University Press, 1994.

Lane, Frederic C. and Reinhold C. Mueller. *Money and Banking in Medieval and Renaissance Venice*, Vol. 1, *Coins and Moneys of Account*. Baltimore: Johns Hopkins University Press, 1985.

Pegolotti, Francesco B. *La pratica della mercatura*. (Cited under Chapter 2).

Sapori, Armando. *La crisi delle compagnie mercantili dei Bardi e dei Peruzzi*. Florence: Leo S. Olschki, 1926.

Swetz, Frank J. *Capitalism and Arithmetic: The New Math of the 15th Century*. La Salle IL: Open Court, 1987.

PART II GENERAL READING

Brady, Thomas A., Heiko A. Oberman, and James D. Tracy, eds. *Handbook of European History, 1400–1600, Late Middle Ages, Renaissance, and Reformation*, Vol. 1, *Structures and Assertions*. Leiden, New York, Koln: E. J. Brill, 1994. A collection of useful and varied articles, two of which are of special relevance and are cited specifically elsewhere.

Miskimin, Harry A. *The Economy of Early Renaissance Europe, 1300–1460*. Englewood Cliffs, NJ: Prentice-Hall, 1969.

——. *The Economy of Later Renaissance Europe, 1460–1600*. Cambridge: Cambridge University Press, 1977.

Munro, John H. "Patterns of Trade, Money, and Credit." In *Handbook of European History, 1400–1600, Late Middle Ages, Renaissance, and Reformation*, Vol. 1, *Structures and Assertions*, edited by Thomas A. Brady, Heiko A. Oberman, and James D. Tracy, 147–96. Leiden, New York, Koln: E. J. Brill, 1994.

Scribner, Bob, ed. *Germany: A New Social and Economic History, 1450–1630*. London: Arnold, 1996. A stimulating collection of essays, the most helpful of which are "Economic Landscapes" (Tom Scott), "The Agrarian Economy" (Werner Rösener), and "Urban Networks" (Tom Scott and Bob Scribner).

CHAPTER 6: THE NEW BUSINESS ENVIRONMENT OF
THE MIDDLE AGES

Brucker, Gene. *Renaissance Florence*. (Cited under Chapter 5.)
Day, John. *The Medieval Market Economy*. Oxford: Basil Blackwell, 1987.
Epstein, Steven A. *Wage Labor and Guilds in Medieval Europe*. (Cited under Chapter 2.)
Jordan, William Chester. *The Great Famine: Northern Europe in the Early Fourteenth Century*. Princeton: Princeton University Press, 1996.
Platt, Colin. *King Death: The Black Death and its Aftermath in Late-medieval England*. Toronto: University of Toronto Press, 1996.
Unger, Richard W. *The Ship in the Medieval Economy, 600–1600*. (Cited under Chapter 2.)

CHAPTER 7: BUSINESS RESPONSES TO
THE NEW ENVIRONMENT

Ashtor, Eliyahu. "The Factors of Technological and Industrial Progress in the Later Middle Ages." *Journal of European Economic History* 18 1 (Spring 1989): 7–36. In this intriguing overview, three factors are cited: diffusion of product improvement through migration of skilled workers, new or improved raw materials, and state intervention, especially from the fifteenth century.
Brucker, Gene. *Renaissance Florence*. (Cited under Chapter 5.)
De Roover, Raymond. *Money, Banking and Credit in Medieval Bruges*. (Cited under Chapter 3.)
——. *The Rise and Fall of the Medici Bank, 1397–1494*. (Cited under Chapter 3.)
——. "The Story of the Alberti Company of Florence, 1302–1348, as Revealed in Its Account Books." *The Harvard Business Review* 32 (Spring 1958): 14–59. Reprinted in *Business, Banking and Economic Thought in Late Medieval and Early Modern Europe*, edited by Julius Kirshner. Chicago: University of Chicago Press, 1974.
Derry, T. K. and Trevor I. Williams. *A Short History of Technology*. London: Oxford University Press, 1960.
Dollinger, Philippe. *The German Hansa*. Stanford, CA: Stanford University Press, 1970.
Edwards, J. R. *A History of Financial Accounting*. (Cited under Chapter 3.)
Gies, Frances and Joseph. *Cathedrals, Forges, and Waterwheels*. New York: Harper Collins, 1994. Although somewhat superficial, this popular, brightly written book is a useful introduction to the subject of technology in medieval Europe.
Harte, N. B. and K. G. Ponting, eds. *Cloth and Clothing in Medieval Europe: Essays in Memory of Professor E. M. Carus-Wilson*. (Cited under Chapter 2.)

Houtte, J. A. van. *An Economic History of the Low Countries, 800–1800*. London: Weidenfeld and Nicolson, 1977.

Kedar, B. Z. *Merchants in Crisis: Genoese and Venetian Men of Affairs and the Fourteenth-Century Depression*. New Haven, CT: Yale University Press, 1976.

Landes, David. *Revolution in Time: Clocks and the Making of the Modern World*. Cambridge, MA & London: Bellknap Press of the Harvard University Press, 1983.

Le Goff, Jacques. *Time, Work, and Culture in the Middle Ages*. Translated by Arthur Goldhammer. Chicago and London: University of Chicago Press, 1980.

Lloyd, T. H. *England and the German Hanse, 1157–1611*. Cambridge: Cambridge University Press, 1991.

——. *The English Wool Trade in the Middle Ages*. Cambridge: Cambridge University Press, 1977.

Mazzaoui, Maureen F. *The Italian Cotton Industry in the Later Middle Ages*. (Cited under Chapter 2.)

Munro, John H. *Textiles, Towns, and Trade*, (Cited under Chapter 2.)

——. "The Origin of the English 'New Draperies': The Resurrection of an Old Flemish Industry, 1270–1570." In *The New Draperies in the Low Countries and England, 1300–1800*, ed. N. B. Harte, 35–128. New York: Oxford University Press, 1997.

Nicholas, David. *The Metamorphosis of a Medieval City: Ghent in the Age of the Arteveldes, 1302–1390*. (Cited under Chapter 4.)

Origo, Iris. *The Merchant of Prato*. Boston: Non Pareil Books, 1986.

Parker, R. H. and B. S. Yamey, eds. *Accounting History; Some British Contributions*. (Cited under Chapter 3.)

Pegolotti, Francesco B. *La pratica della mercatura*. (Cited under Chapter 2.)

Unger, Richard W. *The Ship in the Medieval Economy, 600–1600*. (Cited under Chapter 2.)

White, Lynn. *Medieval Technology and Social Change*. Oxford: The Clarendon Press, 1962.

CHAPTER 8: THE FIFTEENTH CENTURY:
REVOLUTIONARY RESULTS FROM OLD PROCESSES

Ashtor, Eliyahu. *Levant Trade in the Later Middle Ages*. Princeton, NJ: Princeton University Press, 1983.

Bergier, Jean-François. "From the Fifteenth Century in Italy to the Sixteenth Century in Germany: A New Banking Concept?" In *The Dawn of Modern Banking*, 105–30. New Haven, CT: Yale University Press, 1979.

Boxer, C. R. *The Portuguese Seaborne Empire, 1415–1825*. New York: Knopf, 1969.

Clair, Colin. *A History of European Printing*. London and New York: Academic Press, 1976. An excellent country-by-country account of the development of printing and its commercialization from its beginnings in the fifteenth century.

Epstein, S. R. "Regional Fairs, Institutional Innovation, and Economic Growth in Late Medieval Europe." *Economic History Review* 47 (August 1994): 459–82.

Goldthwaite, Richard A. "The Medici Bank and the World of Florentine Capitalism." *Past & Present* 114 (February 1987): 3–31.

Mallett, Michael E. *The Florentine Galleys of the Fifteenth Century.* Oxford: Oxford University Press, 1967.

Mintz, Sidney. *Sweetness and Power: The Place of Sugar in Modern History.* New York: Viking Penguin, 1985. A small but useful part of this book describes the early history of sugar, its technology and uses.

Mollat, Michel. *Jacques Coeur ou l'esprit d'entreprise au xve siècle.* Paris: Aubier, 1988.

Phillips, William D., Jr. *Slavery from Roman Times to the Early Transatlantic Trade.* Minneapolis: University of Minnesota Press, 1985. This work includes a fairly comprehensive review of slavery and slave trading throughout medieval Europe and Africa, and of the forces leading up to the large-scale slave procurement for eastern Atlantic and New World plantations.

Thomas, Hugh. *The Slave Trade: The History of the Atlantic Slave Trade, 1440–1870.* New York: Simon & Schuster, 1997. Although concerned mainly with a much later period, the author also gives an excellent account in the first hundred pages of the early history of slavery in Europe and Africa.

Unger, Richard W. "Dutch Herring, Technology, and International Trade in the Seventeenth Century." *Journal of Economic History* 40 (June 1980): 253–79.

——. "Technical Change in the Brewing Industry in Germany, the Low Countries, and England in the Late Middle Ages." *Journal of European Economic History* 21 (1992): 281–313.

——. "The Scale of Dutch Brewing, 1350–1600." In *Research in Economic History*, Vol. 15, edited by Roger L. Ransome, Richard Sutch, and Susan B. Carter, 261–92. Greenwich, CT and London: Jai Press, 1995.

CHAPTER 9: SOURCES OF CAPITAL IN
THE LATE MIDDLE AGES

De Roover, Raymond. *Money, Banking and Credit in Medieval Bruges.* (Cited under Chapter 3.)

——. *The Rise and Fall of the Medici Bank, 1397–1494.* (Cited under Chapter 3.)

Ehrenberg, Richard. *Capital and Finance in the Age of the Renaissance: A Study of the Fuggers and Their Connections.* Translated by H. M. Lucas. London: Jonathan Cape, 1928. This book focuses almost exclusively on the high finance aspects of the Fugger and other major companies in western Europe through the late Middle Ages and beyond.

Goldthwaite, Richard A. *Wealth and the Demand for Art in Italy, 1300–1600.* Baltimore and London: Johns Hopkins University Press, 1993.

Molho, Anthony. *Marriage Alliance in Late Medieval Florence.* Cambridge, MA: Harvard University Press, 1994.

Riu, Manuel. "Banking and Society in Late Medieval and Early Modern Aragon." In *The Dawn of Modern Banking*, 131–68. New Haven, CT: Yale University Press, 1979.

Strieder, Jacob. *Jakob Fugger the Rich: Merchant and Banker of Augsburg, 1459–1525.* Translated by Mildred L. Hartsough. New York: Adelphi, 1931. Despite its somewhat exuberant style, this book is of special value because of its unusual attention to Jakob Fugger's activities as a businessman rather than as a financier.

Usher, Abbot P. *The Early History of Deposit Banking in Mediterranean Europe*, Vol. 1. Cambridge, MA: Harvard University Press, 1943. This volume is still useful, especially for those interested in early banking in Barcelona.

CHAPTER 10: A NEW AGE FOR BUSINESS

Bautier, Robert-Henri. *The Economic Development of Medieval Europe.* Translated by Heather Karolyi. London: Thames & Hudson, 1971.

Brown, R. Gene, and Kenneth S. Johnson. *Paciolo on Accounting.* New York: McGraw-Hill, 1963.

Ehrenberg, Richard. *Capital and Finance in the Age of the Renaissance: A Study of the Fuggers and Their Connections.* (Cited under Chapter 9.)

Harte, N. B. and K. G. Ponting, eds. *Cloth and Clothing in Medieval Europe: Essays in Memory of Professor E. M. Carus-Wilson.* (Cited under Chapter 2.)

Munro, John H. "The Central European Silver Mining Boom, Mint Outputs, and Prices in the Low Countries and England, 1450–1550." In *Money, Coins, and Commerce: The Monetary History of Asia and Europe*, 119–183, edited by Eddy H. G. van Cauwenberghe. Leuven: Leuven University Press, 1991.

——. *Textiles, Towns, and Trade.* (Cited under Chapter 2.)

Noonan, John Thomas, *The Scholastic Analysis of Usury.* (Cited under Chapter 3.)

Strieder, Jacob. *Jakob Fugger the Rich: Merchant and Banker of Augsburg, 1459–1525.* (Cited under Chap 9.)

Wee, Herman van der. *The Growth of the Antwerp Market and the European Economy (Fourteenth-sixteenth Centuries).* The Hague: Nijhoff, 1963.

INDEX